D0083071

Charlotte Ramsay Lennox

AN EIGHTEENTH CENTURY LADY OF LETTERS

BY

MIRIAM ROSSITER SMALL

ARCHON BOOKS
1969

SBN: 208 00770 9
Library of Congress Catalog Card Number: 69-15692
Printed in the United States of America

PREFACE

JOHNSON'S high esteem for Mrs. Lennox as recorded by Boswell and endorsed by his frequent assistance to her has done as much to keep Charlotte Ramsay Lennox in the dim background of public notice as her novel, *The Female Quixote*, the best of her original works, or as the *Memoirs of Sully*, the most reprinted of her translations. I have found Mrs. Lennox's literary and personal relations not only with Johnson but also with other great figures of her day an interesting part of her life, as I have endeavored to assemble a more complete biography of her than has been before presented. I have also collected and arranged all known editions of her works, and made some estimate of her own writings.

This study was originally presented to the Faculty of the Graduate School of Yale University in partial fulfilment of the requirement for the degree of Doctor of Philosophy. I have since altered and arranged it as additional works of Mrs. Lennox, and manuscripts, have come to my attention and have cast new light upon facts already assembled.

In the preparation of this volume I wish to express my appreciation for the ready help of Miss Emily Hall and other members of the staff of the library of Yale University, also of the staff of the New York Public Library, of the Library of Congress, and of the British Museum. A debt of personal gratitude I am glad to acknowledge to Professor Cecil A. Moore of the University of Minnesota, Allen T. Hazen, and Frederick W. Hilles for suggestion and references; to Mrs. R. B. Adam, Captain Frank L. Pleadwell, Hon. John C. Marshall, secretary of the Royal Literary Fund, Frederick W. Hilles, J. A. Spoor, F. Sidgwick, George P.

Hoff, parish secretary of St. Peter's church in Albany, and Lacy Collison-Morley for granting me access to manuscripts and prints or calling them to my notice; to Professor Chauncey B. Tinker for generously bringing to my attention not only book and manuscript but also ideas bearing upon the subject, from the wealth of his knowledge of the period; and to Professor Karl Young at whose suggestion this study was undertaken and who faithfully guided its writing.

MIRIAM R. SMALL.

Wells College,
Aurora-on-Cayuga, New York,
June, 1935.

CONTENTS

ILLUSTRATIONS

CHARLOTTE RAMSAY LENNOX

CHAPTER I

Life of Charlotte Ramsay Lennox
1720–1765

ON the evening of Saturday, May 15, 1784, Boswell was with Johnson at the Essex Head Club. Johnson was in fine spirits, and in the course of the evening made the following remark to his friends:[1] "I dined yesterday at Mrs. Garrick's, with Mrs. Carter, Miss Hannah More, and Miss Fanny Burney. Three such women are not to be found: I know not where I could find a fourth, except Mrs. Lennox, who is superiour to them all."

This remark indicates what was the most important single fact in Mrs. Lennox's literary life: that from its beginning in 1750 until Johnson's death in 1784 she received the warm approval and assistance of Samuel Johnson. This friendship was of no mean importance when we recall that Johnson had the reputation of being unfriendly to female authors and severe in his judgments upon their works. Perhaps, like Burke, he felt that he lived in an age of female writers and was impatient of the fact. Certainly he is free from the charge of impatience or severity toward Mrs. Lennox, for he generously wrote dedications, reviews, proposals, even a chapter for her. In this age of Johnson, where so many figures of greatness shine, which boasts not only the Doctor himself, and his great biographer Boswell, but also such novelists as Fielding and Richardson, such an actor as Garrick, such a man of letters as Goldsmith, and such a painter as Reynolds, it is not always easy to distinguish the minor

---

[1] Boswell, *Life* (Oxford Press, 1934), iv, 275, 524. Bowles' record of Johnson's conversations at Heale repeats this: "Of Miss Hannah More, Miss Burney & Mrs. Lennox he spoke with great regard but seemed to prefer Mrs. Lennox."

figures except as they are reflected from the greater glory. In this way one comes upon Mrs. Charlotte Ramsay Lennox first, notably in this lavish praise accorded her by Johnson; she was also favorably received by other major figures: praised by Fielding and Richardson, her plays produced by Garrick, an epilogue written for her by Goldsmith, her portrait painted by Reynolds. But as we look more closely at her life and publications it is possible to discern in Mrs. Lennox something more than a lady with literary friendships; she comes before us as an independent author of unflagging industry rewarded with occasional success, and as an attractive woman whose life was rich in experience, though often clouded by penury and domestic unhappiness.

Charlotte Ramsay was born in New York (probably in New York City) in 1720 and remained in America until 1735 when she was sent to England. According to information she herself gave, her father was James Ramsay, Royalist Governor or Lieutenant-Governor of New York in 1720.[2] All contemporary accounts repeat this statement, which is not true. The civil-list, accepted as entirely complete, makes no mention of a James Ramsay; neither does his name appear in any of the detailed colonial histories of the period. It is impossible that anyone holding so high an office as lieutenant-governor should escape mention in all contemporary records. There was, however, an officer, James Ramsay, in Lt. Gen. Bissett's Regiment of Foot, who received his first commission on February 2, 1728-9, and was made First Lieutenant on August 26, 1736.[3] On December 30, 1738, a James Ramsay,

[2] The statistics of the Royal Literary Fund, compiled first in 1792 (see below, p. 57), when she was still alive, give 1720 as the year of her birth and her father as Royalist Governor. The accounts of her death in the *Gentleman's Magazine* for Jan., 1804, and by Nichols in 1812 state that her father was Lieutenant-Governor of New York. Obviously what she wanted believed was that her father held a high office in the New York colony.

[3] *Notes and Queries*, 12th series, viii, 327. "An English Army List of 1740."

THE FIRST ST. PETER'S CHURCH, ALBANY, 1715

probably the same one, was made Captain of one of the four Independent Companies of Invalids stationed at New York.[4] If this were the father of Charlotte, he did not gain a position of any importance until after she had sailed for England.

The only real knowledge we have of these years from 1720 to 1735 is that Charlotte Ramsay was acquainted with life in Albany, in all probability as the daughter of an officer at the fort there. The evidence is found in two of her novels, *Harriot Stuart* (1750) and *Euphemia* (1790), where scenes are laid in America and where there is some description of New York, the trip up the Hudson, and especially of Albany and the country nearby. The last is presented in detail that argues considerable knowledge of the facts; early Albany, its Dutch families, the frequent visitations of the Indians, the formal visits of the governor to renew the treaty with the Six Nations of Indians—all are described with the pictorial vividness of a child observer. Albany in those days was little more than an outpost. A description of it from annals of the time tells that "State Street . . . was occupied by the Dutch church at the foot, a market house below Pearl street, the English church above Pearl, and on a line with the upper side of Lodge street, the battlements of Fort Frederick stood upon a lofty eminence overlooking the city, and stretching nearly across the street, the road to Schenectady winding around its southern angles. The city was surrounded by a wooden barrier. . . . . Within these narrow limits there was a population of about 3,000, and a garrison of 300 more."[5] Among these surroundings Charlotte Ram-

---

[4] *Notes and Queries*, 12th series, vi, 331. See also Appendix I where I have included all the information available on James Ramsay.

[5] Munsell's *Collections of the History of New York*, i, 390. "Albany in 1717." This account is given in connection with the history of St. Peter's Church, founded in 1708. There are no records of the church extant before 1756. The picture opposite is from an India ink drawing of "State Street, Albany, Looking West, 1715. Fort Frederick Built, 1647. English Church Built, 1715." The drawing is in St. Peter's Church.

say probably dwelt until 1735 when she sailed for England never to return to America.

Confused accounts exist as to why she was sent to England. The one probably sponsored by Mrs. Lennox is that given in her obituary notice in the *Gentleman's Magazine* and by Nichols, and coincides with circumstances in her novel *Harriot Stuart*, which seems partially autobiographical: that she was sent over to a wealthy aunt, but on arrival found the aunt incurably insane and no provision made for her. Other authorities supply that she was sent over to complete her education, which was interrupted by the death of her parents who left no property; that she was later patronized by Lady Rockingham and the Duchess of Newcastle.[6] Also:[7]

When she was fifteen years old, her mother being dead, she was sent to England to complete her education. The relation to whose care she was consigned never informed her that her father died during the voyage. Left thus without a protector, Lady Rockingham took her up, receiving her into her household; but an obscure love-affair ended the friendship, and the Duchess of Newcastle became her patroness.

Chalmers adds that her mother died in New York in 1765.[8]

For the period of Miss Ramsay's life between 1735 and 1747 information is meagre. From her later translations we can be sure that she gained a ready knowledge of French. Obviously, too, she read a great deal, probably many of the romances which she afterwards ridicules in *The Female Quixote*. By piecing together a number of allusions we can make out a connected story of her relations with at least one lady of rank, Lady Isabella Finch. In 1747 when her first

[6] Lamb's *Biographical Dictionary* (Boston, 1900-3).

[7] *National Cyclopedia of American Biography* (N. Y., 1896), vi, 51.

[8] Chalmers Alexander, *A General Biographical Dictionary* (Ln., Nichol and Son, 1815), xx, 170-2.

publication, a volume of poems,[9] appeared, it contained the following dedication:

To the Right Honourable the Lady Issabella Finch, First Lady of the Bedchamber to their Royal Highnesses the Princesses.

Madam,

That I presume to lay the following trifles at your Lady-ship's Feet, is not so much the Ambition of having a Patroness distinguish'd for so many shining qualities as your Ladyship, as to have an Opportunity of Acknowledging the Obligations you have conferr'd on me. . . . Yet, Madam, am I truly sensible of the extreme honour your Protection will afford me, since your Approbation is sufficient to stamp a value upon my other-ways Trifling performances. Your Ladyship's early Favour and Indulgence, as it was sufficient to satisfy the most boundless Vanity, gives you the strongest Claim to my Perpetual Gratitude. Suffer me then, Madam, thus publickly to own your Ladyship's Goodness, and to profess myself with the greatest Respect, Your Ladyship's Most oblig'd and grateful Humble Servant, Charlotte Ramsay.

In 1747 Lady Isabella was looked upon as a friend and benevolent patroness from whom favors were to be expected. By 1750 when *Harriot Stuart* was published all this had changed. The most thoroughly despicable character in the book is Lady Cecelia, a lady famous for making promises of court favor and failing to fulfill them. Harriot shows her the manuscript of her poems and is thoroughly deceived by her professed liking for them and her promises of favor. It is only after she has lost all hope of advancement from other quarters because everyone thinks she is Lady Cecelia's protégée that Harriot realizes how bitterly she has been

[9] Nichols, *Literary Anecdotes* (Ln., 1812), iii, 438. "Life of Samuel Paterson:—he opened a bookseller's shop opposite Durham Yard in the Strand, where he published Miss Charlotte Ramsay's (afterwards the celebrated Mrs. Lennox) poems in 1748." The date on the title-page is 1747. See also *Gent. Mag.*, xvii, 548. (Nov. 1747) "Poems by Miss Ramsay pr. 1s. 6d."

duped. Ultimately Lady Cecelia does send Harriot to serve her sister in the country, where she is successful as a companion until she is falsely accused of trying to seduce the French tutor, her enemy because repulsed as her lover. His lies are believed instead of her innocence, and injured virtue is forced to seek a living elsewhere. Lady Mary Wortley Montagu gives these incidents point in her comment upon *Harriot Stuart*:[10]

But while I was indolently perusing the marvellous figures and exhibits, no more resembling anything in human nature than the wooden cut in the Seven Champions, I was roused into great surprise and indignation by the monstrous abuse of one of the very few women I have a real value for, I mean Lady B. F. [note supplies Belle Finch, daughter of Lord Nottingham and sister to the Duchess of Roxboro, the Duchess of Cleveland, Lady Mansfield and Lady Rockingham]; who is not only clearly meant by the mention of the library (she being the only lady at court that has one), but her very name at length, she being christened Cecilia Isabella, though she chooses to be called by the latter. I always thought her conduct irreproachable, I did not think she had an enemy on earth; I now see 't is impossible to avoid them, especially in her situation. It is one of the misfortunes of a supposed court interest (perhaps you may know it by experience), even the people you have obliged hate you, if they do not think you have served to the utmost extent of a power they fancy you are possessed of; which it may be is only imaginary.

With the characters in the novel placed thus, it is easy to conjecture that Miss Ramsay was disappointed of the favor she had anticipated so rosily in 1747 and felt some personal enmity toward the lady who had deceived her. The allusion also lends credence to the suggestion of a sojourn with Lady Rockingham, one of Lady Isabella's sisters, which was closed abruptly by some kind of love-affair.

Social London found occasion for criticism of Miss

---

[10] Lady Mary Wortley Montagu, *Letters*, 2 v. (ed. Lord Wharncliffe, Ln., 1861), ii, 221, March 1, 1752, letter to Countess of Bute.

Ramsay in her next venture, which was on the stage. This time it was Horace Walpole who wrote to George Montagu on September 3, 1748:[11]

> I have just come from the play at Richmond, where I found the Duchess of Argyll etc. . . . . We had a new actress, a Miss Clough; an extremely tall fine figure, and very handsome etc. . . . . Garrick is to produce her next winter; and a Miss Charlotte Ramsay, a poetess, and a deplorable actress.[12]

Since the sole surviving record of Miss Ramsay's stage attempts is so disparaging and so casual, her appearances were probably neither many nor notable.

Although Miss Ramsay's name is still used here in 1748, it is possible that she was married on October 6, 1747, as there is a record in St. George's Church, Mayfair, of the marriage of Alexander Lennox and Barbara Ramsay of St. Anne's, Westminster. Her husband's name was almost certainly Alexander Lennox, for there is a later record of the baptism of her daughter, which gives the parents as Alexander and Charlotte Lennox. There may have been a mistake in her name in this first record. Alexander Lennox was an employee of William Strahan, the London printer, and it was probably through him that Mrs. Lennox was introduced to Johnson,[13] since Strahan and his partner, Andrew Millar, were both friends of Johnson. From the little we know this seems to be the only entirely helpful and auspicious act that Mr. Lennox ever performed for his wife.

Between June, 1749, and January, 1751, Mrs. Lennox's name appeared several times in the section "Poetry" of the

[11] Walpole Horace, *Letters* (ed. Mrs. Paget Toynbee, Oxford Press, 1903), ii, 337.

[12] Walpole's copy of Mrs. Lennox's play *The Sister* is in the possession of Dr. F. W. Atkinson, President of Brooklyn Polytechnic Institute, and bears on the back of the title-page, perhaps in Walpole's handwriting, "the   th Febry 1769 performed but with great difficulty the sense of the house being against it."

[13] *National Cyclopedia of American Biography*, vi, 51.

Gentleman's Magazine.[14] In June, 1749, a long poem addressed "To Mrs. Charlotte Lennox, upon seeing her Poems and Proposals for Printing them" praises the lady's attempts at poetry; in conventional phraseology it refers to her as Ardelia and lauds her "melting lays", fluent fancy", and "rising Muse". In November, 1750, occurs another poem "To Mrs. Charlotte Lennox. On reading her Poems, printing by Subscription, in one volume. 8vo. price 5s." signed E.N. It is more ardent in praise of her verse than the first, comparing her with Sappho to the latter's disadvantage, and concluding with a personal compliment to her beauty:

> Your eyes into our souls that fire convey,
> So well describ'd in thy harmonious lay:
> Your verse creates, your form can fix desire,
> Wishing we read, and gazing we admire.

In the same number of the magazine are printed two poems by Mrs. Lennox herself: "The Art of Coquetry", reprinted from her early volume, and an ode on the birthday of the Princess of Wales, which appears here for the first and only time. In January, 1751, comes a poem occasioned by reading "The Art of Coquetry", entitled "Advice to the Novice in Love", and intended to arm "honest wretches" against the wiles of the "tutor'd fair inspir'd by Charlotte's pen".

This brief flurry of interest in the poems apparently attended upon proposals mentioned above for publishing them by subscription two years after the first edition. After the success of the *Female Quixote* proposals were published again on November 4, 1752. The edition was to appear in March, 1753, and to cost a crown. The sample page, which

---

[14] These poems I have reprinted in Appendices II and III, also "The Art of Coquetry", which I consider her best poem, and the birthday ode of 1750, which appears only in the *Gent. Mag.*

quotes from "On Reading Hutchinson on the Passions", is larger and more ornate than that of the original edition.[15] There is no evidence that this edition or the earlier one advertised was ever published. A modern reader sees no possible reason for republishing. The work is slight both in quantity and value. Love is the prevailing theme, as suffered by Damon, Ardelia, Mira, and their colleagues, with conventional accompaniments of "rising passions", "breathing zephyrs", and "tender lyres". The metres are the quatrain or the octosyllabic couplet, with occasional use of the longer couplet. "The Art of Coquetry", though somewhat conventional, has the most vivacity, but Mrs. Lennox seems to have preferred "Hutchinson on the Passions", as she uses it in *Harriot Stuart*, again in the *Proposals*, and later in the *Lady's Museum*.

The attention attracted by "The Art of Coquetry" was not altogether favorable, for on December 1, 1750, Mrs. Elizabeth Carter writes her friend, Miss Talbot:[16]

Or do you know anything of a Mrs. Charlotte Lennox, who is publishing by subscription? one or two of her poems were printed in the last Magazine. For the edification of some of my young friends, we read one of them on the art of coquetry, at which they were much scandalized. The poetry is uncommonly correct, but the doctrine indeed by no means to be admired. It is intolerably provoking to see people who really appear to have a genius, apply it to such idle unprofitable purposes.

Nor do these seriously righteous ladies find it easy to forget the frivolity of Mrs. Lennox. On Nov. 12, 1753, almost three years later, Miss Talbot writes Mrs. Carter:[17]

[15] A facsimile of these *Proposals* of 1752 is given opposite p. 155 where I discuss the version of the poem.

[16] *A Series of Letters Between Mrs. Elizabeth Carter and Miss Catherine Talbot, from 1741-1770* (ed. Rev. Montague Pennington, Ln., 1809), i, 367.

[17] *Id.*, ii, 146.

But do now write me an essay upon this sort of vanity, and its too frequent consequence, coquetry. Not the art of coquetry like Mrs. Lennox, but an edifying essay proper to be put into the hands of the Muses.

Thus these ladies range themselves with Lady Mary Wortley Montagu in rigorous disapproval of Mrs. Lennox and begin a feminine disapprobation which is steadily and impressively cumulative through her life. Perhaps we have no farther to seek for the reason why she has never been included in any group of the "blues".

Mrs. Lennox's first novel appeared in December, 1750,[18] *The Life of Harriot Stuart*, Written by Herself. It was rather well received by the magazines of the day, but the reception which has given it lasting fame was the celebration conceived by Johnson and recorded for us by the slightly protesting Sir John Hawkins:[19]

Mrs. Lenox, a lady now well known in the literary world, had written a novel intitled, 'The life of Harriot Stuart,' which in the spring of 1751, was ready for publication. One evening at the club, Johnson proposed to us the celebrating the birth of Mrs. Lenox's first literary child, as he called her book, by a whole night spent in festivity. Upon his mentioning it to me, I told him I had never sat up a whole night in my life; but he continuing to press me, and saying, that I should find great delight in it, I, as did all the rest of our company, consented. The place appointed was the Devil tavern, and there, about the hour of eight, Mrs. Lenox and her husband, and a lady of her acquantance, now living, as also the [Ivy Lane] club, and friends to the number of near twenty, assembled. Our supper was elegant, and Johnson had directed that a magnificent hot apple-pye should make a part of it, and this he would have stuck with bay-leaves, because, forsooth, Mrs. Lenox was an authoress, and had written verses; and further, he had prepared for her a

[18] The date on the title-page is 1751, which is also the one usually given. It is announced, however, under the publications for December, 1750, both in the *Gentleman's Magazine* and in the *Monthly Review*.

[19] Sir John Hawkins, *The Works of Samuel Johnson* (Ln., 1787), i, 285-6.

crown of laurel, with which, but not till he had invoked the
muses by some ceremonies of his own invention, he encircled
her brows. The night passed, as must be imagined, in
pleasant conversation, and harmless mirth, intermingled at
different periods with the refreshments of coffee and tea.
About five, Johnson's face shone with meridian splendour,
though his drink had been only lemonade; but the far
greater part of us had deserted the colours of Bacchus, and
were with difficulty rallied to partake of a second refresh-
ment of coffee, which was scarcely ended when the day began
to dawn. This phenomenon began to put us in mind of our
reckoning; but the waiters were all so overcome with sleep,
that it was two hours before we could get a bill, and it was
not till near eight that the creaking of the street-door gave
the signal for our departure .... and I well remember, at the
instant of my going out of the tavern-door, the sensation of
shame that affected me, occasioned not by reflection on any
thing evil that had passed in the course of the night's entertainment, but on the resemblance it bore to a debauch.

This festivity is the first of many attentions which Johnson
bestowed upon Mrs. Lennox during a friendship which continued happily to combine the social and the literary for
thirty years. It definitely places their meeting before 1751
and proves the inaccuracy of part of the account given in
1813 in the memoir of Mrs. Lennox published in the *Lady's
Monthly Museum*.[20] The story, possibly confused with
Johnson's similar treatment of Fanny Burney, may not be
any more accurate than the date, but it deserves inclusion.

It was soon after the publication of the former work
(The Female Quixote, 1752) that she was introduced to Dr.
Johnson as a young lady of considerable genius; but nothing
could exceed the astonishment of Mrs. Lennox at the odd

[20] *Lady's Monthly Museum*, n.s. 14, p. 301 (June, 1813). This magazine was running a series of lives of ladies who had been eminent in
the latter part of the 18th century. Many of them are much more
obscure than Mrs. Lennox. The "life" was regularly the first article
in the magazine and was graced by an engraving of the lady, made
by Cook. It was for this that Cook made the second engraving of
the portrait of Mrs. Lennox, as it is dated June, 1813.

manner in which she was received. The doctor took her on his knee, as if a mere child; after which he carried her in his arms, to shew her his library; and as if resolved to be uniform in his conduct, sent his servant to a pastry-cook, to purchase some cakes for the young lady. Mrs. Lennox found herself greatly embarrassed, but a respect for his character stifled even the idea of resentment, and she preserved an intimacy with him until near the period of his decease.

If Johnson had had the delightful habit of reading Fielding, we might have fancied that this gesture was suggested by old Homer listening to the concert of Orpheus and Sappho in Elysium with Madame Dacier comfortably settled in his lap.

Others than Johnson evinced an interest in *Harriot Stuart*; in a letter dated December 10, 1751, he speaks of Lord Orrery's favorable opinion of "our Charlotte's book".[21]   On November 21, 1751, Mrs. Lennox writes:[22]

Mr. Johnson has informed me of the generous concern you exprest for the severity of my critics, and your good intentions to rescue my book from their censures, and restore me to Mr. Millar's good opinions.

If Mr. Millar's good opinion were necessary for him to publish books, Mrs. Lennox certainly had it, for he printed all her books for the next eight years.

The moderate success of her first novel encouraged Mrs. Lennox to continue in this field and in March, 1752, appeared *The Female Quixote, or The Adventures of Arabella, a* burlesque after the fashion of *Don Quixote*, with a heroine whose head had been turned by reading too many of the long French romances of Scudéri.   This novel was her greatest

---

[21] *Letters of Dr. Johnson* (ed. Hill, N. Y. 1892), i, 26, letter 36.
[22] This letter is noted as Lot 102 of Sotheby's Catalogue for 27 Nov., 1889. It was sold by Pearson & Co. in 1907. I have not been able to trace it further.

success. A second edition appeared in June; there were translations into German, Spanish, and French, and numerous imitations and allusions. Her name did not appear on the title-page until the edition of 1783, but the authorship was generally known and was proclaimed in some of the reviews. The review in the *Gentleman's Magazine*[23] Hill thought was written by Johnson, and I see no reason to question this supposition. It is short—one paragraph—and commendatory. Boswell tells us (with the date ten years out of the way) that Johnson wrote the dedication, which is addressed to the Earl of Middlesex. Besides these contributions he probably wrote one of the chapters. So his share in this book is considerable. Mrs. Lennox, on her part, does verbal honor to the "author of the Rambler" when she quotes his remark that *Clarissa* "has taught the passions to move at the command of virtue" as being "the words of the greatest genius of the present age".

The publication of this quixotic novel brings Mrs. Lennox into contact with another great literary figure of the day, Henry Fielding. The subject unquestionably interested a man who was so strongly under the influence of *Don Quixote* in his own writings, as shown particularly by *Don Quixote in England* and *Joseph Andrews*. This interest is proved by his review of the book, which appeared in the *Covent-Garden Journal* for March 24, 1752, and which is not only the most thorough and favorable review that the book received but is also considered the best book review Fielding ever wrote. It points constantly to the prototype and the contrast is not always to the advantage of the latter. So laudatory and careful a review from a man of genius thoroughly versed in the quixotic increases Mrs. Lennox's literary prestige both in the eighteenth and twentieth centuries. Apparently it led to some personal acquain-

---

[23] *Gentleman's Magazine*, xxii, 146. See below, pp. 78-9.

tance, for in 1754 Fielding mentions her in the *Journal of a Voyage to Lisbon* :[24]

> I then happened to recollect, upon a hint given me by the inimitable and shamefully-distress'd author of the Female Quixote, that I had many years before, from curiosity only, taken a cursory view of Bishop Berkeley's treatise on the virtues of tar-water . . . .

What the distresses were which Fielding knew about it is possible only to conjecture, but all evidence points to her continued poverty in spite of a constant literary activity and considerable recognition. In a later letter she accuses the booksellers of diverting funds from her, and her husband was little help. Mr. Lennox appears never to have been a bread-winner, and even took money from his wife instead of providing it. She always refers to lodgings, and she moved frequently because every time we find an address for her she is in a different part of London or, at least, at a different address. The picture of him we can piece together is slight: working for Strahan the printer, a tidewaiter at the customs,[25] luring his son away from his mother into evil practices, and often living apart from his wife. The pleasantest part of their story belongs to this period when he shares the hardships and pleasures of her existence more nearly than he does later on. Thus Richardson refers to them together in a letter to Lady Bradshaigh :[26]

> The Female Quixote is written by a woman, a favourite of the author of the Rambler: Lennox, her name. Her husband and she have often visited me together. Do not you think, however her heroine overacts her part, that Arabella is amiable and innocent? The writer has genius. She is hardly twenty-four and has been unhappy. She wrote a piece, called Harriot Stuart.

[24] Fielding Henry, *Works. Miscellaneous Writings* (ed. W. Henley), iii, 194.

[25] *Id.*, iii, 290n.

[26] *Correspondence of Richardson* (ed. Barbauld), vi, 243.

Again we have the allusion to her troubles, perhaps here to earlier troubles during those years when we know nothing of her. Richardson is assuredly mistaken as to her age, as she was thirty-two when the *Female Quixote* was published. Whether Richardson ever gave her advice in matters of the heart is uncertain; "she has been unhappy" would suggest confidences. We may surmise that Mrs. Lennox was at one time admitted to that circle which gathered about the oracle at Parson's Green and "could scarcely recall an occasion upon which 'her host had not rehearsed at least one, but probably two or three voluminous letters, if he found her in the humour of listening with attention.' "[27]

Besides sharing this literary friendship, Mr. Lennox brought about his wife's next literary connection, which was with Giuseppe Baretti. A full account of the accidental meeting between Baretti and Mr. Lennox was given in the *European Magazine* at the time of Baretti's death:[28]

About the same time (1753) accident brought him acquainted with a person who was the means of introducing him to the notice of Dr. Johnson, who to the end of his life regarded him with great esteem. The origin of this intimacy has been frequently mentioned by Mr. Baretti to have happened in the following manner: Mrs. Lennox, the authoress of *The Female Quixote*, having an intention to publish a translation of the novels from whence Shakespeare had taken some of his plays, wished to acquire a sufficient knowledge of the Italian language to enable her to execute the work with some degree of credit. To accomplish this point Mr. Lennox, her husband, went to the Orange Coffee-house to learn whether any foreigner was desirous of improving himself in the English language, and by that means receive the same advantage as he should communicate. Mr. Baretti happened to be present when the enquiry was made, and eagerly accepted the offer. After some time he was introduced to Dr. Johnson. An intimacy commenced between

[27] Dobson Austin, *Samuel Richardson* (N. Y., 1902), 136.

[28] *European Magazine* (May, 1789), xv, 349. See also Collison-Morley Lacy, *Giuseppe Baretti* (London, 1909), 81-2 and bibliography.

them, which appears to have continued until nearly the end of Dr. Johnson's life. The incident which occasioned the interruption of their friendship has been already related.

Another account of the relations between Mrs. Lennox and Baretti comes to us from the ill-natured pages of Laetitia-Matilda Hawkins' *Memoirs*. This lady speaks of Mrs. Lennox several times and always in an unpleasant way, although she is no more unpleasant about her than she manages to be about most of her contemporaries. Consequently we cannot accept too confidently the following acid comment:[29]

Mrs. Lennox made a compact with Baretti for mutual assistance in learning each other's native language; but Baretti complained that she fell far short in her part of the treaty. It concluded with a quarrel. He once, in company, bestowed more of his notice on her little girl than she approved, and desiring him to desist, and not to let that child engross his attention; she was answered by his saying, 'You are a child in stature and a child in understanding.' What the measure of the latter was, I do not know but her translation of Sully's Memoirs shows, that however it ended, it began in a praxis on rendering the language, for nothing can be much worse translated than the first pages of it; and I have heard it said, that, in translating Brumoy's *Greek Theatre*, she rendered les enfants perdus by 'the lost children.'[30]   Baretti, I suppose, was generally provoking, where opportunity offered.

Baretti did quarrel with most of his friends, and Mrs. Lennox was no exception. The quarrel here referred to must have come, however, considerably later, as Mrs.

[29] Hawkins Laetitia-Matilda, *Memoirs, Anecdotes, Facts, and Opinions*. (Ln. Pr. for Longman, Hunt, etc., 2 vols. 1824), i, 71.

[30] I have been able to find no "lost children" in the three volumes of Brumoy's *Greek Theatre*. The nearest approach is in *Hippolitus* act iv, sc. 4 (i, 291), when Theseus says "Oh Gods! have I then lost my children?", a translation of the French (i, 353), "Dieux! aurois-je perdu mes enfants!"

Lennox's daughter was not born until 1765. For some years they apparently enjoyed a friendship of advantage to both. Baretti's first important work in English, *The Italian Library* etc., appeared in 1754. As he had written in English as early as 1751, it must have been greater practice and familiarity that he sought, whereas Mrs. Lennox probably knew no Italian before their meeting. Her publication, however, came before his, and in May, 1753, we find announced in the *Gentleman's Magazine*

Shakespear Illustrated. 2 vols. 5s. Millar. By the author of the Female Quixote. These volumes contain nine entertaining novels, and a play by Plautus, elegantly translated from the Italian, French, Latin and Danish; the author exhibits them as the original stories, on which the following plays of Shakespear are founded. [Table of contents.] A parallel is afterwards drawn between the play and the novel, and the difference is critically remarked.

These two volumes were followed by a third in February, 1754. If the anecdote in the *European Magazine* is correct as to date and Mrs. Lennox did not meet Baretti until 1753, we have a record of amazing industry and quickness in her thus translating the six sources from the Italian given in the first two volumes and the one in the third within the year. The translations are, in style, neither awkward nor hasty, and are executed with a certain amount of ease. That the criticism she contributed is not acceptable is not to be wondered at. Obviously the actual labor of locating the sources, translating, and criticizing must have taken so much of her time between the production of the *Female Quixote* in March, 1752, and *Shakespear Illustrated* in May, 1753, that she had little opportunity for careful study and reflection.

This important and practically untried move in Shakespearean criticism, the study of sources, was undoubtedly undertaken at the suggestion of Johnson, who, although he had been compelled by Tonson's claim to copyright to give up his edition of Shakespeare proposed in 1745, had not lost interest in the subject, as may be seen by the appearance of two articles on Shakespeare's plays in *The Rambler* in 1751. If he was still contemplating an edition of the plays in which, as his proposals of 1756 indicate, there should be a comparison of each play with its source it is but natural that he should wish to be spared the painstaking drudgery such a task would require. Mrs. Lennox, on the other hand, under pressure of want and pleased by any suggestion of Johnson, was only too willing to engage upon a literary enterprise which might later be connected with his edition, and would certainly place her among the already redoubtable list of Shakespearean commentators. The labor involved did not daunt her. Neither did the criticism of the plays for which she was little suited. What she did was to seize upon the accepted canon of criticism and apply it ruthlessly and whole-heartedly, remaining blind to the beauty and humanity of Shakespeare. Johnson could not have entirely approved of these criticisms and he actually made little use of her book when he came to his own edition; but he wrote the dedication to the Earl of Orrery, and the influence he had with the *Gentleman's Magazine* may have had something to do with the favorable mention there and the space granted for an entire reprint of the criticism on *Romeo and Juliet*.

There is further evidence of Johnson's influence over Mrs. Lennox and over the trend her work was taking during this decade in an ode written to Charlotte Lennox by Baretti, dated at London, May 30, 1754, and still existing in a manuscript book found at Casale, Italy, by Captain Pleadwell and now in his possession. In this ode[31] Baretti praises her love poetry and urges her to continue writing of love, not to turn away from the pastoral drama of her early poems. He states that he knows it is Johnson who is opposed to him and who is guiding her away from writing of love to more austere subjects. In this mention of Johnson's influence in

[31] See below, pp. 158-60.

connection with Charlotte's poetry Baretti may refer to the changes she has made in her poem so often reprinted, "On Reading Hutchinson on the Passions," which is shortened, made less personal, more restrained, in the 1752 version of the *Proposals* to suit with the objection he here raises.

We are especially turned to the changes in the *Proposals* for the reason for Baretti's remarks to Charlotte since the only pastoral she ever attempted after the conventional phraseology of name and detail in her early poems was a drama, a tale of pastoral love entitled *Philander*, which was not published until 1757, though its inception may date from the time of this ode. Baretti's influence may be seen here since in the dedication Charlotte admits the first hint came to her from the *Pastor Fido* of Guarini. Besides this possible influence on the writing of *Philander* the ode is chiefly interesting for its pleasantly Gallic flattery and the stress it lays upon Johnson's responsibility for the serious and moral turn Mrs. Lennox was taking, in the poem reprinted in the *Proposals* in particular, in her work during this decade in general, leaving behind her forever the frivolity of the "Art of Coquetry" and the gaiety of the *Female Quixote.*

During the next eight years the Monthly Catalogues of Books from the Magazines emphasize Mrs. Lennox's slavery to the booksellers. Only two original compositions come from this period; the rest were translations or compilations, all reminding the readers of her most successful book by this legend on the title-page, "by the Author of the *Female Quixote*". The *London Evening-Post* for November 1, 1755, announced the *Memoirs of Maximilian de Bethune, Duke of Sully, Prime Minister to Henry the Great . . . To which is added, (being never before printed) The Trial of Ravaillac, for the Murder of Henry the Great.* It was dedicated to the Duke of Newcastle, and the dedication was written by Johnson. Aside from the facts that all internal evidence points to his authorship and that Mrs. Lennox would naturally turn to him for the dedication of so important a translation there are two references connecting the work with him.   Boswell writes to Percy[32]

I return you the list of Mr. Johnson's writings with many thanks.   I must tell you however that he allowed Levet to dictate to you several errours, as for instance the Conquest of Goree, and the Preface to Sully.   He corrected these errours *himself* to me.

The "errour" here is probably preface for dedication, as the only preface is long and translated from the French edition.   T. T. makes the same "errour" in his additional anecdotes of Dr. Johnson:[33]

He composed the preface to . . . . Sully's Memoirs, . . .

The review of it in the *Literary Magazine* is one of those which Boswell gives as acknowledged by Johnson.[34]   It was favorably reviewed also in the *Monthly Review*[35] and is the most important of all Mrs. Lennox's translations, being a standard historical work.   It passed to fourteen editions in all: eight English, two Scotch, one American, and three both English and Scotch.   The last was that of the Bohn French classics series in 1856.   Not all bear Mrs. Lennox's name on the title-page but all are substantially her translation, though there was an attempt to disguise the opening pages especially in the pirated Scotch editions.   The later editions, however, both English and Scotch, acknowledge her as translator.

Even though it may have been hackwork, the translation of a work so well known must have done much to keep the author of the *Female Quixote* before the public, and perhaps added a certain weight and authority to her reputation.   The

---

[32] *The R. B. Adam Library relating to Dr. Samuel Johnson and his Era* (Ln. and N. Y., 1929), i.

[33] *Gentleman's Magazine* (Feb., 1785), lv (1), 87.

[34] *Life*, i, 309.

[35] *Monthly Review* (May, 1756), i, 312-4.

same ladies who were offended by the frivolity of *The Art of Coquetry* were exclaiming over Sully's *Mémoires*. In 1751 Miss Talbot wrote to Mrs. Carter:[36]

I am still bewitched by the *Mémoires de Sully*. I wish you may meet with it, for it is extremely worth reading. I know none that shews one the world in a more entertaining and instructive way, and numberless are the reflections that every page suggests to me.

On the heels of this translation came the *Memoirs of the Countess of Berci*, announced in April, 1756. This translation from the French of an old romance revamped was not noticed particularly; the *Critical Review* expressed a wish[37] that if the author were going to take from the French she would take something of importance. Mrs. Lennox profited by this advice and her next translation, announced in the *Gentleman's Magazine* for April, 1757, was the *Memoirs for the History of Madame de Maintenon and of the Last Age. Translated from the French by the Author of the Female Quixote.* The original was by De La Beaumelle, and had appeared two years before. This was by no means so successful a venture as Sully had been, and although the reviews were lengthy and fairly favorable, it did not pass to a second edition. The dedication is to the Countess of Northumberland, but all but the last sentence and signature is printed on a leaf which is a cancel. Whether Mrs. Lennox intended to dedicate the work to some one other than the Countess of Northumberland or whether she wrote a dedication herself and then received one from Johnson which she substituted is conjectural. Although nowhere attributed to Johnson, it enjoys something of the Johnsonian balance of idea and dignity when the "exalted understanding, superiority of genius, universal benevolence, and unfeigned piety" of Madame de Maintenon are compared to the same "quali-

[36] *Letters between Mrs. Elizabeth Carter and Miss Catherine Talbot* (Ln., 1809), ii, 47.
[37] *Critical Review* (May, 1756), i, 312-4.

ties, which, in you, madam, adorn the most eminent rank, add
lustre to the noblest line of ancestors, and give dignity to
wealth." It might well be Mrs. Lennox's own attempt to
write a dedication patterned after those Johnson had written
for her, if it is not by Johnson himself. Although less laudatory than the other reviews, the one in the *Monthly Review*[38]
has the most claim to attention, since it was written by Goldsmith. He criticizes the length, the "amphibious" mixture
of history and romance, the quoted conversations which cannot be authentic, but grants it the virtues of skilful writing
and liveliness. He ends by taking a fling at Voltaire:

We are at a loss to account for Mr. Voltaire's calling
the present performance a Romance; he, of all men, should
have been cautious of thus stigmatizing a work which bears
so strong a resemblance to *The Age of Lewis XIV*.

There is no recommendation of the translation in this
review as there is in Johnson's review of the Sully *Memoirs*;
in fact, the translator is not mentioned and there is nothing
to show that Goldsmith was writing for someone he knew
unless it is his final emphasis on the probable popularity of
the work, on its entertaining and amusing qualities, after the
strictures with which he begins.

The year 1758 finds Mrs. Lennox again in the monthly
catalogues, this year no longer with translations but with
original works. The first, *Philander*, was announced in the
London Chronicle for Dec. 1, 1757, and is a slight poetic
drama based on the Italian of Guarini and perhaps inspired
by the ode of Baretti mentioned previously. In spite of the
"uncommon elegance and purity"[39] of the style and the
"proper, soft, and delicate" sentiments it roused little interest
and was soon forgotten. The dedication was addressed to

[38] *Monthly Review* (July, 1757), xvii, 80-1, art. 3. For Goldsmith's
authorship cf. Nangle Benjamin, The *Monthly Review First Series*
1749-1789. Index to Contributors and Articles. (Oxford, 1934), 227.
[39] *Critical Review* (Nov., 1757), iv, 468.

Lord Charlemont, a great friend of Beauclerk's[40] and later of other members of the Club.   If the dedication of Maintenon to the Countess of Northumberland sounded, in one paragraph, like the work of Johnson, it is difficult to find any part of this dedication which does not suggest that author who once said to Reynolds: "There are two things which I am confident that I can do very well: One is an introduction to any literary work, stating what it is to contain, and how it should be executed in the most perfect manner; the other is a conclusion showing from various causes why the execution has not been equal to what the author promised to himself and to the public."

The dignity of the apology and the measured, steady development of the thought remind one of the best of Johnson's prefatory writing.   The external evidence to bear out what the text strongly indicates is of the very slightest,—indication rather than evidence.   Johnson had written many of Mrs. Lennox's dedications and was to write many more; there is no reason to believe that he had lost interest in her endeavors during these particular years.   Lord Charlemont was an intimate friend and political colleague of Lord Rockingham;   since it was from the house of Lady Rockingham that Charlotte Ramsay was dismissed, she might be particularly anxious to have the skill and dignity of Johnson to aid her in such an address.   Boswell himself says that he found it impossible to locate all the dedications Johnson wrote and comments upon the large number he turned off for his friends.   At the least, nothing definite influences one against the belief that Johnson wrote it.

Mrs. Lennox's other production of this year was her novel, *Henrietta*, announced in the *London Evening-Post* for Febru-

---

[40] Beauclerk writes to Lord Charlemont, Nov. 20, 1773: "Johnson shall spoil your books, Goldsmith pull your flowers, and Boswell talk to you; stay then if you can."   Hardy Francis, *Memoirs of the Political and Private Life of James Caulfield, Earl of Charlemont*, 2d. ed. (Ln., 1812), i, 347.

ary 2. It was carefully done and the first real composition of hers since *Shakespear Illustrated*. Easily second in rank among her novels, it lacks the originality and humor of the *Female Quixote*, but it excels them all in strength of character-drawing and in plot. It was well received as one of the "genteel" novels of the day, and although the second London edition did not appear until 1761, this time with a dedication to the Duchess of Newcastle, there was a Dublin edition in 1758 and there were two French translations of it issued in 1760. This novel shows at last where Mrs. Lennox has placed herself; like all her work from this time on it is strongly moral, and no situation is so tense as not to admit the inclusion of judicious moralizing. Although *Henrietta* is not so weak as to fall into a type, it foreshadows the Richardsonian convention which Mrs. Lennox, like so many women novelists of the day, is adopting, a rather colorless repetition of *Clarissa* and her sentiments without the remarkable analysis of feelings which was Richardson's especial gift. It shows an advance, however, in that the aura of romanticism that lent unreality to *Harriot Stuart* and the *Female Quixote* has disappeared and characters, especially people of fashion, are treated more incisively. As if Mrs. Lennox had lost her shallow girlish illusions of the glamor of wealth and fashion and saw the world about her more truthfully, if less rosily.

Her industry is unflagging. Almost before *Henrietta* is printed we find her contemplating a new work. The following letter to Dr. Thomas Birch informs of this as well as of the expressed approbation of that worthy but uninspired author :[41]

[41] From Sloane mss. 4312 in the British Museum. The Rev. Thomas Birch (1705-1766) was a well-known preacher and translator. In Boswell's *Life*, i, 159, we find the following: "it is circulated that Johnson considered Dr. Birch as a dull writer, and said of him: 'Tom Birch is as brisk as a bee in conversation; but no sooner does he take a pen in his hand, than it becomes a torpedo to him, and benumbs all his faculties.' That the literature of this country is much indebted to Birch's activity and diligence must certainly be acknowledged."

Sir,

I beg leave to return you my thanks for your agreeable present, and to assure you that I think myself highly honoured by the favourable mention you are pleased to make of me and my little writings: I wish you may approve of my plan for a new work which I am advised to publish by subscription, I send you one of my proposals and shall be extremely obliged to you if you will recommend my undertaking.   I am

Sir

Your obliged, and very
humble Servant

Charlotte Lennox

March 16, 1759.
at Mr. Austin's Engraver.
in great George Street
Hanover Square

What the "agreeable present" was I do not know.   It may, of course, have been financial assistance, but the tone of the letter does not imply that.   More probably it was the *Royal Society*, a history which had been painstakingly compiled by Dr. Birch in 1756-7,—at least it reads as though it had been a painstaking compilation.   The "favourable mention" may refer to one of the reviews of *Henrietta*, all of which were favorable.   I should choose the one in the *Critical Review*[42] as the one referred to, since it is longer and alludes more to her other writings than the others.

The "new work" was weighty enough to win the approval of even so learned a person as Dr. Birch.   As announced in 1760 it was *The Greek Theatre of Father Brumoy* in three volumes quarto.   It must have been a tedious task, possibly imposed by Millar and executed for the money of which she seems to have been in pressing need.   Her health was not good and in order to get the work done collaborators were called in, or offered their services.   The most distinguished

---

[42] *Critical Review* (Feb., 1758), ii, 122-30.

was Johnson, who furnished two of the essays in the last volume. As Boswell puts it:[43]

He, however, from that liberality which never failed, when called upon to assist other labourers in literature, found time to translate for Mrs. Lennox's English version of Brumoy, 'A Dissertation on the Greek Comedy', and 'The General Conclusion of the Book'.

The dedication signed by Mrs. Lennox is to the Prince of Wales, and, like the dedication of *Philander*, sounds as if it were written by Johnson. As Mrs. Lennox was ill and did little of the third volume herself, it is likely that she would get as much help as possible in the final tasks, and where would she more naturally turn for a dedication than to Johnson?

Her most substantial assistant was John Boyle, the Earl of Cork and Orrery (1707-1762), known today for *Remarks on the Life and Writings of Dr. Jonathan Swift*, that curious mingling of personal estimate of the Swift he knew and blind criticism of the writer of *Gulliver's Travels* and the *Battle of the Books*, who had offended his rigid moral principles. Berkeley said of him: "He would have been a man of genius, had he known how to set about it," but Johnson did not go so far: "He would have been a liberal patron if he had been rich." Mrs. Lennox had already dedicated *Shakespear Illustrated* to him, having perhaps shared Johnson's faith in his liberality and being more sanguine of his riches. His former translation of Pliny's *Epistles* and some acquaintance with him through Johnson made him a natural person for Mrs. Lennox to call on for assistance at this juncture. He wrote a preface in which he offered a compliment to the *Female Quixote* and *Henrietta*, and translated three essays at the beginning. The preface is adequate, but his translation is less easy than Mrs. Lennox's; hers, too, is least able in this work, where it is flowery in

[43] *Life*, i, 345.

the beginning and careless toward the end of the second volume when her illness made it difficult for her to continue. Johnson's is rather free and has a characteristic majesty and weight. The most skilful is that toward the beginning of the third volume done by a "young gentleman" who remains unidentified. One section each in the third volume is done by Dr. Gregory Sharpe, an excellent classical and oriental scholar and prebendary of Salisbury Cathedral; by Dr. James Grainger, friend of Bishop Percy, physician, poet, and translator, of whom Johnson said "he would do any good in his power"; and by John Bourryau, a pupil of Grainger's, whom he accompanied to the West Indies as tutor and companion. Mrs. Lennox's association with what the *Monthly Review* called her "noble and able Coadjutors" proves that she had come to enjoy, not fame since the *Female Quixote*, but a solid literary respectability and approbation.

Mrs. Lennox speaks for herself through the following letter to the Duchess of Newcastle:[44]

Madam,

As Your Grace has been pleased to permit me to dedicate some of my Works to You,[45] I take the opportunity of a new edition of my *Henrietta* to solicit that favour now. The first edition was so hurried, Madam, that I had not time to make an application to Your Grace, I therefore sent it into the world without any dedication, for having in my own mind devoted it to so illustrious a Patroness, any other name would not satisfy my ambition. The favourable reception this performance has met with, both at home, and abroad, where it has been translated several times, gives me more confidence to intreat that Your Grace will allow me to lay it at your feet: it is a debt of gratitude Madam which I am impatient to pay; I shall never forget Your goodness, Madam, nor the generosity with which Your Grace relieved my distress last Winter, and surely providence seem'd willing to give

[44] British Museum. Newcastle Papers. Add. Mss. 33067.

[45] Sully's *Memoirs* was dedicated to the Duke of Newcastle, but no work of Mrs. Lennox's other than *Henrietta* remains with a dedication to the Duchess.

success to the benevolent intention of Your Grace's present, I have been in the Country almost ever since, and the air, together with proper exercise has restored me to a very tollerable degree of health.

I have the comfort to hear from Mr. Stone that Your Grace continues Your favourable intentions with regard to Mr. Lennox, and this hope supports me in my present slavery to the Booksellers, whom I have the more mortification to see adding to their heaps by my labours, which scarce produce me a scanty and precarious subsistence. If Your Grace will do me the honour to signify Your pleasure to me with regard to the Dedication of *Henrietta*, a Message directed for me at the Mineral Water Warehouse in Bury Street St. James's, will come safe to my hands.

I am with the deepest respect

> Madam
> > Your Grace's
> > Most grateful and devoted Servant.
> > > Charlotte Lennox.

London Bury Street
October 6, 1760.

The Duchess accepted the proposed dedication of *Henrietta*, for it appeared in the second edition. As Mrs. Lennox had been ill and felt gratitude to the Duchess for her assistance we may suppose that she was eager that the dedication should be worthy of her benefactress and in spite of her "very tollerable degree of health" might be glad to have help in so important and delicate a compliment. What more natural at this time than for her to turn again to Johnson for the type of writing of which he had declared himself master and which he obviously regarded less as a burden than as an easy and generous favor to grant? The text of the dedication (see below, p. 127) with its echo in one sentence of an idea expressed by Johnson three years earlier in a review, the balance of the last sentence and the sentence containing "enlarged your knowledge, or refined your sentiments" argues for the belief that here Johnson again wrote for Charlotte.

The allusion to Mr. Lennox shows that they are still living together and that Mrs. Lennox is appealing for a favor for him. The immediate juxtaposition of Mrs. Lennox's "slavery to the booksellers" suggests that Mr. Lennox is still employed with Strahan or one of the booksellers in the "Trade" and that the favor was for the Duke's help in one of the attempts of such men as Tonson and Millar to obtain injunctions in the House of Lords against Donaldson and his kind, who were beginning to sell cheap editions of the classics of their own printing.[46] But since these arguments had little connection with the prices paid authors, Mrs. Lennox may be referring to an intention of the Duchess to procure for Mr. Lennox an appointment which would provide more than a "scanty and precarious subsistence" for his family, and her "slavery" is surely no misnomer for her frequent and lengthy translations; the *Memoirs* of Sully, the Countess of Berci, and Maintenon, the *Theatre of Father Brumoy*, all within four years, would mean toilsome days, without a novel and pastoral drama of her own creating.

From the *Female Quixote* through the *Theatre of Father Brumoy*, eight publications in all, Andrew Millar, according to Johnson "the Maecenas of the age", one who had "raised the price of literature", had been Mrs. Lennox's publisher and he was noted for his generosity to authors; but that may be remembered of him with more justice at the time of *Tom Jones* or the *Seasons* than in 1759, when he was declared bankrupt.

After Millar's bankruptcy Mrs. Lennox was connected with another bookseller, who is known to have lent money to Johnson from 1741-1760. This bookseller was John Newbery, of St. Paul's Churchyard, whom Prior describes thus:[47]

[46] Collins A. S., "Some Aspects of Copyright from 1700-1780." *The Library* (June, 1926), vii, 67-81.

[47] Prior, *The Life of Oliver Goldsmith*, 2 vols. (Ln., 1837), i, 340.

His ingenuity and amiable qualities rendered him soon generally respected. Writers of the first character sought his acquaintance, and in his friendship not infrequently found occasional alleviation of their most pressing wants. Among these were Dr. Johnson . . . and similar loans of which the evidences remain, were rendered to . . . Mrs. Lennox.

These loans were, no doubt, in connection with her magazine, *The Lady's Museum,* "consisting of a course of Female Education and Variety of Other Particulars for the Information and Amusement of Ladies," the first number of which appeared on March 1, 1760,[48] and the last on January 1, 1761, all eleven numbers published by Newbery. The publication of this magazine indicates that the actual rest taken to improve her health was short and if, as she tells the Duchess of Newcastle, she was in the country during much of the early part of that year she nevertheless prepared this magazine monthly for the press, doing much of the work herself. She made several translations for it, wrote some introductory comments for most of the numbers under the title of *The Trifler,* in which, in the fashion prevalent after Steele's Clarindas and Chloes, a young lady despite her blameless virtue and the most moral intentions is led astray, seduced, and her happiness forever gone with her chastity, while she derives, we feel sure, no small comfort from lamenting in public in order that other damsels may take warning. In this magazine first appeared Mrs. Lennox's novel, *Harriot and Sophia,* reprinted by Fletcher in 1762 as *Sophia.* The most conventional and least original of her novels, it has some interest today in that the two sisters, Harriot and Sophia, and their worldly and weakly sympathetic mother faintly suggest the two sisters, Elinor and Marianne, and the emotional Mrs. Dashwood of Jane Austen's *Sense and Sensibility.* A French translation was published in 1770.

In 1764 another part of *The Lady's Museum* was reprinted, the *History of the Count de Comminge,* under the title,

---

[48] Announced in *London Chronicle* Feb. 19, 1760, and every month thereafter through Feb. 28, 1761.

The History of the Marquis of Lussan and Isabella. A shift in names, a rapid change of plot at the end, and the inclusion of another episode are the only differences.

The Lady's Museum and the two romances reprinted from it mark the end of Mrs. Lennox's literary production for some years—until 1768-9. During this lapse of publication her children were born. On April 28, 1765, was baptized in St. Paul's Church, Covent Garden, Harriot Holles, the daughter of Alexander and Charlotte Lennox. The name Harriot may have been a family name connected with the earlier, happier days in America; at any rate Mrs. Lennox had used it twice already in her novels. The Holles, doubtless in compliment to Thomas Pelham-Holles, Duke of Newcastle, indicates Mrs. Lennox was still acknowledging favors from that house. Mrs. Lennox's son was born soon after her daughter although I have been unable to find any record of his baptism. References indicate that he was a little younger than the daughter, still a noisy "little boy" in 1777. Judging from the circumstances and occupations of Mrs. Lennox, I should think it most probable that he was born in 1766 or 7, although there is a possibility that he was not born until 1770-1, for during those years Mrs. Lennox's literary activity lapsed again.

With the birth of her children comes the end of Mrs. Lennox's early and most important period of literary production. Glancing back, we see that almost every year since 1749 marks the publication of some work by her. Four of these were translations, two were partly translation but contained some independent writing; the rest were her own compositions. Her works had been brought out by two printers of high repute, Millar and Newbery. She had been patronized by Lady Isabella Finch and the Duchess of Newcastle, perhaps by the Countess of Northumberland. Johnson is known to have written three dedications for her and he may have assisted with one or two more. When she was ill and unable to continue with the translation of Father Brumoy's *Greek Theatre* he came to her assistance with two

essays.   He gave her a banquet after the publication of her
first novel and crowned her with laurel.   He suggested the
task of collecting the sources of Shakespeare's plays and
contributed a chapter to the *Female Quixote*.   The same
printers and some of the same patrons served for both.
Acquaintance with the Earl of Cork and Orrery, Baretti,
Newbery, and Richardson they had in common.   According
to the following anecdote related by Fanny Burney in 1778
he introduced her to Richardson :[49]

I find she, among others, waited upon Dr. Johnson upon
her commencing writer, and he told us that, at her request,
he carried her to Richardson.   'Poor Charlotte Lennox!'
continued he: 'when we came to the house, she desired me
to leave her, for, says she, "I am under great restraint in
your presence, but if you leave me alone with Richardson I'll
give you a very good account of him"; however, I fear poor
Charlotte was disappointed, for she gave me no account
at all!'

Inauspicious as this meeting sounds, Richardson's own
letter[50] shows that the acquaintance was continued and states
his opinion that the writer of the *Female Quixote* has
genius.   By this novel Mrs. Lennox succeeded in winning
the commendation of both Fielding and Richardson and
although in its tendency toward burlesque it comes closer to
the type of *Joseph Andrews* than to *Pamela* the allusion to
Clarissa and the *Rambler* shows that as early as 1752 Mrs.
Lennox had declared herself of the moral school of Johnson
and Richardson.   Johnson paid her the honor of quoting
from her works in the *Dictionary*.   Under the definition of
"talent" he gave as illustration of its correct use "Persons
who possess the true *talent* of raillery are like comets; they
are seldom seen, and all at once admired and feared.—Female
Quixote."   Possibly she was one of the "very few" in this
anecdote Northcote relates :[51]

[49] D'Arblay, *Diary and Letters* (ed. Austin Dobson), i, 86.
[50] See below, p. 85.
[51] Northcote, *Memoirs of Sir Joshua Reynolds* (Phila., 1817), 119.

Several ladies being in company with Dr. Johnson, it was remarked by one of them, that a learned woman was by no means a rare character in the present age; when Johnson replied, 'I have known a great many ladies who knew Latin, but very few who knew English.'

We are able to gain some idea of Mrs. Lennox's appearance from the portrait done of her by Reynolds in 1761. In Sir Joshua's "Pocket-book" for January, 1761,[52] she is on the list of sitters and there is a note in the Diary of January, 1761,[53] "Mrs. Lennox send to Mr. Selwin." This must have been George Selwin, the well-known wit and friend of Horace Walpole, who sat for his portrait in the same year. As he was a patron of Reynolds the note may refer to the portrait or it may mean that the latter was interceding with Selwin for aid for Mrs. Lennox. That he himself assisted her we know from an allusion later:[54]

Or Mrs. Lenox, another literary lady, but less learned than Mrs. Carter—for her translations of the Greek are through the French—and less favoured by fortune than most about her. She is just now in great distress, as the apartments which have been granted her in Somerset House are about to be pulled down in the course of Sir William Chambers's projected rebuilding, and she will pour out her griefs and fears in Sir Joshua's sympathizing ear, or to Johnson, who, tyrant as he is to the strong, has always a kindly heart for the weak and suffering.

The portrait, though listed as "unfinished,"[55] shows a lady with some pretensions to beauty, even at the age of forty-

---

[52] Leslie and Taylor, *Life and Times of Sir Joshua Reynolds* (Ln., 1865), i, 200.

[53] From the Diary in the library of the Royal Academy.

[54] Leslie and Taylor, *Id.*, ii, 10.

[55] Graves and Cronin, *A History of the Works of Sir Joshua Reynolds* (Ln., 1899), ii, 579. The description here confuses Mrs. Lennox's portrait with that of another Mrs. Lennox or of a Lady Lennox. The diary note is printed in iv, 1480.

one. Two engravings were made from it: one by Bartholozzi in 1793 for Harding's *Shakespeare Illustrated*[56] in
which Mrs. Lennox is shown as twelfth in a group of
Shakespearean critics; another by Cook in 1813 for the
memoir of Mrs. Lennox in the *Lady's Monthly Museum*.
The latter I am reproducing here. Fanny Burney, Mrs.
Thrale, or Miss Hawkins, all of whom decry Mrs. Lennox's
charm and abilities, might remind us that Horace Walpole
said,[57] "Mr. Reynolds seldom succeeds with women" and
that Johns Williams,[58] a contemporary critic, wrote, "To his
male sitters he was tolerably accurate, but with the ladies he
was a most unlicensed flatteur; and according to the evidence
of his valued canvass, it was of little significance to observation whether the Omnipotent had made a Grace or a Trulla,
as he uniformly arrayed each with the dignity of the
Queen of Heaven and the fascinating smiles of Hebe."
Besides the portrait the only evidence of the charms of
Mrs. Lennox comes from the early poems to her in the
Gentleman's Magazine. One is tempted to find an argument for them in the general disfavor with which she was
regarded by the women of the period while the men unite
in finding her worthy of regard, assistance, or sympathy.

By 1765 Mrs. Lennox had made a name for herself in
literary London. Having left behind her in 1735 the colony
of New York, the familiar Hudson, the fort at Albany, a
mother with whom she was uncongenial, and a military father
whom she idolized, she had been thrown upon her own
resources at an early age. She had tried the stage and writing poetry. From the beginning her attempts at writing had
met with encouragement and praise. Her first novel won
her the attention and continued kindness of the man who
was to gain a peculiar ascendency over the ideas and literature of his age. Her next novel earned general acclaim
and the commendation of the two leading novelists of the

---

[56] In the Barton Collection of the Boston Public Library.
[57] Leslie and Taylor, *Life and Times of Reynolds*, i, 170.
[58] Williams, *Memoirs of the Royal Academicians* (Ln., 1796), 68.

Sir J. Reynolds Pinxt.   H.R. Cook Sculp.

COOK ENGRAVING OF REYNOLDS' PORTRAIT OF MRS. LENNOX

day, however opposed they were to each other.   Her portrait was painted by the popular court painter, and her name was connected with translations of importance in which she was assisted by men of learning and position.   At a time when periodicals were rife, she, too, was responsible for one for a twelvemonth.   She had married at twenty-seven a man who at first shared her interests, but who became not only less congenial but also more of a burden so that she felt responsible for the financial support of the family.   Domestic duties now claimed her, and we know little more of her until the end of the decade.

CHAPTER II

Life of Mrs. Lennox (cont.), 1765–1804

MRS. LENNOX'S next venture was writing for the stage. The following letter to Garrick shows that she had known him for some years and had reason to expect friendly assistance from him.[1]

Sir,

The success which has lately attended writers for the stage, and some of them too, of my own sex, has encouraged me to write a comedy, which I beg you will read with your usual candor, and that indulgence you have always shown for my writings. You will find that I have pursued a hint you gave me some years ago, which has furnished me with one of the most interesting incidents in the whole piece; you may depend upon it that every alteration, and amendment which you judge necessary, will be readily, and thankfully admitted. I am so fully persuaded of your justice and benevolence, that I do not think you will reject my play unless you find it wholly destitute of merit, and by accepting it you will confer a great obligation upon me, and put it in the power of my friends to serve me, in a way which they have often wishd to serve me, and often recommended to me. But what ever be your determination Sir, I earnestly entreat you to acquaint me with it soon; suspence is a most uneasy state of mind, and on this occasion, delay will be productive of great inconveniencies.

> I am
>
> Sir
> Your obligd humble
> Servant
>
> Charlotte Lennox

I have not yet written the concluding lines, but that can be done, when the piece has received your corrections. Somerset-house October 25, 1768

[1] British Museum Add. Mss. 29300 (in pencil—"to David Garrick"). Printed in *The Private Correspondence of David Garrick* (Ln., 1831), i, 319.

Still under the pressure of want, Mrs. Lennox seems hopeful that the stage may be more remunerative than translations. Garrick did not accept her play, but it was brought out at the rival theatre of Covent Garden on February 18, 1769. The play was entitled *The Sister* and was based upon her novel *Henrietta*. Garrick's hint may have been that the novel had dramatic possibilities or that Mrs. Autumn was a possible comic character for the stage. The performance was so unusually distressing that it was widely commented upon in newspapers and magazines. This account appeared in *Lloyd's Evening Post* the following Monday:

On Saturday night, during the performance of the first act of the new comedy, called *The Sister*, part of the audience shewed great marks of disapprobation, which interrupted the piece for some time; it went on, notwithstanding great opposition, until the beginning of the fifth act, when the noise was so great that the actors were unable to proceed in their parts. After some time Mr. Powell addressed the house, hoping they would be so kind as to give the play a patient hearing, at the same time assuring them, that if it was found unworthy of their encouragement, it should be performed no more; this produced an intermission of the disturbance until the conclusion of the comedy, when it seemed to be almost universally condemned. Mr. Smith, however, entreated permission to give it out for this evening, but we are assured the Author, having heard the reception it met with has entirely withdrawn it from the stage.

That the attack was premeditated and malicious is shown by the following anecdote told by Langton:[2]

Dr. Goldsmith, upon occasion of Mrs. Lennox's bringing out a play, said to Dr. Johnson at the Club, that a person had advised him to go and hiss it, because she had attacked Shakespeare in her book called *Shakespeare Illustrated*. Johnson. 'And did you not tell him he was a rascal?' Goldsmith. 'No, sir, I did not. Perhaps he might not mean what he said.' J. 'Nay, sir, if he lied, it is a different thing.'

[2] *Life*, iv, 10.

Colman, who was present, slily said (but it is believed Dr.
Johnson did not hear him,) 'Then the proper expression
should have been,—Sir, if you don't lie, you're a rascal.'

Far from hissing it Goldsmith wrote the epilogue for it,
said by Forster to be the best epilogue he ever composed.
In it he does mock the moral trend of the play, which belongs
in the school of sentimental drama, but the general tone of it
is friendly.   I have not certainly discovered who was responsible for the attack, but Johnson said later that Mrs. Lennox
suspected Cumberland, the dramatist who was famous for
his jealousy and irritability for many years before Sheridan
pilloried him as Sir Fretful Plagiary.

Mrs. Lennox had been granted apartments in Somerset
House, perhaps through the generosity of the Duke of Newcastle, and she continued to live there until 1773, when it was
being remodelled.   She apparently called for aid upon other
members of the Club than Garrick or Goldsmith, because it
is to this time that reference is made by Leslie and Taylor:
". . she will pour out her griefs and fears in Sir Joshua's
sympathizing ear, or to Johnson, who, tyrant as he is to the
strong, has always a kindly heart for the weak and suffering."

The decade of 1770 found her literary activity lapsing.
In 1774 appeared her last translation from the French:
Memoirs and Penitential Prayers, written by the Duchess de
la Vallière.   This was much shorter than her other translations, only one volume octavo, and was indifferently noticed
in the magazines.   In spite of her first crushing failure she
turned to the stage again, and once more made her approach
through Garrick.[3]

Sir,

enclosed is the letter we agreed I should write, but in sending it you, I must beg leave to declare, (for the sake of my
reputation for candor, which I do not think I have ever yet
forfeited) that what relates to Mrs. Yates, tho' wrote ex-

[3] Victoria and Albert Museum, Forster Collection, *Garrick Letters*,
vol. 28, folio 28.

pressly for her perusal, are my real sentiments. Mr. Colman can tell you that I spoke in the same manner to him, and at a time, when it was heresy to say she was equal to her great theatric rival Mrs. Barry; I was a bold and daring schismatic, and always maintaind she was superiour to her. This indeed following the rules of politeness would not be fit to say to you, if Mrs. Barry held the same rank in your house which she did last winter, but as things are, I conceive I am at liberty to speak my sentiments. You will perceive that this article of flattery is a nice point with me. I own it —I would not for any consideration fall under the suspicion of it—it is true, that when I praise it is with warmth, with a kind of enthusiasm—such is my natural temper, but I mean what I say, and it is well worth a life of habitual sincerity, to purchase the pleasure of being beleived [*sic*] when one gives vent to the effusions of one's heart, as at present when I tell you that your disinterested, kind, and noble manner of proceeding with   proves you to be as good a Man, as you are a great Actor.   and I think no flight of flattery can go beyond that plain and simple truth.

I am, Sir, your much obligd humble servant,

Charlotte Lennox

August 4, 1774.

The version of this letter printed in Garrick's *Correspondence*[4] supplies the words "Sir Joshua Reynolds's nephew's play" after "proceeding with". In that volume this letter of Mrs. Lennox's immediately follows the letter of Reynolds to Garrick, dated August 2 and asking Garrick to produce this play, and Garrick's own notes on the play. A mistaken association because of this proximity is the only reason I can see for the editor's interpolation here. It could not possibly refer to Garrick's action as early as this, for his first response was to tell Reynolds he could not produce it for two years, and after Reynolds' angry reply of September 4, he wrote on September 5 a conciliatory letter, which might suit better Mrs. Lennox's description of a month before. A postscript on this letter of September fifth as reproduced

---

[4] *The Private Correspondence of David Garrick*, i, 647-8.

from the manuscript in the Massachusetts Historical Society shows that he had not yet received the manuscript of the play to be read.[5]   Consequently Boaden's guess is misleading and Mrs. Lennox's reference must be to some other act of Garrick's.   The name of either of two people might be supplied here, Cumberland or Samuel Foote.   During this decade the former was constantly acknowledging Garrick's fairness and generosity.   But Mrs. Lennox's description of Garrick's kindness and nobility characterizes his treatment of Samuel Foote more accurately than that of anyone else.   After 1769 Foote was threatening to mimic Garrick at the Shakespeare Jubilee, and alternately threatened him and borrowed money from him during the succeeding years.[6] Apparently he had borrowed from him in the autumn of 1774, as he writes on September 15, from France:[7]

You need not doubt but I shall be happy to hear from you: my epistolary debts it will be always in my power to pay; the others I pay when I can: is it in man to do more?

These two names are only suggestions where Mrs. Lennox has herself left no clue; and I mention them without the assurance I feel in correcting the interpolation of "Sir Joshua Reynolds's nephew's play".

The letter Mrs. Lennox enclosed I have not found in manuscript, but as printed in the *Correspondence* it reads as follows:[8]

August 4th, 1774.

Sir,

I need not tell you, who are so good a critic in the French drama, that Racine's "Bajazet" is allowed by all good judges to be one of the best of his tragedies; my own humble

---

[5] *Pineapples of Finest Flavour* (ed. D. M. Little, Cambridge, Mass., 1930), 68.

[6] Davies Thomas, *Memoirs of the Life of David Garrick* (Ln., 1781, 3d ed.), ii, ch. 48.

[7] *Private Corr. of David Garrick*, ii, 5.

[8] *Id.*, i, 647-8.

opinion coinciding with this general one, I resolved to translate it, and by hazarding a few alterations, adapt it to the taste of an English audience. The principal female character in this play, if acted by Mrs. Yates, would alone, I think, ensure its success. The haughty, the impassioned, the beautiful Roxana, seems drawn expressly for such an actress. She is in her look and acting the very image of the poet's thought, and I had her in my eye in every line that I translated of this part. The alterations I propose to make will be in the fifth act, which is not busy enough for our taste. I think it might be turned entirely new, and by one of those sudden revolutions, common enough in the Turkish government, Bajazet, instead of being murdered, might be placed upon the throne. As for Roxana, if the general plan of the play makes it necessary that she should die, her death might be rendered more affecting by some circumstances of terror and pity, which are not found in the original.

Upon the whole, Sir, I submit it to your judgment; give it a reading, and if you think it may be made fit for representation, I will be guided by your advice in every alteration to be made in it.

> I am, Sir, your very humble servant,
>
> Charlotte Lennox.

In May of that year Garrick had been writing to Mrs. Yates to persuade her to come to Drury Lane for two years in the place of Mrs. Barry, but in his last communication about it[9] "Mrs. Yates had two ladies with her, and would not accept of the terms." Evidently the letter succeeded in its purpose, for Mrs. Yates acted at Drury Lane the next two winters.

Mrs. Mary Ann Yates was an actress of distinction who had been with Garrick in 1754 and whom he thought splendid in the tragic rôles. Apparently he wanted her for leading parts in French adaptations the coming winter and asked Mrs. Lennox to write a letter which would influence her to come. There was some friendship between the two women, according to the early biographies of Mrs. Lennox, but the only definite information I have found was the

---

[9] *Private Corr. of Garrick*, i, 627.

comment of the Rev. William Beloe, who considered himself most fortunate in meeting the actress soon after he came
up to London[10] "for at her house he immediately became
acquainted with some of the most distinguished literary
characters of the time.   There he met Murphy, Home, the
author of Douglas, Richard Cumberland, Hoole, ... old
Macklin, Mrs. Lennox, Mrs. Brooke, and various other eminent individuals, all of whom alas! have now paid the last
awful debt of nature!"   If the recollections of Mr. Beloe are
accurate, Mrs. Lennox had widened her circle of friends to
include many of the people connected with the stage at the
time, a natural concomitant to her interest in play-writing.

The adaptation of *Bajazet* is not to be found in any available contemporary records of the stage; consequently it may
be fairly taken for granted that Garrick disapproved of the
project or was too busy with other plays to consider producing it.

His failure to produce two plays Mrs. Lennox had offered
him did not create any coolness between them, for the next
year he had evidently suggested another attempt to her and
reproached her with indifference to the suggestion.   The
following letter to Garrick indicates clearly Mrs. Lennox's
continued dependence upon her own literary projects for
support and her desire to write for the stage.[11]

August 20th, 1775.

Sir,

When your letter was left for me, I was confined to my
bed by a fever: I am now better and hope to be able to
attend your summons to the Adelphi.   Indeed you wrong me
if you suppose I did not take pains.   It is true I depended
upon your assistance; you permitted me to do so, and I
well know how easy it is for you to make that piece as pleas-

[10] Beloe William, *Sexagenarian* (Ln., 1817), i, 401.

[11] *Private Corr. of Garrick*, ii, 77.   The "others" referred to in the
letter may have been Colman and Goldsmith, who wrote the prologue
and epilogue for *The Sister*, both of whom had written successful
plays.

ing as any we have had for a long time.   I am not indiffer-
ent to theatrical rewards; could I obtain them, they would
assist me to bring up my little boy and my girl; but having
once failed, when I had to a certain degree pleased myself,
and several others whose judgment I relied on more than my
own, I am grown diffident, so diffident that, if I have any
genius, I dare not trust it.   A little success would embolden
me, and this success I hope to owe to you; and I shall always
be ready to acknowledge to others, with the same sincerity
that I do now to you, that if from this piece I should have
any share either of reputation or profit, it will be entirely
your gift.

> I am, Sir, your much obliged servant,
>
> Charlotte Lennox.

Unaccustomed to rebuffs Mrs. Lennox was leaning heavily
upon Garrick's experience before she risked another misfortune before the public.   He must have accorded her that
assistance she asked, because on the evening of November
9th, 1775,[12] *Old City Manners* was given at the Drury Lane
theatre.   This adaptation from *Eastward Hoe!* by Ben
Jonson, Marston, and Chapman was favorably received and
ran for several nights successively, then intermittently
through December.   Mrs. Lennox was as good as her word
and in the printed edition which appeared on November 28,[13]
she advertised after the title-page:

It is with great satisfaction that Mrs. Lennox takes this
opportunity to acknowledge her obligations to Mr. Garrick,
for recommending to her, the Alteration of *Eastward Hoe*,
and for his very friendly assistance throughout this Comedy.

Earlier in this same year of 1775 were published "Proposals for Printing by Subscription, dedicated to the Queen,
a new and elegant Edition of the Original Works of Mrs.
Charlotte Lennox."   These proposals were advertised during
March in four newspapers, but I have been able to find no
copy of them extant, though Bishop Percy is said to have

[12] *Lloyd's Evening Post* (Nov. 10, 1775).
[13] *Public Advertiser* (Nov. 28, 1775).

had one.   They were written by Johnson, and Boswell gives
us some idea of the contents:[14]

In his diary, January 2, I find this entry: 'Wrote Charlotte's Proposals.'   But indeed, the internal evidence would
have been quite sufficient.   Her claim to the favour of the
publick was thus enforced: 'Most of the pieces, as they
appeared singly, have been read with approbation, perhaps
above their merit, but of no great advantage to the writer.
She hopes, therefore, that she shall not be considered as too
indulgent to vanity, or too studious of interest, if, from that
labour which has hitherto been chiefly gainful to others, she
endeavours to obtain at last some profit for herself and her
children.   She cannot decently enforce her claim by the
praise of her own performances; nor can she suppose, that,
by the most artful and laboured address, any additional notice
could be procured to a publication, of which Her Majesty has
condescended to be the Patroness.'

It was probably in connection with this edition of her works
that Mrs. Lennox wrote Reynolds in 1773:[15]

Addressed To   Sir Joshua Reynolds
Leicester Square.

Sir

So many years have interven'd since I had the pleasure
of your acquaintance, that I know not whether there is not
some impropriety in asking a favor of you—but I depend
greatly upon that benevolence in your character, which I had
formerly an opportunity of observing and which if report
be true you still possess in a very high degree.   It is in your
power to assist me in a little affair in which my interest is
concern'd—if you will give me a quarter of an hour, I will
explain the nature of my request to you, and if you will likewise let me know in a line by the penny post, what day,
and what hour it will be convenient for you to see me you
will greatly oblige

Sir/   Your very humble servant

Charlotte Lennox.

[14] *Life*, ii, 289.
[15] This letter, A. L. S. 2 sheets quarto, is in the collection of R. B.
Adam, Buffalo.   I owe this copy to the courtesy of Mrs. Adam.

My compliments to
Miss Reynolds
Great Tower Hill

The corner of Muscovey Court.
May 20 1773.

N.B. The favor above requested, was to give Mrs. Lennox designs for Copper Plates to adorn a new Edition, with great improvements, of the Female Quixote.

Sir Joshua gave her more than the requested "quarter of an hour"; or the brief interview may have led to a renewal of their friendship, because Reynolds dined with her once in that year :[16] "Besides Sir Joshua's regular club and tavern dinners . . . . and his evenings with the blues, Mrs. Montagu, Mrs. Ord, and Mrs. Vesey (and once with Mrs. Lennox)." The note explaining that the request was for copper plates for a new edition of the *Female Quixote* was added in a different handwriting, perhaps by an early possessor of the letter. The new edition of the *Female Quixote* was in all probability a part or the nucleus of the edition of her original works for which Johnson wrote the proposals. As it never appeared it is impossible to know what answer Sir Joshua made. The next edition of the *Female Quixote* appeared in 1783 in the *Novelist's Magazine* and was adorned with plates signed "Strothard del., Walker sculp.", except the third which had "Heath sculp.".

Since Mrs. Lennox's literary ventures were so scattered after 1765 we are not surprised to find that she was earning money in other ways. Our information comes from Miss Hawkins' *Memoirs*; and although it is sketchy and animated by prejudice it offers some detail of Mrs. Lennox's life at this period. In the reference already quoted from Miss Hawkins she relates how Mrs. Lennox quarreled with Baretti because he took more notice of her little girl than she approved. Other references show that she was for a

---

[16] Leslie and Taylor, *Life of Reynolds*, ii, 52.

time in charge of the daughters of Saunders Welch. This gentleman was a police-magistrate of the city, a successor and friend of Fielding, a man of property and of literary tastes. He[17] "lived to see his house the resort of persons distinguished in the elegant arts, and the *belles lettres*"; and "away from business, he was not only the associate of men of genius, but, in some instances, their patron." His eldest daughter, Mary or Maria, was very beautiful but not talented. She married Nollekens the painter, and[18] "on the authority of her sister, . . . she is the original of Johnson's Pekuah in Rasselas. If the intimate attention of such a man was an honour, she consequently had much to boast of, and indeed he treated both the ladies as he might have done nieces." Anne, the other daughter, is described by Boswell in 1778 as[19] "a young lady of uncommon talents and literature" and Miss Hawkins supplies that she was as plain as her sister was handsome.[20] "Neither of the young ladies, I must confess, had a fair chance for what is called success in life. When taken from a nurse, I believe they had an antiquated *gouvernante*, a French woman of the old school, who managed the one very ill and the other not at all. The beauty was, after some experimental plans, put under the care of Mrs. Lennox, a lady of too eccentric a genius to render any service to a young person of less than moderate intellect and whose ideas were bounded by the fashions of dress." Unsuited as Mrs. Lennox may have been to the elder daughter, she was more congenial with the younger, and[21] "little Nanny cultivated the friendship, and enjoyed the intimate conversation of Johnson and his friends, Charlotte Lennox, Baretti, Paradise, Sir Joshua Reynolds, the family of Mr. Wilton, and many others of the first colloquial talents of the time." Miss Hawkins did not, however, approve of Mrs.

---

[17] Hawkins L. M., *Memoirs* (Ln., 1824), i, 51, 53.
[18] *Id.*, i, 57.
[19] *Life*, iii, 217.
[20] Hawkins, *Memoirs*, i, 53-4.
[21] *Id.*, i, 63-4.

Lennox. She was in the habit of visiting her father's court and recalled[22] "one occasion we expected amusement, for which we had only the disgusting substitution of Mrs. Charlotte Lennox's *manual* conflict with her maid." She further revealed Mrs. Lennox's domestic difficulties when telling of Anne Welch:[23]

Her natural quietness of temper made her a cool spectator of many circumstances that would have implicated others. Her intimacy with Charlotte Lennox who, though one of Johnson's favorites, was, I think, as little entitled to favour as most women, afforded her opportunity of observing with a contemplative eye, obliquities which to many would have been intolerable. When residing with her sister in the house of Mrs Lennox, notwithstanding the want of all order and method, all decorum of appearance, and regularity of proceeding, she endeavored to extract from the mind of her hostess what was good, and smiled at all the rest. But it must have been a *dernier ressort* to place her, or any female, in a family thus ill-ordered, and with a woman whom I saw in a court of justice fairly pitted against a low female servant, who had endeavored to obtain a compensation for ill words and hard blows received from her mistress.

This second reference to the court scene fairly illustrates Miss Hawkins' flair for the unpleasant. Her phrase about Mrs. Lennox, "as little entitled to favour as most women" might be broadened to "people" and taken as a motto for the memoirs. Surely Mrs. Lennox was not so ill fitted to guide young ladies as Miss Hawkins implies, for, besides bringing up a daughter of her own, she had enunciated in *The Lady's Museum* through 1760-1 many ideas on the education of daughters, ideas which should have accorded with the most exemplary of that day. It is always possible that she was more efficient in theory than in practice. Through these allusions appears still another bond between Mrs. Lennox and Johnson, a mutual interest in the Misses Welch;

[22] Hawkins, *Memoirs*, ii, 13.
[23] *Id.*, i, 70.

Mrs. Lennox's care of them may have come from Johnson's suggestion or they may simply have met in the same circles, since Mrs. Lennox was ranked among "the first colloquial talents" of the day.

Mrs. Lennox is rarely mentioned among the "blues". Leslie, in his life of Reynolds, is the only writer who gives us any picture of Mrs. Lennox as one of that literary circle.[24] Since she knew and apparently conversed with Garrick, Goldsmith, and Reynolds, it is surprising if she was not occasionally present at evening gatherings,—those evening conversaziones at Mrs. Ord's where Leslie mentions her as the fourth after Mrs. Montague, Mrs. Chapone, and Mrs. Carter in the "deep-blue" section of the circle, the group more serious and less charming than that of Mrs. Vesey, Mrs. Thrale, and Mrs. Cholmondeley. Her comparative absence from the social records may be most easily accounted for by her penury; as Leslie says, she was less favored by fortune than those about her. That she ranked with the leading literary ladies of the time is proved by her inclusion as one of the nine living Muses of Great Britain in the engraving bearing that title which appeared in the *Ladies' Pocket-Book* of 1778.[25] The painting is by Richard Samuel, a portrait painter and engraver, and an exhibiter in the Royal Academy from 1772-1779. His "Portraits in the Characters of the Muses in the Temple of Apollo" was exhibited in 1779,[26] and the inference is that the engraving was taken from that portrait. The "Muses" were "Miss Carter, Mrs. Barbauld, Mrs. Angelica Kauffman, on the Right hand; Mrs. Sheridan, in the Middle; Mrs. Lenox, Mrs. Macaulay, Miss More, Mrs. Montague, and Mrs. Griffith on the Left hand."

[24] Leslie and Taylor, *Life of Reynolds*, ii, 10.

[25] The engraving is in the print collection of the British Museum. I owe the reproduction here to the kindness of F. Sidgwick, esq., of Sidgwick and Jackson.

[26] Graves A., *The Royal Academy of Arts*, 1769-1904 (Ln., 1906), vii, 11.

Samuel Adm   *Pine Sculp*

The **NINE LIVING MUSES** of **GREAT BRITAIN**.

Mrs Carter, Mrs Barbauld, Mrs Angelica Kauffman, in the Right hand; Mrs Sheridan, in the Middle; Mrs Lenox, Mrs Macaulay, Miss More, Mrs Montague, and Mrs Griffith, on the Left hand

We have few comments on her from the ladies of the day, and these are usually connected with her work. Thus Mrs. Carter and Miss Talbot did not approve of *The Art of Coquetry* and Lady Mary Wortley Montagu was shocked by her attack upon Lady Isabella Finch in *Harriot Stuart*. She also disapproved of the *Female Quixote*, but Miss Talbot found it "whimsical, and not at all low" and Miss Highmore and Miss Mulso (Mrs. Chapone) spoke of "Lady Arabella" as familiarly as of a friend. Fanny Burney quotes Mrs. Thrale:[27] "But Mrs. Thrale says that tho' her books are generally approved, nobody likes her." She supports Mrs. Thrale by the gusto with which she relates the ill-success of Charlotte's first meeting with Richardson. Her other comment shows no warmer liking for Mrs. Lennox. This is not to be wondered at, since she was in the awkward position of explaining Johnson's expressed preference for Mrs. Lennox over three of his favorites, one of them herself. She is giving an account of the visit of Mr. Turbulent in 1791:[28]

He was eager to inquire of me who was Mrs. Lenox? He had been reading, like all the rest of the world, Boswell's Life of Dr. Johnson, and the preference there expressed of Mrs. Lenox to all other females had filled him with astonishment, as he had never even heard her name.

These occasional sallies of Dr. Johnson, uttered from local causes and circumstances, but all retailed verbatim by Mr. Boswell, are filling all sorts of readers with amaze, except the small part to whom Dr. Johnson was known, and who, by acquaintance with the power of the moment over his unguarded conversation, know how little of his solid opinion was to be gathered from his accidental assertions.

Like many other friends of Johnson after they had seen themselves in Boswell's *Journal of a Tour to the Hebrides* and *Life*, she is uneasy in that startlingly vivid light, and

[27] D'Arblay, *Diary and Letters* (ed. Dobson), i, 86.
[28] *Id.*, iv, 476.

resentful of the man who gave these anecdotes to an inquisitive public.

During the next few years we have evidence of the continued friendship between Johnson and Mrs. Lennox. In 1777 we find her writing to Johnson:[29]

Sir

You cannot imagine the pleasure it gave me to hear you say you would come and eat apple dumplings of my making. You may be sure I will hold you to your promise, but alas! apples will not be ripe this long time, and I am impatient for your company. Suppose you were to try my hand at a gooseberry tart—if I might venture to say it without being thought vain, I could tell you that my tarts have been admired—indeed you will make me very happy by naming a day for another visit to my cottage, and I will take care that you shall not be tried with the noise of my little boy, who I am sensible was very troublesome when you was here. Mr. Lennox is so desirous of recovering his property out of the hands of the booksellers, that he gives me leave to take any measures that shall be judged proper—it will be necessary to have the advice of some gentleman of the law, I am not known to Mr. Murphy,[30] but if you will be so good to mention my affairs to him, and let me know where he lives, I will call upon him. The person who leaves this at your house, will call again for an answer, which if you please may be left with your servant for him. Dear Sir if you write me a line, tell me in one word if there are any hopes of a reprieve for poor Dr. Dodd. I was sadly shock'd when I heard of the determination of the Council.

I am Sir Your oblig'd
humble Servant

Charlotte Lennox

Marybon June 17 (1777)
No. 7 Nottingham Street near
    Marybon Church

[29] *The R. B. Adam Library relating to Dr. Samuel Johnson and his Era.* (Ln. and N. Y., 1929) Miscellaneous Autographs, iii, 152-3.

[30] Mr. Murphy is without doubt Arthur Murphy (1727-1805), actor, playwright, and barrister. He took up law in 1757 and retired from the bar in 1788. He was a friend of Johnson.

Dr. Dodd was the famous preacher of London who had forged the name of Lord Chesterfield to a bond, but who had won the interest and sympathy of many prominent people. Johnson wrote a sermon which Dr. Dodd preached in Newgate on June 7th, and also wrote a petition to the king for him.[31] But the mayor pressed the case and Dr. Dodd was hanged at Tyburn on June 27th, 1777. Not only Mrs. Lennox but also many others of Johnson's circle must have been "sadly shock'd" at this summary enforcement of the sentence. The trial took up a great deal of space in the periodicals of the day, especially in the *Gentleman's Magazine.*

This letter bears out Miss Hawkins' strictures on Mrs. Lennox as a successful guide to the young; but if there was a "want of all order and method" in her home there were the compensations of tasty apple dumplings and gooseberry tarts.

The mention of Mr. Lennox being desirous of getting his property out of the hands of the booksellers and of his needing the advice of a gentleman of the law is elucidated by the following letter from Mrs. Lennox to Johnson recently published by the Rylands Library and placed by the editor, rightly, I think, in 1778.[32]

Marybon May 29 (1778)

Sir

Although I have no answer to my last letter, yet I venture to write again about my little affairs, and beg you will let me know when I may call upon you—I saw Mr. Dodsley yesterday, and he told me they had printed another edition of Sully's Memoirs—I apprehend they had no right to do this without my consent, it is more than fourteen years since that book was first published; and about a year ago, I offerd to give them my corrected copy for a reasonable consideration, which Dodsley in the name of the partners refusd—and now

[31] *Papers Written by Dr. Johnson and Dr. Dodd in 1777.* Printed from the originals in the possession of A. Edward Newton (ed. R. W. Chapman, Oxford, 1926).

[32] *Bulletin of the John Rylands Library* (Manchester, 1932), xvi, 56, Letter XXV.

they have reprinted it without consulting me although by the late decision concerning literary property the copy is mine—I am advisd to publish it for myself in numbers, and if the partners expect to sell another edition, I have some reason to hope that I may have success by publishing it in this manner, as the purchase will be so much easier—but I must be speedy, for Dodsley owned the book was almost ready—it will be necessary I suppose to draw up a little address to the publick explaining my reasons for publishing Sully myself, and in this manner—this favour I earnestly entreat of you—as likewise that you will appoint a day for my calling upon you—if the bearer is so fortunate as to find you at home he will bring me your answer, but if that should not happen I send my direction again lest my former letter should be lost

I am Sir
Your most hum^e Servt

C. Lennox.

No 7 Notingham Street,
near the Church Marybon.
To Doctor Johnson
Bolt Court Fleet Street.

Mr. Lennox's "property" is obviously his wife's earlier works, which under the statute of 1709 would return to her ownership after fourteen years. The decision of the House of Lords given Feb. 22, 1774, against perpetual copyright, upon the appeal of Donaldson in behalf of the Scotch editors, had so changed the position of such firms as Dodsley's that authors were beginning to reclaim their property. Mrs. Lennox would naturally seek Sully's *Memoirs*, since it was the one of her translations that had been twice pirated in cheap editions in Scotland. As there are two editions of Sully's *Memoirs* printed by J. Rivington, J. Dodsley, etc. in 1778 and as one is in 5 vols. instead of the 6 vols. 1763 and one 1778 edition and bears on the title-page, instead of simply "Translated from the French.", "Translated from the French, by the Author of the Female Quixote . . . A New Edition." we may assume that through Johnson's intervention and the efforts of Mr. Lennox and A. Murphy Dodsley's were persuaded to take Mrs. Lennox's "corrected copy for a reasonable consideration" and bring it out as a new edition, allowing the edition which "Dodsley owned . . . was almost ready" and which probably was released before Mrs. Lennox's opposition succeeded in becoming formidable, to stand.

Another letter from Mrs. Lennox to Johnson is in the Rylands collection:[33]

Mary-bon Monday (1778)

Dear Sir

Mr. Lennox thinks a hundred and fifty Copies will be sufficient, we are both greatly obligd to you for so kindly undertaking to manage this little affair—permit me only to hint that as it is of great consequence to me to have the book presented to His Majesty, before I am quite forgot, the sooner you begin to treat with Mr. Strahan the better.

I am Sir
Your grateful humble
Servt
Charlotte Lennox

Doctor Johnson
N[r] eight Bolt Court
Fleet Street

As Mrs. Lennox is still in Mary-bon and it is after Johnson has moved to Bolt-Court it is after 1776 and before 1784; otherwise I see no reason for putting the letter in a specific year or for assuming the book is the *Memoirs of Sully* as Wright does in editing the letter. The hundred and fifty copies would scarcely be a number chosen for as proven a success as Sully's *Memoirs*; it is little likely that a book that had been in the public eye for so long a time, in so many formats, dedicated to the Duke of Newcastle, would be chosen to have presented to the king; the second edition of Sully's *Memoirs* put out by Dodsley in the year 1778 as a new edition and with the "author of the Female Quixote" on the title-page indicates an amicable arrangement of

[33] *Bulletin of the John Rylands Library* (Manchester, 1932), xvi, 57, Letter XXVI.

Mrs. Lennox's altercation with him and removes the occasion for her printing of the *Memoirs*. On the other hand, Johnson had written "Charlotte's proposals" in 1775 for an edition of her original works dedicated to the Queen and I am inclined to think that the "hundred and fifty Copies" refer to the first volume of the proposed edition, which would probably include her *Poems* and first novel *Harriot Stuart*, neither of which had passed to a second edition in spite of the *Proposals* twice published for printing the poems by subscription. The number would in no sense be inappropriate for the complete edition, which would assuredly be a trial venture as compared with Sully's *Memoirs*. Since the proposed edition was never advertised and there is no copy recorded or to be found, we must assume that Mr. Strahan was not successfully "treated with" and the "hundred and fifty Copies" were never printed.

In 1779 Johnson mentions Mrs. Lennox in one of his letters to Mrs. Thrale. In the letter of October 21,[34] Johnson has been commenting on Cumberland's hatred for Miss Burney, who has done nothing to occasion it except write a successful book. Mrs. Thrale in her answer may have remarked upon Cumberland's ambition and jealousy of all rivals, for on October 28 Johnson writes:

C———— L———— accuses . . . . of making a party against her play. I always hissed away the charge, supposing him a man of honor; but I shall now defend him with less confidence. *Nequid nimis.* Horace says that *Nil admirari* is the only thing that can make or keep a man happy. It is with equal truth the only thing that can make or keep a man honest. The desire of fame not regulated, is as dangerous to virtue as that of money. I hope C———— scorns his little malice.

Baretti, in a marginal note, supplies Charlotte Lennox for "C———— L————."[35] Mrs. Piozzi, Malone, and S. Lysons, in copies of the *Piozzi Letters* annotated by them, all say that Cumberland is the person accused.

[34] *Letters of Dr. Johnson* (ed. Hill, 1892), ii, 112, 115.
[35] *Life* (Oxford, 1934), iv, 10, 477.

Besides Johnson's expression of his high esteem for Mrs. Lennox in 1783 already quoted, there is only one other reference to their friendship.　In his diary for March 18, 1782, is the entry:[36] "On Thursday night I slept with great tranquility.　On the next night (15) I took diacodium and had a most restless night.　Of the next day I remember nothing but that I rose in the afternoon, and saw Mrs. Lennox and Seward."

A great light must have gone out of Mrs. Lennox's life when Johnson died.　Though other famous men of the day had assisted her none had been so constantly a friend. From the banquet given in 1750 to hail her at the beginning of her literary career to his loyalty to her as compared with Mrs. Carter, Miss Hannah More, and Fanny Burney in 1783 he had shown himself not the tyrant and arbiter but the counsellor and generous patron.

Mrs. Lennox's remaining literary attempts are few.　In 1784 she writes to Dodsley, the bookseller, a letter, whose contents give further proof that the altercation over Sully's *Memoirs* was amicably settled:[37]

Kensington May 10 . 84

Sir

If you are willing to treat with me for a work of the novel kind, which I sketched out some years ago, and which I have since been employd upon at different times—let me know what day, and at what hour you will be at home—and I will call upon you—I am at present at Kensington, where I propose to stay all the summer, but as I frequently go to town, it will be no inconvenience to me to call at your house—pray let me have your answer immediately. direct for me at Mr. Annis's on the Terrace Kensington.

————I am Sir
Your humble Serv[t]

Charlotte Lennox

[36] *Johnsonian Miscellanies* (N. Y., 1897), i, 102.

[37] This letter, which has never before been published, I owe to the courtesy of Professor Frederick W. Hilles of Yale University, who owns it.　It is directed "To Mr. Dodsley, Bookseller Pall-Mall."

This "work of the novel kind" was probably *Euphemia,* which was published, not by Dodsley but by his successor, Cadell, in 1790. Mrs. Lennox's phrase is apt, for it contains little action, but is deliberate and reflective. The scene is laid in Albany, and in her old age Mrs. Lennox recalls vividly the fort at Albany and events of Colonial days. The novel was well received and favorably reviewed in the magazines.

Two other publications have been attributed to Mrs. Lennox. One, the *Memoirs of Henry Lennox,* 1804, bears on the title-page "By the Hon. Miss Lenox" and the only evidence for its being by Mrs. Lennox is that it was originally entered in the British Museum Catalogue under her name. The contents are episodic memoirs of imaginary people, the whole very loosely connected. Both external and internal evidence of this being by Mrs. Lennox is so slight that I think it may be dismissed at once. The other, *The History of Sir George Warrington; or, the Political Quixote,* presents more of a problem.[38] Mrs. Lennox was in dire need of money all the last years of her life, but she does not seem to have been an invalid until after 1802. Having turned to her literary efforts for support during much of her life, she might make another attempt, even after the age of seventy. Two copies extant of this novel have on the title-page "By the Author of the Female Quixote". A third, and the only other one I know of, has "By the Author of the Benevolent Quixote". This is also marked as a second edition. From bibliographical evidence all three come from the same issue of the same edition, but the title-pages of the third are different. I should be inclined to give this book to Mrs. Lennox. It is even more rambling than *Euphemia,* but indulges in the same type of moral reflection. In style and general trend of thought it sounds more like her other novels than like the only one I have been able to find by the author of the *Benevolent Quixote, Matilda and Elizabeth.*

[38] For more detailed bibliographical discussion of two copies of this book see Appendix V.

The latter is a weak, conventional tale with nothing to recommend it. *The Political Quixote* has faults of structure and conception; it has little continuity and too much sentimental comment; but it has some firmness of diction and strength of handling which, though far below Mrs. Lennox at her best, still make it possible to ascribe it to her.

What we know of Mrs. Lennox's last years gives us a sad picture of distress, penury and loneliness. Most of the information I have obtained through the Royal Literary Fund, a Society founded by David Williams in 1790 and supported by John Nichols the printer, Dr. Alexander Johnson, Alexander Blair, John Gardner the painter, and others who joined later.[39]

The following particulars are presented by permission of the Royal Literary Fund. This Society observes a strict rule of secrecy as to the names of the beneficiaries of the Fund, but, in this instance, Mrs. Lennox herself made known that she received assistance from this Society. *vide* Nichols' *Literary Anecdotes*, iii, and the *Dictionary of National Biography*.

The statistics which the Society has are as follows:

Charlotte Lennox, daughter of Colonel Ramsay, Royalist Governor of New York in 1720.

Born in New York.   1720.

Died in London Jan. 4th 1804.

London Address.   56 Queen Anne Street, East.

Case introduced to the Literary Fund by the Revd. W. Beloe, Dr. Richard Johnson, and Lady Chambers.

Grants made to Mrs. Lennox.

May 4, 1792.   Ten Guineas.

Aug. 1793.   Twelve Guineas.   'For the express purpose of enabling her to send her son to Virginia, and thence to Baltimore, where the young man's friends reside.'

[39] I owe this information to the kindness of the Hon. J. C. Marshall, the present secretary, who gained permission from the Society for me to make the information public, provided the notice above is placed before it.

Nov. 1793.   One Guinea 'To cover additional cost of passage of her son to America.'

Jan. 1802.   Ten Pounds 'on account of her urgent distress.'

Jan. 1802.   Ten Pounds additional.

Mar. 1802.   Seven Guineas.

Jan. 1803.   Ten Guineas. 'on account of her distress.'

Aug. 1803.   Thirteen Guineas. 'One guinea a week to be paid until the next Meeting.'

Oct. 1803.   Allowance continued.

Nov. 1803.   Eight Guineas.

Dec. 1803.   Three Guineas.

Jan. 1804.   Mrs. Lennox died.

Mrs. Lennox's case was the twelfth dealt with by the society, and the small size of the grants made to her is accounted for by the fact that this society had been but recently formed, a small number of gentlemen subscribing 1.1.0 each annually.

Of the people who introduced Mrs. Lennox's case to the attention of the Fund the Reverend Mr. Beloe had met Mrs. Lennox at Mrs. Yates' home when he first came to London. He was rector of All Hallows, London Wall, from 1796 to 1803, when he became Keeper of the Printed Books of the British Museum, a post from which he was dismissed in 1806 for having unwittingly allowed depredations. He did several translations, besides *Anecdotes of Literature*, in which he deals with rare and scarce books to which he had access while at the Museum. Lady Frances Chambers was the wife of Sir Robert Chambers, a judge and an intimate friend of Johnson. His learning and ability were highly respected and Boswell mentions him always with esteem. Mrs. Lennox may have met Lady Frances in earlier days. Dr. Richard Johnson I have found nothing about. It is to him that the following letter is addressed. This letter and the following are in the records of the Royal Literary Fund. They are here printed, with the permission of the Society, for the first time.

Sir,

It is with great confusion that I take the liberty to importune you, who know me only by name, with this application, and my distress may be easily imagined, when it forces me to break through decorums which I always wished to observe—but I am a Mother, and see an only child upon the brink of utter ruin. Driven as he was first, to desperation by a most unnatural father, and then deserted, and left exposed to all the evils that may well be expected from the dreadful circumstances he is in—I would preserve him if I could. Alas! I do not pretend to excuse his fault, but if his story was candidly told, that fault great as it is, would with the severest Judge meet compassion as well as blame. I have in vain used my utmost endeavors to mortgage the poor income I hold from a husband whose fortune I have made by the sacrifice of my own, in order to raise money to send this unfortunate youth to my relations in the United States of America, who will receive him kindly. I have been informed, Sir, that Mrs. Blair, your Daughter, is endeavoring to promote my subscription—the generous efforts of that Lady, tho' they were to be as successful as Her most benevolent heart could wish would come too late to preserve my unhappy son—the last ship that will go to America till next March, will sail in a week—the money for the passage must be paid before he goes on board, and the very lowest terms that are offered are out of my reach.

I have been once relieved by a benefaction from the Literary fund; if by your interest, Sir, I could procure some assistance in this hour of distress, my grateful heart will be impressed with the strongest and most lasting sense of your goodness, to which I shall owe all the remaining comfort of my life. I am

Sir

Your obligd, and most
obedient servant

Charlotte Lennox.

August 22, 1793.

Mrs. Lennox found some relief for her anxious distress in the generous help of the Literary Fund, which enabled her to send this son to America. What his fault was—and his father's—I have been unable to discover. Court records and convictions for these years throw no light on the subject. I can only conjecture that Mr. Neville, the husband of the heroine in *Euphemia*, is drawn from the unworthy Mr. Lennox. Besides being generally overbearing and disagreeable, he takes his son out against his wife's wishes and exposes him to the dangers of dissipated, reckless living. Mr. Lennox is curiously removed from the situation here, as if there were no possibility of getting help from him, though for the first time it sounds as if he were capable of giving it. From all indications he has nothing more to do with his family except for the "income". From being a burden financially he has become actively a force for evil and Mrs. Lennox blames him for his son's downfall. The only further trace of the son is conjectural. A copy of the Bartholozzi engraving of Mrs. Lennox's portrait in the New York Public Library is mounted upon a card bearing the name "Richard Walzl. No. 48 N. Charles St. Baltimore". Beneath the picture is the note "from an old print". The fact that Mrs. Lennox's son came to Baltimore suggests that he may have preserved this picture of his mother.

The other letter from the Literary Fund represents Mrs. Lennox in a less desperate but more pitiable situation. It is from the Lady Frances Chambers to the Rev. Dr. Williams, founder of the Literary Fund, and is here made public for the first time.

Copy of letter from Lady Frances Chambers to the Revd. Dr. Williams. Founder of the Literary Fund.

Sir,

The enclosed note I was favoured with the end of last month in consequence of having been desired by the late Mr. Bennet Langton to collect any small sums of half guineas or less for the immediate relief of Mrs. Charlotte Lennox who is in great distress for the common necessaries of life and is too ill, and now too old to be able to assist herself in any way—she has not been able to go out of her lodging this three months and but today I have been informed that she is at a cabinet makers in Dartmouth Street,

Westminster, but I do not yet know the number tho I shall make a point of seeing her in a few days. I sent by the person Mr. Langton appointed the little matter I had collected—and did not wish to apply to the Literary Fund till I had his approbation—alas his recent death and the distress of his family has for the present left Mrs. Lennox's cause in my hands and I have today sent a gentleman who was going that way with a note to Mr. Nichols. Sir Robert Chambers says that he means to subscribe two guineas a year to the Charity and I mean to call and pay it in Pall Mall very soon—In the meantime Sir I have the pleasure to find that Mr. Johnson recommends for the first time since he became a subscriber, and I trust that something will be done for Mrs. Lennox who has not any relations or friends who seem to think that she has claims on them—indeed I believe she has lost in her daughter the only friend she had a claim upon.

I am, Sir, your obedient humble servant.

Frances Chambers.

56 Queen Anne Street, East. Wednesday Jany 20th 1802.

Again Mrs. Lennox received the desired assistance from the Fund, which subsidized her regularly until her death in 1804. From the fact that her address is given as 56 Queen Anne Street, East, Lady Frances' address above, she must have been under the immediate protection of that lady during the last years, if she was not actually removed to her home. After the early references to "my girl" and "her little girl" this allusion to the death of Harriot Holles Lennox is all we know of her. The *Gentleman's Magazine* for May, 1797, records the death on May 11, of Alexander Lennox at Gellston, Scotland. Although Alexander Lennox is scarcely a remarkable name in Scotland, there remains a possibility that this is Mrs. Lennox's husband. The failure to mention either husband or son in this letter implies that they were both dead or had entirely deserted Mrs. Lennox. The likelihood is that the husband was dead and the son had lived up to his early promise and proved certainly a thankless, if not a worthless, child.

Through this letter we discover that still another of the members of the Literary Club had befriended Mrs. Lennox. If Langton had accepted from Johnson the legacy of assisting Mrs. Lennox he had proved himself equally generous and loyal. Langton's acquaintance with Mrs. Lennox may have dated from happier days when she was well-known though impecunious and he counted her among the "blues" with whom he was a favorite.[40]   Boswell gives us this anecdote about him: "Johnson told Burke, 'I had seen, at a Blue-stocking assembly, a number of ladies sitting around a worthy and tall friend of ours, listening to his literature.' 'Ay, (said he) like maids round a May-pole.' "

Besides Langton and Lady Frances Chambers we glean from Nichols that the Rev. William Beloe and the Rt. Hon. George Rose befriended Mrs. Lennox in her poverty and sickness. The latter was a prominent court official, a friend of Pitt's and of the king, who several times visited him. He must have had literary tastes because in 1799 Lord Marchmont left him a fine collection of books and in 1804 he was made a trustee of the British Museum. In 1762, when he was first trying his fortune in London, he was befriended by William Strahan, the printer. That may have been the time that he first met Mrs. Lennox,—through her husband or through their mutual acquaintance, Strahan.

In spite of this assistance Mrs. Lennox's last years were destitute and unhappy. Singularly lonely, she had lost husband and son with unpleasant memories of the selfish desertion and worthlessness of the one and the disgrace of the other. Her daughter died just as her mother was most dependent upon her for companionship and care. Separated from all her immediate relations or denied by them, destitute, and an invalid reduced to live upon the charity of others, Mrs. Lennox lingered on after her days of usefulness, after her early friends had ."all gone into the world of light".

[40] *Life* (Oxford, 1887), v, 33 n.

Surely for her the opening of a new century must have been

> —days, which are at best but dull and hoary,
> Mere glimmering and decays.

She died in Dean's yard, Westminster, on the 4th of January, 1804, and, according to Nichols,[41] "lies buried with the *common soldiery* in the further burying-ground of Broad Chapel, undistinguished even by a headstone to say where she lies."

As we look back over Mrs. Lennox's life, we are impressed by its length and her untiring industry. She began to publish when Thomson had just finished working over the *Seasons* and when Johnson was still only the author of two poems, of the *Life of Savage* and of *Irene*; and her last book was advertised in the same newspapers as Southey's and Coleridge's poems. In spirit and idea she belonged with the middle of the century, an older generation than Hannah More and Fanny Burney, though she is occasionally mentioned in the same breath, and she has much in common with the school of moral sentiment. Her great success came from an original imitation of *Don Quixote* done at a time when the quixotic character was much in vogue. Her later, less refreshing, more didactic works established for her a reputation of dignity and worth; and, although she never catered to ordinary popular taste—as did Mrs. Eliza Haywood—, she was sufficiently in the popular trend to win favorable reviews from the critics. Considered a person of learning and genius, she never sacrificed her high literary associations and interests, even in her penury. Her friends are to be found among the men of the time rather than the women, but the loyalty of these friends attests her admirable character as well as her charm. Her continued literary respectability and her many illustrious friends may have done much to alleviate the sorrows of unceasing and unremunerative toil, domestic misfortunes, and constant poverty.

[41] Nichols, *Literary Anecdotes*, vii, 435; iii, 201.

CHAPTER III

The Female Quixote *and Other Quixotic Imitations of the Eighteenth Century*

CHARLOTTE LENNOX'S most enduring claim to literary notice rests on her novel, *The Female Quixote*. It is an imitation of Cervantes' satire upon the romances, *Don Quixote*. In appropriating part of his title, Mrs. Lennox openly acknowledges her indebtedness to Cervantes, and begins a series of "Quixote" novels which appear sporadically through the next four or five decades.

The leading character of *The Female Quixote* is a young lady, Arabella, the daughter of a marquis who meets with ill-treatment at court and retires into the country with a young wife. Soon after the retirement Arabella is born, and the wife dies three days later. The young lady is brought up absolutely away from the world so that at the age of seventeen, when the story begins, she has known nothing of life except what she sees upon her father's estate. She has been taught by masters from London and is proficent in French and Italian, music and dancing.[1] "Nature had indeed given her a most charming Face, a Shape easy and delicate, a sweet and insinuating Voice, and an Air so full of Dignity and Grace as drew the Admiration of all that saw her." All would have been well, had not the marquis allowed her free use of his library,[2] "in which, unfortunately for her, were great Store of Romances, and, what was still more unfortunate, not in the original *French*, but very bad Translations." These romances told her all she knew of life, and she conceived that people of her own time

[1] Lennox, *The Female Quixote* (Ln., 1752), i, 4.
[2] Two of the most famous of these French romances were *La Cléopâtre* in 23 volumes by La Calprénède (1642), and *Le Grand Cyrus* in 10 volumes by Mlle. de Scudéri (1650). *Cléopâtre* was translated into English by Richard Loveday, and *Cyrus* by F. G. Gent (1653). About 1660 there were a great many translations, all vastly inferior to the French originals.

still lived and acted as did the heroes and heroines of these tales. The novel consists of the strange mistakes she makes because of this obsession.

Arabella's maid, Lucy, adds much to the humor of the situations. She is honest and well-intentioned, but entirely bewildered by her mistress' ideas and strange language. She finds that to be her mistress' *confidante* and live up to the heroine's "women" of the romances is a strain upon her unimaginative and untutored mind. Arabella's first experience is with a young man whom she sees in a country church, a Mr. Hervey, who she imagines must be deeply enamoured of her. Lucy is properly warned not to accept bribes for carrying letters—a new idea to Lucy, who rather hesitates to sign away such a pleasing prospect and who succumbs to the temptation when it is finally offered. Mr. Hervey is glad to escape to London after he has had his note returned unopened, and has experienced the unpleasantness of being held and threatened as a "ravisher" by two of Arabella's men, when he was only riding up to gain a nearer view of and, if opportunity offered, exchange a word or two with the fair lady.

Mr. Glanville, the hero of the tale, enters early. He is the cousin of Arabella and comes to visit the marquis. He falls in love with his beautiful cousin in spite of her strange ideas, and proceeds to suffer from her whims and the ridiculous light in which they make her appear to others. He is properly reproached for his own ignorance.[3]

For Heaven's sake, Cousin, replied Arabella, laughing, how have you spent your Time; and to what Studies have you devoted all your Hours, that you could find none to spare for the Perusal of Books from which all useful Knowledge may be drawn; which give us the most shining Examples of Generosity, Courage, Virtue, and Love; which regulate our Actions, form our Manners, and inspire us with a noble Desire of emulating those great, heroic, and virtuous Actions which made those Persons so glorious in their Age, and so worthy Imitation in ours?

[3] Lennox, *Female Quixote*, i, 69.

Glanville inadvertently expresses a willingness to remedy his omission, whereupon his cousin has four long romances brought in from the library to the dismay of the poor hero,[4]

counting the Pages, he was quite terrified at the Number, and could not prevail upon himself to read them: Therefore, glancing them over, he pretended to be deeply engaged in reading, when, in Reality, he was contemplating the surprising Effect these Books had produced in the Mind of his Cousin; who, had she been untainted with the ridiculous Whims they created in her Imagination, was, in his Opinion, one of the most accomplished Ladies in the World.

The succeeding scene is amusing. Glanville joins his cousin at the window to enjoy a spring twilight. Unfortunately she insists on turning the conversation to the romances, and attempts to discuss them with him. He manages to keep up his pretence for several speeches, but ends by making a fatal blunder which shows he read nothing after all, and Arabella leaves him in scorn and disgust.

Glanville has a rival in the person of Sir George Bellmour, a country knight whom they meet at the races (which Arabella insists upon designating as the Olympic Games, endowing the jockeys with high ancestries quite unsuspected by them). His attempts at wooing Arabella are somewhat hindered by the presence of Charlotte Glanville, sister of Mr. Glanville, a typical coquette of the town, shallow and sophisticated, in contrast to whom, despite her fancies, Arabella seems charmingly natural, innocent, and sweet-natured. Sir George has the advantage of having read all the romances and he takes advantage of Arabella's folly, to the annoyance of Glanville, who dislikes to see Arabella made ridiculous. The sixth book is the most amusing of all, for here, by Arabella's request, Sir George after the manner of the true hero gives an account of his life. The story itself is not only delightfully burlesqued, but the situation draws added humor from the presence of Sir Charles Glanville, the father of Glanville and uncle and guardian of Arabella,

[4] Lennox, *Female Quixote*, i, 72.

an outspoken, practical-minded, impatient old gentleman. He tolerates the tale,—though he is considerably bewildered by the glorification of Dolly Acorn, the milkmaid, into a heroine—until Sir George reaches the account of his ten months of melancholy in the forest.[5]

Give me Leave, Sir, said Sir Charles, to ask, If you eat in all this Time?
Alas! Sir, replied Sir George, Sighs and Tears were all my Sustenance.

This is too much for Sir Charles, who bursts into roars of laughter, believing now that the whole thing is a magnificent jest. Arabella's natural good sense receives a slight shock at the extravagance, and she rather lamely objects that in true romances the subject of eating is not discussed, but that of course the hero lives from the resources of Nature. Sir George defeats his own end, of winning Arabella, by the close of his tale which convinces our heroine that he has been false to his former lady. She sees nothing for him to do but seek out his earlier love and win her at all odds.

Arabella's second unfortunate experience is with an under-gardener, Edward, whom she sees often gazing pensively into the fish-pool in the garden. In her eyes he immediately becomes a prince in disguise, who is sighing away his heart for love of her. He is dismissed for stealing carp, but tries to get Arabella to intercede for him. He starts for her chamber with the steward on an evening when Glanville and his sister are dining at Sir George's. Arabella, conceiving that the two men have come to carry her away, makes Lucy keep them out, and flees across the fields to Lucy's brother's home. Half way there she faints and is rescued by a gentleman in a coach to whom she tells a fantastic tale. When the Glanvilles return a search is begun, and Edward is the first to find Arabella, who is delayed in her flight because the coach has broken down. When Glanville comes up his cousin refuses to return with him because she has just seen

---

[5] Lennox, *Female Quixote*, ii, 98.

him talking to Edward, whom she calls her "ravisher". She takes that inopportune moment to enlarge upon the similar experiences of Parthenissa and Cleopatra, and is induced to return home only when she finds that her new protector considers Cleopatra a "whore". She continues to accuse Glanville of complicity until his constant attendance causes her to relent in the following fashion:[6]

Go, therefore, Glanville, go, and endeavor your Justification; I desire you should effect it, no less than you do yourself; and, if my Prayers can obtain from Heaven this Favour for you, I shall not scruple to offer some in your behalf. Arabella, when she had pronounced these Words blushed excessively, thinking she had said too much: but, not seeing any Signs of extreme Joy in the Face of Glanville, who was silently cursing Cleopatra, and the Authors of those Romances that had ruined so noble a Mind; and exposed him to perpetual Vexations, by the unaccountable Whims they had raised—Why are you not gone, said she, while I am in an Humour not to repent of the Favour I have shown you?

Arabella has an inordinate idea of the power of her favor over life and death. When she hears that Mr. Hervey is ill, she speaks thus to Lucy:[7]

I am not cruel enough to wish his Death; say that I command him to live, if he can live without Hope.

A somewhat similar message goes to Sir George in his indisposition. Again Arabella says to Lucy:[8]

I will despatch you To-morrow Morning with my Orders to him, to live, or, at least, to proceed no farther in his Design of dying, till he has farther Cause.

When Glanville is seriously ill at her home, she condescends to tell his sister that she does not desire his death, to the indignation of Charlotte. She finally goes to see him

[6] Lennox, *Female Quixote*, i, 174-5.
[7] *Id.*, i, 17.
[8] *Id.*, i, 271.

in person to command him to live, and is much displeased
with his negligence as a lover when he is worse the next day!

Arabella's errors become more flagrant when she goes out
in the world. Her cousin, Charlotte, at length can stand
the country no longer and they go to Bath. There they
meet two fops, Selvin and Trivel. Selvin considers himself
very learned, but is silenced and awed by the stream of
historic lore which flows from Arabella's lips, disclosing
details in the lives of the ancients of which he has never
heard. He begins to be skeptical of his own knowledge of
the classics, when he discovers such tremendous gaps in his
information, and he conceives a great admiration for the
lady. She imagines herself carrying on affairs with both
the gentlemen, and writes them in a most condescending way,
urging them to take no violent measures in regard to her.
This results in her receiving a letter from each in which
he disavows any affection for her, a bewildering and dis-
illusioning experience for Arabella, and one which Charlotte
rather maliciously enjoys. Charlotte is not depicted as having a generous nature :[9]

As Miss Charlotte had a large Share of Coquetry in her
Composition, and was fond of Beauty in none of her own
Sex but herself, she was sorry to see Lady Bella possessed of
so great a Share; and, being in Hopes her Brother had
drawn a flattering Figure of her Cousin, she was extremely
disappointed at finding the Original so handsome.

When Mr. Selvin attempts an entrance to Arabella's room,
she again imagines a rape is intended and faints. This last
act makes trouble for Lucy, who is expected to recount
every motion which occurred while her mistress was unconscious, and finds it difficult, since nothing took place of the
nature that Arabella expects and suggests.

The ladies of Bath, envious of Arabella's wealth and
beauty, laugh and sneer at her peculiarities which are especially noticeable in her dress, for she copies the descriptions of

[9] Lennox, *Female Quixote* (Ln., 1752), i, 118-9.

gowns from the romances. There is one exception, a
countess, highly intelligent, generous and courteous, who
takes pity on Arabella. Lady Mary Wortley Montagu does
not help to identify this countess as she did the one in
Harriot Stuart:[10] "Tell me who is that accomplished countess
she celebrates. I left no such person in London." She is
at once attracted by the girl's unusual sweetness, sense, and
charm, and begins to enlighten her as to the mistaken ideas
under which she is living. Just as Glanville hopes for the
entire restoration of his cousin to normal ways of thought,
the countess is called away and the progress ceases.

The Glanvilles next take Arabella to London, where she
further embarrasses Mr. Glanville by an absurd mistake in
Vauxhall gardens. They come upon a young woman dis-
guised as a man, with a soldier, both somewhat intoxicated.
Arabella immediately thinks this is a heroine like Statira,
Candace, or one of a thousand others, in disguise for some
noble purpose. She advances to aid the girl, and a large,
jeering crowd gathers before Glanville despairs of convincing her of her error by argument and forces her to come
away by telling her that the soldier is the girl's true lover
whom she has at last found again.

The climate of London causes Arabella to retire to Rich-
mond; here Sir George makes his last attempt to impose
upon her credulity. He hires an actress to pretend she is
Cynecia, Princess of Gaul, a fair lady deserted by Glanville,
who, nevertheless, still loves him and wishes to win him back;
he hopes that this will prejudice Arabella against her cousin.
The plot is succeeding until one day our fair lady goes to
Twickenham to see Cynecia. She is with a company of
ladies, and upon their return they see several men on horse-
back approaching. Once again Arabella suffers from her
obsession of the "ravishers", and emboldening herself and

---

[10] *Letter and Works of Lady Mary Wortley Montagu* (ed. Wharncliffe, 1861), ii, 280. Letter to the Countess of Bute, July 23, 1755.
Lady Mary attributes *The Female Quixote* to Sally Fielding and calls
it "sale work".

her companions by citing the virtuous example of the Roman Clelia who plunged into the Tiber to preserve herself from the ravisher, Sextus, she follows her precedent and, before the ladies can restrain her, jumps into the Thames. While she is recovering from the illness caused by the shock, a "Divine" comes to see her and, learning from Glanville the cause of her unusual speeches, he attempts to reason her out of her delusions. In one chapter full of great wisdom and argument, the Doctor succeeds in convincing Arabella that the ideas of the romances are not only out-of-date and impractical, but also inconsistent with actual life, and sometimes false and evil. In a few hours of conversation he does what several months of contact with ordinary people and methods of life have failed to do. Meanwhile a duel between Sir George and Glanville has caused the former to confess his ruse and Glanville has received him into apparent favor, but not on the same basis as before:[11] "For tho' not of a vindictive temper, it was one of his maxims, That a Man who had once betray'd him, it would be an error in Policy ever to trust again." Sir George's wound makes it essential that he remain in Arabella's house until he recovers, and this gives Miss Glanville a desired opportunity to practice her charms upon him. She is at length victorious and wins him; at the same time Arabella admits to Glanville the love she has long felt for him. The story closes upon the two marriages with this distinction drawn between them:[12]

Sir George . . . . . was accordingly married to that young Lady [Miss Glanville] at the same Time that Mr. Glanville and Arabella were united. We chuse, Reader, to express this Circumstance, though the same, in different Words, as well to avoid Repetition, as to intimate that the first mentioned Pair were indeed only married in the common Acceptation of the Word; that is, they were privileged to join Fortunes, Equipages, Titles, and Expence; while Mr. Glanville and Arabella were united, as well in these, as in every Virtue and laudable Affection of the Mind.

[11] Lennox, *Female Quixote*, ii, 298.
[12] *Id.*, ii, 324-5.

These closing words imply a moralizing tendency which is not found in the earlier part of the novel, but which creeps in toward the end. It is not sufficient to slow the action of the work or to change the tone, but it is significant that we find *The Female Quixote* closing on the note which *Henrietta* and the later novels maintain throughout. Its introduction may come from an unconscious influence of Johnson or it may be the more conscious result of readings and conversations at Parson's Green with the great sentimental moralist of the day.

As a burlesque *The Female Quixote* is successful. Arabella's actions are sufficiently absurd to rouse wonder and often mirth; frequently they are ingeniously devised, and seldom are they beyond the range of possibility. The humor is most successful when it is obtained by presenting Arabella's idiosyncrasies in their effect upon some stolid and unimaginative person whom they leave in hopeless confusion. Such is the scene between Arabella and the unfortunate servant of Sir George, who is completely puzzled by the language with which he is greeted.[13]

I know what thou wouldst say, said she: Thou wouldst abuse my Patience by a false Detail of thy Master's Sighs, Tears, Exclamations, and Despair.

Indeed, Madam, I don't intend to say any such Thing, replied the Man.

No! repeated Arabella, a little disappointed, Bear back his presumptuous Billet, which, I suppose, contains the melancholy Account; and tell him, He that could so soon forget the generous *Sydimiris* for *Philonice,* and could afterwards be false to that incomparable Beauty, is not a Person worthy to adore Arabella.

. . . . . . Arabella, supposing he meant to importune her still more, made a Sign with her Hand, very majestically, for him to be gone; but he, not able to comprehend her Meaning, stood still, with an Air of Perplexity, not daring to beg her to explain herself; supposing she, by that Sign, required something of him.

[13] Lennox, *Female Quixote*, ii, 125.

Why dost thou not obey my Commands? said Arabella, finding he did not go.

I will, to be sure, Madam, replied he; wishing at the same time secretly, she would let him know what they were.

Lucy suffers most frequently, for it devolves upon her to bear her mistress' messages or to carry out her ideas and explain them. It is Arabella's intention that Lucy shall relate her life history to Sir George, a task which appears quite impossible to the maid and which she escapes through the departure of the gentleman while Arabella is endeavoring to coach her for an elaborate narration. Sir Charles also serves to set off the follies of Arabella, for his bluff, practical, unimaginative mind is constantly reduced to amazement at her absurdities. He is ready more than once to decide that she is insane, but is usually persuaded otherwise by his son or by seeing Arabella again when she is not riding her hobby. It is but natural that she should not only amuse but also horrify people by her apparent desire for bloodshed and her light treatment of death; it is partly explained by the following creed which she herself states:[14]

The Law has no Power over Heroes; they may kill as many Men as they please without being called to any Account for it; and the more Lives they take away, the greater is their Reputation for Virtue and Glory . . . . . The Blood that is shed for a Lady, enhances the Value of her Charms; and the more Men a Hero kills, the greater his Glory, and, by Consequence, the more secure he is.

Which recalls the words of Don Quixote:[15]

Where hast thou ever read or seen that knight-errant that hath been brought before the judge, though he committed never so many homicides and slaughters?

[14] Lennox, *Female Quixote*, i, 195-6.
[15] Cervantes, *The History of Don Quixote* (tr. Thomas Shelton, London, 1900), i, 63.

Talgol in *Hudibras* claims the same exemption:[16]

> For he was of that noble Trade
> That Demi- gods and Heroes made,
> Slaughter and knocking on the head;
> The Trade to which they all were bred;
> And is, like others, glorious when
> 'Tis great and large, but base if mean,
> The former rides in triumph for it;
> The latter in a two wheel'd Chariot,
> For daring to prophane a thing
> So sacred with vile bungling.

We do not get many touches of eighteenth century life in *The Female Quixote*. The fact that Arabella occupies the center of the stage almost continually accounts for this lack of eighteenth century atmosphere; it would be impossible to present very much of contemporary life and still keep up Arabella's delusion till the end of the novel. What we get is necessarily second-hand. Thus Glanville comments upon city manners and belles:[17]

... I wish some of our Town Beauties were, if not altogether of your Opinion, yet sufficiently so, as to make it not a Slavery for a Man to be in their Company; for unless one talks of Love to these fair Coquets the whole time one is with them, they are quite displeased, and look upon a Man who can think anything, but themselves, worthy his Thoughts or Observation, with the utmost Contempt. How often have you and I, Sir George, pursued he, pitied the Condition of the few Men of Sense, who are sometimes among the Croud of Beaux, who attend the Two Sister Beauties to all Places of polite Diversion in Town? For those Ladies think it a mortal Injury done to their Charms, if the Men about them have Eyes or Ears for any Object but their Faces, or any Sound but that of their Voices: So that the Connoisseurs in Music, who attend them to Ranelagh, must stop their ears,

[16] Butler, *Hudibras* (ed. A. R. Waller, Cambridge, 1905), 36.
[17] Lennox, *Female Quixote*, i, 226-7.

like Ulysses, when the Siren Frasi[18] sings; and the Wits, who gallant them to the Side-box, must lay a much greater Constraint upon themselves, in order to resist the Soul-moving Garrick; and appear insensible while he is up on the Stage.

The "Two Sister Beauties" are undoubtedly the Gunnings, Maria and Elizabeth.[19] "These are two Irish girls, who are declared the handsomest women alive . . . however, they can't walk in the Park, or go to Vauxhall, but such mobs follow them that they are generally driven away." "The world's still mad about the Gunnings . . . people go early to get places at the theatre when it is known they will be there." They came to London in 1751 and in the spring of 1752 married, Elizabeth the Duke of Hamilton, and Maria the Earl of Conventry. As Walpole says, the world talked of nothing else. Though marvelously beautiful, the sisters were supposed to be "lacking in sense and knowledge of the world".

There are allusions to the popular places at Bath, the pump-room and the Assembly, but little attention is given to the picture of the time. The best description of this sort is the scene at Vauxhall Gardens, where we gain an idea of the place and the people who frequent it, with local color in the girl, the soldier, and the noisy crowd which swarms about at the first slight disturbance which Arabella creates.[20]

Miss Glanville ever curious and inquisitive, demanded the Cause why the Company ran in Crouds to that particular Spot; and received for Answer, That a Gentleman had drawn his Sword upon a Lady disguis'd in a Man's Habit.

Oh Heav'ns! cry'd Arabella, this must certainly be a very notable Adventure. The Lady has doubtless some very extraordinary Circumstances in her Story, and haply upon

[18] An opera singer known as "the Frasi", very popular at the time, but not of good repute. "Young Churchill has got a daughter by the Frasi; Mr. Winnington calls it the *opera comique*: the mother is an opera girl; the grandmother is Mrs. Oldfield (the actress)." *Letters of Horace Walpole* (ed. Toynbee), ii, 40.

[19] *Id.*, iii, 59, 87-8.

[20] Lennox, *Female Quixote*, ii, 248-9.

Enquiry, her Misfortunes will be found to resemble those
which oblig'd the beautiful Aspasia to put on the same Disguise, who was by that Means murder'd by the cruel Zeno-
dorus in a Fit of Jealousy at the Amity his Wife exprest for
her. But can I not see this unfortunate Fair One, added
she, pressing in spite of Mr. Glanville's Intreaties thro' the
Croud—I may haply be able to afford her some Consolation.
. . . . The disguis'd Lady whom she was endeavouring to
approach, had thrown herself upon a Bench in one of the
Boxes, trembling still with the Apprehension of the Sword,
tho' her Antagonist was kneeling at her Feet, making Love
to her in Mock-Heroics for the Diversion of the Company.
. . . . . Lovely Unknown, said she to her with an Air of
extreme Tenderness, tho' I am a Stranger both to your Name
and History, yet your Aspect persuading me your Quality is
not mean, and the Condition and Disguise in which I behold
you showing that you are Unfortunate, permit me to offer
you all the Assistances in my Power, ...
Mr. Glanville was struck dumb with Confusion at this
strange Speech, and at the Whispers and Scoffs it occasion'd
among the Spectators.

The literary allusions seem to be introduced with a purpose; as there are only two, I shall quote them here.
When Sir George has finished the tale of his life, Sir Charles
remarks,[21]

Ods-heart! it is pity you are not poor enough to be an
Author; you would occupy a Garret in Grub-street, with
great Fame to yourself, and Diversion to the Public.
Oh! Sir, cried Sir George, I have Stock enough by me, to
set up an Author To-morrow, if I please: I have no less than
Five Tragedies, some quite, others almost finished; Three or
Four Essays on Virtue, Happiness, etc., Three thousand
Lines of an Epic Poem; half a Dozen Epitaphs; a few
Acrostics; and a long String of Puns, that would serve to
embellish a Daily Paper, if I was disposed to write one.
Nay, then, interrupted Mr. Glanville, you are qualified for
a Critic at the Bedford Coffee-house; where, with the rest of
your Brothers, Demy-wits, you may sit in Judgment upon
the Productions of a Young, a R———, or a Johnson. Rail
with premeditated Malice at the Rambler; and, for the want

[21] Lennox, *Female Quixote,* ii, 119-120.

of Faults, turn even its inimitable Beauties into Ridicule: the Language, because it reaches to Perfection, may be called stiff, laboured, and pedantic; the Criticisms, when they let in more Light than your weak Judgment can bear, superficial and ostentatious Glitter; and because those Papers contain the finest System of Ethics yet extant, damn the queer Fellow for over-propping Virtue; an excellent new Phrase! which those who can find no Meaning in, may accommodate with one of their own; then give shrewd Hints, that some Persons, though they do not publish their Performances, may have more Merit than those that do.

This defence of Johnson may be animated by some tangible criticism of him and his work; perhaps it strikes at Fielding, Foote, and the school of scoffers who ridiculed the moral utterances of Richardson and his friends. The latter and Johnson are again mentioned.[22]

Truth is not always injured by Fiction. An admirable Writer of our own Time, has found the Way to convey the most solid Instructions, the noblest Sentiments, and the most exalted Piety, in the pleasing Dress of a Novel and, to use the Words of the greatest Genius in the present Age, 'Has taught the Passions to move at the Command of Virtue.'

Mrs. Lennox has inserted footnotes to the effect that the "Writer" is Richardson, the "Novel" *Clarissa,* and the "greatest Genius" the Author of the *Rambler.*

Such statements leave no doubt as to the literary faction toward which Mrs. Lennox was leaning in 1752. Already she was under the protection of Johnson, who, according to Boswell,[23] wrote the dedication to the Earl of Middlesex. This gentleman had presented Mrs. Lennox's birthday ode to the Princess of Wales in 1750. The brief dedication I shall reproduce in full.

[22] Lennox, *Female Quixote,* ii, 314.
[23] *Life* (1934), i, 367. Boswell gets the date of the novel ten years too late.

TO THE RIGHT HONOURABLE
THE
EARL OF MIDDLESEX.

My Lord,

Such is the Power of Interest over almost every Mind, that no one is long without Arguments to prove any Position which is ardently wished to be true, or to justify any Measures which are dictated by Inclination.

By this subtil Sophistry of Desire, I have been persuaded to hope, that this Book may, without Impropriety, be inscribed to Your Lordship; but am not certain, that my Reasons will have the same Force upon other Understandings.

The Dread which a Writer feels of the public Censure; the still greater Dread of Neglect; and the eager Wish for Support and Protection, which is impressed by the Consciousness of Imbecillity; are unknown to those who have never adventured into the World; and I am afraid, my Lord, equally unknown to those, who have always found the World ready to applaud them.

'Tis, therefore, not unlikely, that the Design of this Address may be mistaken, and the Effects of my Fear imputed to my Vanity: They who see Your Lordship's Name prefixed to my Performance, will rather condemn my Presumption, than compassionate my Anxiety.

But, whatever be supposed my Motive, the Praise of Judgment cannot be denied me; for, to whom can Timidity so properly fly for Shelter, as to him who has been so long distinguished for Candour and Humanity? How can Vanity be so completely gratified, as by the allowed Patronage of him whose Judgment has so long given a Standard to the National Taste? Or by what other means could I so powerfully suppress all Opposition, but that of Envy, as by declaring myself,

My Lord,
Your Lordship's
Obliged and most Obedient
Humble Servant,

The AUTHOR?

The commendatory review of *The Female Quixote* in the *Gentleman's Magazine* was probably also written by Johnson, as Hill suggests.[24]   Because the internal evidence argues for his authorship I shall give part of the review here:

. . she believed the business of the world to be love, every incident to be the beginning of an adventure, and every stranger a knight in disguise.

The solemn manner in which she treats the most common and trivial occurrences, the romantic expectations she forms, and the absurdities which she commits herself, and produces in others, afford a most entertaining series of circumstances and events.   Mr. Fielding, however emulous of Cervantes, and jealous of a rival, acknowledges in his paper of the 24th, that in many instances this copy excels the original; and though he has no connection with the author, he concludes his encomium on the work, by earnestly recommending it . . . .

Besides the dedication and review Johnson wrote the greater part of Book IX, chapter 11, or the next to the last chapter in the book,[25] the one in which the "Divine" by reason persuades Arabella of the folly of her former ideas and restores her to normal good sense, and which is entitled "Being in the Author's Opinion, the Best Chapter in this History."   This is the only chapter which has been located as an example of the "odd chapters" in Fanny Burney's remark on making a list of Johnson's miscellaneous works:[26]

. . . it will be very difficult, as I dare say he hardly knows himself what he has written; for he has made numerous prefaces, dedications, odd chapters, and I know not what, for other authors, that he has never owned,

[24] *Gentleman's Magazine* (March, 1752), xxii, 146.   *Life* (1887), i, 367.

[25] "Another piece of Dr. Johnson's escaped all his biographers until Rev. J. Mitford pointed out the last chapter of Mrs. Lennox's *Female Quixote* as being by internal evidence written by him." Nichols' *Literary Illustrations* (London, 1817-58), vii, 161.

[26] *Diary and Letters of Madame D'Arblay* (ed. A. Dobson, London, 1904), ii, 206.

The Rev. J. Mitford was the first to call attention to the probability of this chapter's being written by Johnson. In the *Gentleman's Magazine* for August, 1843, he introduces the subject, citing the high opinion Johnson held of Mrs. Lennox, and the very obvious praise which she twice introduces in *The Female Quixote*. In January, 1844, he continues his thesis and reprints the chapter under discussion. He bases his statement upon external and internal evidence: the external being the praise of Johnson in the novel, the heading of the chapter, Johnson's esteem for Mrs. Lennox; the internal, the difference in style and subject from the rest of the work. The last point would be heartily endorsed by any careful reader of the novel. The tone differs radically from that of the rest of the book. As for Mrs. Lennox's own expression of gratitude by the term "the greatest genius of the present age" and the note explaining that this is Johnson the obvious compliment argues that the chapter was given by Johnson and that Mrs. Lennox here inserts an acknowledgment to him. Certainly the clause including the compliment to Johnson sounds like an insertion, as the passage reads more reasonably and smoothly without it:[27]

Yet though I cannot forgive these Authors for having destroyed so much valuable Time, yet I cannot think them intentionally culpable, because I cannot believe they expected to be credited. Truth is not always injured by Fiction. An admirable Writer of our own Time, has found the Way to convey the most solid Instructions, the noblest Sentiments, and the most exalted Piety, in the pleasing Dress of a Novel [and, to use the Words of the greatest Genius of the present Age, 'Has taught the Passions to move at the Command of Virtue.'] The Fables of AEsop, though never I suppose believed, yet have been long considered as Lectures of moral and domestic Wisdom . . . .

If Johnson wrote the reference to Richardson as he very probably did, since it repeats what we often find him saying

[27] Lennox, *Female Quixote*, ii, 314.

about that writer, Mrs. Lennox added the words after "Novel" and the footnotes explaining the allusions as referring to Richardson, *Clarissa*, and "The Author of the Rambler." Or the whole sentence may have been inserted by Mrs. Lennox.

The opening paragraph of the chapter (ii, 299) and the closing one (ii, 322) bear no distinctive marks of being by Johnson, and it would seem probable that these were written by Mrs. Lennox to connect the chapter with those preceding and following. With these three exceptions, I should certainly agree that the chapter is by Johnson. Many passages are his, not only in style but also in subject matter. For instance, we have here a thought which seven years later is the main theme of *Rasselas*.[28]

Tho' it is not easy, Madam, said he, for anyone that has the Honour of conversing with your Ladyship to preserve his Attention free to any other Idea, than such as your Discourse tends immediately to impress, yet I have not been able while you was speaking, to refrain from some very mortifying Reflections on the Imperfection of all human Happiness, and the uncertain Consequences of all those Advantages which we think ourselves not only at Liberty to desire, but oblig'd to cultivate.

The following passages contain a depth of thought and a balance of expression which are not found elsewhere in the novel but which are generally conceded to be characteristic of Johnson.[29]

The only Excellence of Falshood . . . is its Resemblance to Truth; as therefore any Narrative is more liable to be confuted by its inconsistency with known Facts, it is at a greater Distance from the Perfection of Fiction; for there can be no Difficulty in framing a Tale, if we are left at Liberty to invert all History and Nature for our own Conveniency. When a Crime is to be concealed, it is easy to cover it with an imaginary Word. When Virtue is to be

[28] Lennox, *Female Quixote*, ii, 300.
[29] *Id.*, ii, 316, 317, 320.

rewarded, a Nation with a new Name may, without any
Expence of Invention, raise her to the Throne. . . . . It is
the Fault of the best Fictions, that they teach young Minds
to expect strange Adventures and sudden Vicissitudes, and
therefore encourage them often to trust to Chance. A long
Life may be passed without a single Occurrence that can
cause much Surprize, or produce any unexpected Consequence of great Importance; the Order of the World is so
established, that all human Affairs proceed in a regular
Method, and very little Opportunity is left for Sallies and
Hazards, for Assault or Rescue; but the Brave and the
Coward, the Sprightly and the Dull, suffer themselves to be
carried alike down the Stream of Custom.

. . . . . It is impossible to read these Tales without lessen-
ing part of that Humility, which by preserving in us a Sense
of our Alliance with all human nature, keeps us awake to
Tenderness and Sympathy, or without impairing that Compassion which is implanted in us as an Incentive to Acts of
Kindness. If there be any preserved by natural Softness,
or early Education from learning Pride and Cruelty, they
are yet in danger of being betrayed to the Vanity of Beauty,
and taught the Arts of Intrigue.

It is a compliment to Johnson but a defect in plot that
the words he wrote were more effective than any amount of
actual experience in correcting the heroine's romantic attitude toward life about her. It would be more convincing if
this were done gradually through some of her actual experiences instead of suddenly at the end, but the emphasis is
intended to be placed more upon the burlesque than upon
character, and for the former it is essential that Arabella's
whims be maintained throughout.

These whims are frequently too heavily stressed. The
constant repetition of the same type of speech by Arabella
becomes tiresome. We weary of Statira and Candace, Parthenissa and Artamenes, and the lengthy accounts of their
pursuits, speeches, and escapes. When the contrast with the
actual condition is great enough, it is amusing, but it is
hard to maintain such piquant situations and frequently the
story lags. We become as peevish and out of patience as

Glanville, when Arabella again and again shows herself impervious to outside influences and embarks upon her pet theories, utterly oblivious to her environment and the opinions of others. It is hard at such times to credit the statement, which is several times repeated, that, when away from her hobby, Arabella shows herself possessed of sense and intelligence. Yet Arabella is lovable. She is always generous, and in actual experience tender and kind toward others. She is charmingly innocent and unsophisticated despite her reading and there is nothing unlovely in the dream world in which she lives. We feel her sweetness especially when she is brought into contact with women of fashion such as Miss Glovers, who lacks all refinement of thought and feeling, or Miss Glanville, who is more than once embarrassed by her cousin's frank unworldliness and lack of subterfuge. Whatever Arabella may do or say, she is always sincere, honest, and brave. She takes an unselfish pleasure in her cousin's beauty and a trusting innocent interest in Miss Glovers' welfare. Miss Whitmore has said[30] that Arabella is more womanly than Clarissa or Sophia Western, and that there is a reality about her sweetness and innocence which shows that the author understood the nature of the romantic girl. It would be difficult to maintain her superiority to Clarissa and Sophia, but she has, despite the burlesque intention and the improbability of the events, a naturalness which makes her vivid and appealing.

Of the other characters, Lucy shares the naturalness of her mistress. Austin Dobson has said[31] that "the Glanvilles and Sir Charleses and Sir Georges of Mrs. Charlotte Lenox are little more than shrill-voiced and wire-jointed 'high-life' puppets." Sir George and Charlotte Glanville are both types from the society life of the day and are rather dimly drawn; even more dim are Miss Glovers and Mr. Hervey. Sir Charles is only somewhat individualized, but neither he nor his son is wooden. Mr. Glanville is, to be sure, often pas-

---

[30] Whitmore Clara, *Woman's Work in Fiction* (N. Y., 1910), 32-36.
[31] Dobson Austin, *Eighteenth Century Vignettes*, 1st series, 67.

sive, but he makes himself felt as something more than a puppet. His constant attendance upon Arabella makes him frequently a sufferer, often the actual victim of her whim. Although he endures these humiliations with a patience hardly credible in man, the naturalness of his reactions within, which usually coincide with the reader's, makes him a sympathetic character.

The Female Quixote met with great success in its own day. It passed to a second edition by June, 1752, three months after the first edition had appeared. The title-page of this says "revised and corrected", but practically no changes are made. An edition appeared in Dublin in 1752 also, and another from there, called on the title-page "The Third Edition," in 1763. Both the Dublin editions are printed from the first London edition. The title-pages of volume i and volume ii have minor differences of set-up in both the first and second editions, London, and in the third edition, Dublin. (See Appendix VI.) In 1783 it was included in the *Novelist's Magazine*, the two volumes printed in one, with four plates. Although with the arrival of new types of the novel in Mrs. Radcliffe and Jane Austen, interest in it waned, another English edition appeared in 1799, and the last, after Mrs. Lennox's death, in 1810 in Mrs. Barbauld's *British Novelists*, a series printed again in 1820. This makes eight editions in English within about sixty years. The earliest translation was in 1754 when it was put into German under the title, *Don Quixote im Reifrocke*, and published in one volume at Hamburg and Leipzig. It was not translated into French until 1773, but there was a second edition of this translation in 1801. The last translation was into Spanish in 1808 by Don Bernardo Maria de Calzada. The various prefaces of these translations all recognize it as an important English novel, recommended by variety and wit. Most of them refer to its being in the tradition of *Don Quixote*; the French preface of 1801 mentions the fact that the burlesque has less point now that the old romances are no longer read.

That *The Female Quixote* was popular through the latter half of the eighteenth century we have other proof than the number of editions and translations. Through letters or other writings of various people we find that Arabella is well known and that quixotism has become a by-word. Immediately after its publication we begin to hear of it. Writing to Mrs. Elizabeth Carter, March 14, 1752, Miss Talbot says,[32] "I have been reading a book which promises some laughing amusement, 'The Female Quixote'; the few chapters I read to my mother last night while we were undressing were whimsical enough and not at all low." Writing later, April 22, 1752, to the same lady, she says, "Arabella, as a little book, is highly diverting, and much in fashion." It must have been in contrast to seven volumes of *Clarissa* that *Arabella* seemed a "little book".

Mrs. Delany in a letter to Mrs. Dewes, 30 April, 1752, writes,[33] "We have begun the Female Quixote. I like the design, and am glad to get into good company again."

Apparently it was "much in fashion". Joseph Warton writes his brother, "Dearest Tom", on June 7th, 1753, and among other literary scraps remarks,[34] "I want to see Charlotte Lennox's book."

Richardson in a letter to Lady Bradshaigh, February 24, 1753, thus comments,[35] "The Female Quixote is written by a woman, a favorite of the author of the *Rambler* . . . . . Do you not think, however her heroine overacts her part, that Arabella is amiable and innocent? The writer has genius." Not without condescension, this is still a generous tribute from the popular novelist of the day and the man who would seem least constituted to appreciate a burlesque.

[32] *A Series of Letters Between Mrs. Elizabeth Carter and Miss Catherine Talbot* (ed. Pennington, Ln., 1809), ii, 69, 76.

[33] *The Autobiography and Correspondence of Mary Glanville, Mrs. Delany* (ed. Lady Llanover, London, 1861), iii, 116.

[34] *Biographical Memoirs of the late Rev. Joseph Warton* (ed. Wooll, Ln., 1806), 217.

[35] *The Correspondence of Samuel Richardson* (ed. Mrs. Barbauld, Ln., 1804), vi, 243.

Miss Highmore shows that our heroine has acquired a definite connotation in eighteenth century parlance, when she writes to Miss Mulso (later Mrs. Chapone),[36] "I had some very odd adventures since I saw you, not unworthy of a Lady Arabella, which happily I may relate, when we have the pleasure of meeting again, when in return, I shall, questionless, claim your history." The last part of this quotation is in the style of Arabella, who always demanded a lady's "history", and with whom "questionless" was a favorite word.

Lady Mary Wortley Montagu is less complimentary than the other ladies of the time. She thinks that the novel is by Sally Fielding, and writes thus to the Countess of Bute on July 23, 1755:[37] "The Art of Tormenting, the Female Quixote, and Sir C. Goodville are all sale work. I suppose they proceed from her pen, and heartily pity her, constrained by her circumstances to seek her bread by a method, I do not doubt she despises." On September 22, 1755, she writes the Countess again of the same books: "I take them to be Sally Fielding's, and also the Female Quixote: the plan of that is pretty, but ill-executed."

If we jump two decades we still find the novel a well-known book, its title carrying a distinct significance. Francis Gentleman, criticizing *The Recruiting-Officer* in his periodical, *The Dramatic Censor* (1770), uses this expression:[38] "Sylvia, the capital lady, has spirit and sense; but the former runs her into female quixotism, and the latter often dwindles into licentiousness." Mrs. Thrale, from Rome, 25 March, 1786, thus emphasizes her strictures upon Boswell:[39] "—for, if Boswell was Plutarch, nothing but the sayings of Johnson could he record—like 'Arabella's' maid in the *Female Quixote,*

[36] *The Correspondence of Samuel Richardson* (ed. Barbauld, 1804), ii, 312.

[37] *Letters of Lady Mary Wortley Montagu* (ed. Wharncliffe), ii, 280, 283.

[38] Gentleman Francis, *The Dramatic Censor* (London, 1770), i, 77.

[39] *Dr. Johnson's Mrs. Thrale* (ed. A. Hayward and J. Lobban, Edinburgh and London, 1910), 256.

we should all be at a loss to keep a register of his actions, for even her ladyship's smiles might be mentioned, as she suggests; but dear Dr. Johnson did not afford us many of them." The allusion here is to Arabella's frequent injunctions to Lucy, as when she says:[40] "Only you must be sure, as I said before, not to omit the least Circumstance in my Behaviour, but relate everything I did, said, and thought upon that Occasion."

Jane Austen read it more than once and took pleasure in it. On Jan. 7, 1807, she writes to her sister, Cassandra:[41]

'Alphonsine' did not do. We were disgusted in twenty pages, as, independent of a bad translation, it has indelicacies which disgrace a pen hitherto so pure; and we changed it for 'The Female Quixotte,' which now makes our evening amusement; to me a very high one, as I find the work quite equal to what I remembered it. Mrs. F. A., to whom it is new, enjoys it as one could wish; the other Mary, I believe, has little pleasure from that or any other book.

Macaulay, writing of Dorothy Osborne in 1838, shows that the book was still current:[42] "But her favorite books were those ponderous French romances which modern readers know chiefly from the pleasant satire of Charlotte Lennox."

The last mention of this sort comes in the middle of the last century. Lord Wharncliffe prefaces his edition of the letters of Lady Mary Wortley Montagu (1861) with some introductory anecdotes, among which we find this.[43] "For she (Lady Mary) possessed, and left after her, the whole library of Mrs. Lennox's Female Quixote—Cleopatra, Cassandra, Clelia, Cyrus, Pharamond, Ibrahim etc.,—all, like the Lady Arabella's collection, 'Englished', mostly by persons

[40] Lennox, *Female Quixote*, i, 188.

[41] Austen, *Letters* (ed. R. W. Chapman, Oxford, 1932), i, 173.

[42] Macaulay, *Works* (ed. Lady Trevelyan, Ln., 1871), vi, 291. Review of Courtenay's *Life of Sir William Temple*.

[43] *Letters of Lady Mary Wortley Montagu* (ed. Wharncliffe), i, 55.

of honour." He goes on to tell us that the Lady Mary liked them immensely, which may be one reason why she was so niggardly of praise of the *Female Quixote.*

In her liking for romances Lady Mary belongs more with the ladies of the seventeenth century than with those of the eighteenth. Dorothy Osborne, amiable, witty, charming, is an enthusiastic reader of them as they appear although she, too, finds the French superior to their English translations and imitations. Thus she writes of *Parthenissa* by Lord Broghill, that it contains nothing "new or *surprenant*":[44] "Another fault I find, too, in the style—'tis affected . . . and though he makes his people say fine handsome things to one another, yet they are not easy and näive like the French, and there is a little harshness in most of the discourse that one would take to be the fault of a translator rather than of an author. But perhaps I like it the worse for having a piece of *Cyrus* by me that I am hugely pleased with, and that I would fain have you read." Her letters to William Temple from 1652-1654 contain many allusions to *Cleopatra* and *Cyrus*, which she reads avidly and sends on, volume by volume, to him in London.

Another lady, whose enthusiasm for them comes down to us more indirectly, is Mrs. Pepys. Thus on December 7, 1660,[45] "I fell a reading Fuller's History of Abbeys, and my wife in the Great Cyrus till twelve at night, and so to bed." In 1666 she is still reading and re-reading, for on May 12 "At noon home, where I did find my wife troubled still at my checking her last night in the coach in her long stories out of Grand Cyrus, which she would tell, tho' nothing to the purpose, nor in any good manner."

Arabella was not, then, the first to afflict her companions with long tales from the romances. Other ladies made the heroines matter of allusion; thus the Countess of Hartford

[44] *Letters from Dorothy Osborne to Sir William Temple* 1652-54 (ed. Parry, 1888), 66, 152, 177, 236-8.

[45] *The Diary of Samuel Pepys* (ed. Wheatley, Ln., 1923), i, 280; ii, 272.

writes to the Countess of Pomfret in 1740 of the Great-duke of Tuscany:[46] "what will become of his duchess; who I have heard Lord Brooke and others say, is one of the most beautiful and amiable women upon earth? She seems to run a risk of wandering through the world like another Mandane or Statira, and furnishing some future Scudéry or Calprénède with materials for a romance as long as that of the Grand Cyrus or Cassandra."

A faint foreshadowing of Arabella may be noticed in the Leonora of Addison's "Lady's Library", for there he finds "The Grand Cyrus; with a pin stuck in one of the middle leaves . . . . Clelia; which opened of itself in the place that describes two lovers in a bower." And of Leonora he remarks, "As her reading has lain very much among romances, it has given her a very particular turn of thinking, and discovers itself even in her house, her gardens, and her furniture." He laments, "What improvements would a woman have made, who is so susceptible of impressions from what she reads, had she been guided to such books as have a tendency to enlighten the understanding and rectify the passions, as well as those which are of little more use than to divert the imagination?"

This feminine predilection for romance is reflected through casual references in other well-known works of the first half of the century. In *The Rape of the Lock* Belinda's chamber has

> —to Love an altar built
> Of twelve vast French romances, neatly gilt.

The fire in her Lilliputian majesty's apartment which brings disgrace upon Gulliver is caused "by the carelessness of a maid of honour, who fell asleep while she was reading a romance." Gay anticipates the delusions of Arabella when he makes Polly say to MacHeath, "Nay, my Dear, I have no

[46] *Correspondence between Frances, Countess of Hartford (Afterwards Duchess of Somerset), and Henrietta Louisa, Countess of Pomfret*, between the years 1738-1741 (Ln., 1806), ii, 116.

reason to doubt you, for I find in the Romance you lent me, none of the great heroes were ever False in Love." The Miss Williams of *Roderick Random* is betrayed into her folly by the ideas she had gleaned from the romances:[47]

There was so much of knight-errantry in this gentleman's coming to the relief of a damsel in distress, with whom he immediately became enamoured; that all I had read of love and chivalry recurred to my fancy, and I looked upon myself as a princess in some region of romance, who, being delivered from the power of a brutal giant or satyr by a generous Oroondates, was bound in gratitude, as well as led by inclination, to yield my affections to him without reserve.

An actual instance of a lady's action being influenced by her reading is related by Boswell, where Johnson explains the unreasonable behavior of Mrs. Porter, riding first ahead and then back on their grotesque journey to the church to be married:[48] "Sir, she had read the old romances, and had got into her head the fantastical notion that a woman of spirit should use her lover like a dog."

Perhaps Johnson understood Mrs. Porter's eccentric behavior more easily because he himself had not escaped the spell of the romances. Dr. Percy told Boswell that[49] " 'when a boy he [Johnson] was immoderately fond of reading romances of chivalry, and he retained his fondness for them through life; so that (adds his Lordship) spending part of a summer at my parsonage-house in the country, he chose for his regular reading the old Spanish romance of *Felixmarte* of Hircania, in folio, which he read quite through. Yet I have heard him attribute to these extravagant fictions that unsettled turn of mind which prevented his ever fixing in any profession.' " Although the romance here referred to is closer to the subject of satire in *Don Quixote* than in the

[47] Smollett, *Roderick Random* (Ln., ed. Saintsbury. The Navarre Society), ii, 4.
[48] *Life*, i, 96.
[49] *Id.*, i, 49.

Female Quixote, the idea of a false influence is similar. If Johnson discussed this subject with Mrs. Lennox, it may be that from some hint in these conversations developed the plan and execution of *The Female Quixote.* The sentiment that romances were harmful reading for young ladies had, as we can see from the above quotations, been growing through the century. Mrs. Lennox was not even the first of her sex to be strong-minded enough to censure the misguided taste. Mrs. Chapone, the blue-stocking of[50] "repulsive exterior" but of "superior attainments and extensive knowledge", took the dignified Mrs. Elizabeth Carter to task for her confessed weakness for them in a letter written July 31, 1750.[51]

Indeed I am a little surprised that you, who are impatient with Mr. Richardson's prolixity, should ever descend to the most tedious, as well as unedifying kind of reading in the world, I mean a romance. I make no scruple to call romances the worst of all the species of writing; unnatural representations of the passions, false sentiment, false precepts, false wit, false honour, and false modesty, with a strange heap of improbable, unnatural incidents mixed up with true history, and fastened upon some of the great names of antiquity, make up the composition of a romance; at least of such as I have read, which have been mostly French ones. Then the prolixity and poverty of the style is unsupportable. I have (and yet I am still alive) drudged through Le Grand Cyrus, in twelve huge volumes, Cleopatra, in eight or ten, Polexander, Ibrahim, Cleli, etc. . . . . . but this was in the days when I did not choose my own books, for there was no part of my life in which I loved romances.

In spite of Mrs. Carter's and Lady Mary's liking for the romances learning and literary solidity seem to have been against them. The popularity of Mrs. Lennox's effective satire undoubtedly crystallized the currents of criticism which had been rising.

[50] Wraxall, *Historical Memoirs of My Own Time* (ed. Richard Askham, London, 1904), 93.

[51] *The Works of Mrs. Chapone* (N. Y., 1818), i, 34-6.

Mrs. Lennox showed a nice sense of the temper of her time in her choice of the kind of quixotism her heroine was to illustrate. Any burlesque depending for its effect upon the reader's knowledge of a literary type necessarily limits the audience, but the audience of *The Female Quixote* was as little limited as conceivable with such dependence. Aside from the fact that many names and plots of the romances had become part of ordinary knowledge, it is possible to enjoy the book without much knowledge of them. Arabella quotes enough to give us a general idea of their romantic situations and unnatural dialogue. On the other hand, emphasis on Arabella's fads and little attention to eighteenth century background render the atmosphere exotic, and the long monologues of Arabella wear the thread of the narrative thin to the reader at a loss for her allusions. Paucity of incident increases the dependence upon vivacity and trenchant wit of dialogue. The conversations are forced and the descriptions labored more than once for the enlightened reader; consequently the unenlightened more frequently finds his interest dwindling. There is unquestionable skill in the handling of plot, the story is connected and not episodic, and many amusing and unusual incidents rouse universal interest. Nevertheless its happiest reception would be with the eighteenth century man or woman who had once enthusiastically buried himself in the romances; who perhaps still cherished a secret pleasure in their far-away unreality, but had allowed them to take much the same well-bound un-used library position Scott's romances command in the library of today; and who enjoyed a true eighteenth century familiarity with *Don Quixote*.

Don Quixote had seized the imagination of the eighteenth century in a way peculiar to that age, although even today when we think of great imitations of *Don Quixote* we may not recall first the title-page of *Joseph Andrews* but turn to the seventeenth century *Hudibras*. Ralpho, Talgol, Hudibras, the Lady,—these stand next to Don Quixote and Rozinante and Sancho and Dulcinea. The beating of Ralpho harks back to Don Quixote tilting at the wind-mills or Sancho taking the beatings for his master's folly. But if the figures in *Hudibras* come nearer in time to *Don Quixote*, a large and famous group looms in the distance of the eighteenth century, gentler and more gracefully whimsical than the figures that gallop vigorously but sometimes awkwardly through the octosyllabics of Butler; for that reason to many a little more in the tradition of the sentimental fantastic old knight himself. There to the tune of Lillibulero appears Uncle Toby with Corporal Trim, engrossed in an explanation of the redoubts of Namur. Close behind him Walter Shandy is still standing at the turn of the stairs discoursing upon the peculiar power of names. Dr. Primrose, sane and tolerant, friendly old gentleman, suddenly rises up tumultuous, red-faced, fiery-worded because some one has inadvertently dangled before him the red flag of Whiston and second marriages. Lismahago, appearing eccentrically half way through *Humphry Clinker*, is a curious blend of Ichabod Crane and Don Quixote. In this same novel Humphry Clinker, wandering around England with Matthew Bramble, endures humiliations and misunderstandings much after the manner and spirit of Sancho. Knight and squire have their replicas respectively in Tom Jones and Partridge, in Roderick Random and Strap, in Joseph Andrews and Parson Adams, though the resemblance with the first two pairs lies chiefly in the fact that they wander and have adventures; and with the last in the quixotism of Parson Adams, as when he encounters the prosperous hog-keeping minister, Parson Trulliber. It is Fielding who is most under the influence of Cervantes in form and title and who, by his own originality, often escapes the spirit and atmosphere in actual creation.

These famous quixotic characters from well-known novels are not the only influences of Cervantes' masterpiece in this century. There grew up a school of imitations in title and general plan, of which Mrs. Lennox's was the most successful. Fielding is the first to bring over the title in his *Don Quixote in England*, begun in 1728 and performed in 1733 at the Haymarket Theatre. He has here transplanted Don Quixote and Sancho to England and presented them at an English inn, encountering an English squire, an English lawyer and doctor, an English knight, and an English election. He has retained most of the characteristics of the two figures, and in so doing has kept so close to the original that the imitation suffers in consequence. We meet the same Sancho and Don Quixote, but the removal from their early background has divested them of much of their charm. Fielding himself realized this, as he makes an apology for it in his preface. The important thing to consider here is that Fielding not only fell under the spell of the quixotic character and took advantage of its humorous possibilities, as did Sterne, Smollett, and Goldsmith, but he also actually borrowed the figures of Don Quixote and Sancho and sought to recreate them in England. Mrs. Lennox therefore had this as an example, and was following in a path already trod by Fielding. It is significant that he should have written a long and favorable review of Mrs. Lennox's ingenious attempt at imitating the model from which he also had drawn.

This review of her novel by Fielding in the *Covent-Garden Journal* for March 24, 1752, treats at length the whole question of the comparative merits of the original and this imitation. Mr. Jensen, in his edition of the *Covent-Garden Journal*, finds it Fielding's best executed review: "He knew his Cervantes thoroughly and was imbued with the comic spirit of *Don Quixote*; consequently his review of Mrs. Lennox's very clever imitation of this type is sympathetic, acute and even brilliant." The review, still interesting today, I shall give in part here.[52] Fielding calls Mrs. Lennox's book an imitation of *Don Quixote* and points out first in what respects Cervantes is superior: (1) because he is original; (2) because he wrote for instruction and reformation as well as diversion;

[52] *The Covent-Garden Journal* by Sir Alexander Drawcansir (ed. Gerald E. Jensen, New Haven, 1915), i, 108, 279-282.

(3) the character of Don Quixote himself, as well as that of Sancho Pancha are superior to those of Arabella and her Maid;

(4) some of the Incidents in the Original are more exquisitely ridiculous than any which we find in the Copy. And these, I think, are all the particulars in which an impartial Critick can give the preference to the Spaniard. And as to the two last, I cannot help observing, they may possibly be rather owing to that Advantage, which the Actions of men give to the Writer beyond those of Women, than to any Superiority of Genius. Don Quixote is ridiculous in performing Feats of Absurdity himself; Arabella can only become so, in provoking and admiring the Absurdities of others. In the former case, the Ridicule hath all the Force of a Representation; it is in a Manner subjected to the Eyes, in the latter it is conveyed, as it were, through our Ears, and partakes of the Coldness of History or Narration.

The two writers are equal in preserving the affection of the reader for the principal characters.

Both characters are accordingly represented as Persons of good Sense, and of great natural Parts, and in all Cases, except one, of a very sound Judgment, and what is more endearing, as Persons of great Innocence, Integrity and Honour, and of the Highest Benevolence. Again the Fidelity and Simplicity of Sancho Pancha are well match'd by these Qualities in Arabella's Handmaid. Tho' as I have before observed, I do not think the Character of Sancho is here equalled. It is perhaps a Masterpiece in Humour of which we never have, nor ever shall see the like.

Mrs. Lennox has excelled Cervantes in the following particulars: (1) it is more probable that the head of a young lady be turned in this way than an old man's, and the attendant circumstances are well represented to render such a result likely in this case; (2) Arabella is more endearing than Quixote.

This will undoubtedly be the case between a beautiful young Lady and an old Fellow, where equal Virtues in both become Candidates for our Favour; (3) the Situation of

Arabella is more interesting. Our hearts are engaged very early in good wishes for the success of Mr. Glanville; a character entirely well-drawn, as are indeed many others; for in this Particular, the English author hath doubtless the Preference; (4) she has presented a more regular Story with a complete Plan, while *Don Quixote* is composed of loosely-connected Adventures which might come in any order at all; (5) the Incidents, or, if you please, the Adventures, are much less extravagant and incredible in the English than in the Spanish Performance. The latter, in many Instances, approaches very near the Romances which he ridicules. (Such are the stories of Cardenio and Dorothea, Ferdinand and Lucinda, etc.) In the former their [*sic*] is nothing except the Absurdities of the Heroine herself, which is carried beyond Common Life; nor is there any Thing even in her Character, which the Brain a little distempered may not account for. She conceives indeed somewhat preposterously of the Ranks and Conditions of Men; that is to say, mistakes one Man for another; but never advances towards the Absurdity of imagining Windmills and Winebags to be human Creatures, or Flocks of Sheep to be Armies.

I might add more on this subject, but I will pursue it no further; having already, I apprehend, given a larger dose to Malice, Envy, and Ignorance, than they will care to swallow; but I cannot omit observing, that tho' the Humour of Romance, which is principally ridiculed in this Work, be not at present greatly in fashion in this Kingdom, our Author hath taken such Care throughout her Work, to expose all those Vices and Follies in her Sex which are chiefly predominant in our Days, that it will afford very useful Lessons to all those young Ladies who will peruse it with proper Attention.

Upon the whole, I do very earnestly recommend it, as a most extraordinary and most excellent Performance. It is indeed a Work of true Humour, and cannot fail of giving a rational, as well as very pleasing Amusement to a sensible Reader, who will at once be instructed and very highly diverted. Some faults perhaps there may be, but I shall leave the unpleasing Task of pointing them out to those who will have more Pleasure in the Office. This Caution, however, I think proper to premise, that no Persons presume to find many: For if they do, I promise them, the Critic and not the Author *will be to blame.*

The very extravagance and absurdity Fielding criticizes
have kept *Don Quixote* alive today, while *The Female
Quixote* has faded from popular knowledge. The former
excels notably in invention of incident and in vividness of
character. Samson, the barber, the vicar—these are all real
to us, while Don Quixote and Sancho hold our affection
unalterably. It is larger in scale and consequently achieves
a greater ultimate effect. There is much to be said, however, for *The Female Quixote* as an imitation. The idea is
definitely taken from the earlier work; a person is induced
to a distorted view of life from too much reading of unnatural
romances. There, however, the resemblance practically
ceases. Mrs. Lennox is absolutely independent in the invention of the rest of her plot. No incidents are copied
from Cervantes. She shows ingenuity in creating situations
suitable to the age and surroundings in which Arabella lived.
These situations are neither so brilliant nor so daring as
the ones Cervantes presents, but they are, in general, successful. Thus incident, character, and style she has created for
herself, with the possible exception of one small item in
connection with style. Don Quixote, when talking in the
manner of the romances, uses the word "questionless" so
often that it becomes a characteristic expression. This is a
favorite word of Arabella's, which she, too, employs when
talking in her grand style.

We realize more poignantly the originality of Mrs. Lennox's work when we compare it with Smollett's imitation,
The History of Sir Launcelot Greaves, which appeared peri-
odically in the *British Magazine* ten years later (1760-1).
The tale borrows from Cervantes not in idea but in actual
incident and character. Thus Sir Launcelot is not induced
to his disguise by too much reading of romance but as a
result of disappointment in love and a feigned madness.
The rest of the story is a transplanting of a few adventures
from *Don Quixote* to an eighteenth century background with
local color and a character or two which are creations of

Smollett. Such a creation is Captain Samuel Crowe, the
retired sailor, with his fund of nautical expression.

The borrowings from *Don Quixote* are obvious. There
is the squire, Timothy Crabshawe, who is as sentimentally
attached to his ill-natured Gilbert as ever was Sancho to his
ass. Sir Launcelot rides Bronzomarte, while Don Quixote's
famous steed was Rozinante. Crabshawe always seems to be
the one who suffers most and is constantly complaining of
his hard fate to his master. They have occasional arguments which are reminiscent of the conversations which
Sancho had with his master; such a one is Crabshawe main-
taining the thesis that cowardice is as much a distemper as
madness and therefore should no more be subject to punishment. He is particularly eloquent on this point, as his
master has just threatened him with a flogging. In spite
of his sufferings, Timothy is as unerringly loyal to his master
as is Sancho. The bachelor Samson is dimly suggested by
Squire Sycamore's attitude as the Knight of the Griffin.
Miss Aurelia Darnel is almost as much idealized by her
lover as is Dulcinea. The knight's watch of his armor is
taken over by Smollett and used to great effect in the case
of Captain Crowe and the enthusiastic beginning of his
noviciate.

To all this paraphernalia dragged in rather promiscuously
from *Don Quixote*, Smollett has added eighteenth century
characters and scenes which might occur in any of his other
novels. Such are Tom Clarke, the eager young lawyer, and
Dolly Cowslip, Mr. Ferret and Justice Gobble, to say nothing
of the parliamentary struggle between Mr. Isaac Vander-
pelft and Sir Valentine Quickset, the fox-hunter. There is
a long description of King's Bench prison, which is quite
evidently there for its own sake and not for any share it
has in advancing the story. There are frequent digressions,
and we do not feel that we have a consistent story or plot.
The characters are delightfully humorous, and a certain
piquancy is gained by the introduction of Sir Launcelot and
his hobby. The imitation, however, is not a real burlesque,

nor is any definite point chosen to be presented satirically as in the other two novels mentioned. Smollett has simply lifted out of Cervantes certain characters and incidents which seem to him especially fertile in humorous possibilities. These he has used advantageously, and has succeeded in presenting a distinctly amusing tale. There is no relation between Smollett's imitation and Mrs. Lennox's. They illustrate opposite methods of profiting by an old burlesque: Mrs. Lennox takes the general idea and enlarges upon that, making a consistent story, independent in character and plot; Smollett fails to have any main idea, but borrows characters and incidents which appeal to him and, giving them different names and slightly different motives, presents them in connection with some eighteenth century creations of his own, thus succeeding in evolving an entertaining but incoherent medley.

The first literary influence from *The Female Quixote* is to be seen in an obscure play never acted but published in 1758. This was called *Angelica*;[53] *or Quixote in Petticoats*. It was dedicated to Garrick who had refused to produce it because it was too much like *The Tender Husband*; the advertisement stated that "the character of Angelica and the heroic part of Careless, is not only borrow'd, but entirely taken, from the female Quixote, of the ingenious Mrs. Lenox." The play, which is in two acts, is a combination of stock scenes from the sentimental drama of the time and of borrowings from *The Female Quixote*. These occur only when Angelica and Careless are on the stage together; Angelica is frankly an attempt at recreating Arabella by having her quote Mandana and Statira and by emphasizing two of her ideas: that distance and formality are required of a lover, even for ten years; and that a lady has absolute power of life and death over her lover.

[53] *Angelica; or Quixote in Petticoats*. A Comedy, in Two Acts. London; Printed for the Author, and sold by the Booksellers of London and Westminster, 1758. [LC]

Angelica. No! live Careless! and, if possible, forget a weakness, I cannot but condemn.—But remember that your death will be a fault which I cannot resolve to pardon.

The two borrowings do not make for unity: there are passages like the above which sound like Mrs. Lennox and there are other passages where Gripe, the old miser, is talking which are clumsy and coarse. This coarseness as well as the advertisement show that Mrs. Lennox herself had no hand in the drama and that her novel had created such a stir that some hack-writer thought it material for a play.

The next literary influence of *The Female Quixote* is found in a farce by George Colman, *Polly Honeycombe*,[54] given at Drury Lane December 5, 1760. Polly is the child of an honest tradesman and has been corrupted by much reading of the sentimental novels of the day, especially Richardson's. In his preface, Colman remarks that he will "conclude my preface with an extract from the catalogue of one of our most popular circulating libraries; from which extract the reader may, without any great degree of shrewdness, strain the moral of this performance." The "Extract" is a seven-page list of works which were popular in 1760. Three of Mrs. Lennox's appear there: *Harriot Stuart, Henrietta*, and her translation of the *Memoirs of the Countess of Berci*. Polly's father regards the Circulating Library with about the same degree of favor as does Sir Anthony Absolute. Polly is led to indulge in an affair with a young man whom she conceives to be a gentleman but who turns out to be the nephew of her servant. It is a slight piece but rather humorous, and undoubtedly owes its conception to Mrs. Lennox's novel.

The first book to imitate Mrs. Lennox in her partial use of the Quixote title was announced in the *Monthly Review* for December, 1754 (ix, 445, art. liv): "The Spiritual Quixote;

---

[54] *The Dramatick Works of George Colman* (Ln., T. Becket, 1777), iv, 1-60. For further comparison of *Polly Honeycombe* with *The Female Quixote*, see Austin Dobson, *Eighteenth Century Vignettes*, 3rd series, 84-88.

or, the entertaining history of Don Ignatius Loyola, founder of the order of Jesuits: of whom it may, with the strictest truth be said, that he was one of the most extraordinary men that ever the world produced. Containing also an account of the embellishment, government, and surprising progress of that powerful order. Tr. from the French of Mons. Rosiel de Silva. 2 vols. 12 mo. 4s. sewed Bouquet." The review comments on the fact that Ignatius compares himself to Amadis of Gaul and refers to "these original spiritual knights-errant". The book shows, however, merely a super-ficial imitation of title.

In 1761 appeared[55] *Tarrataria, or Don Quixote the Second*, "a Romantic Poetical Medley, in Two Cantos. By a Travel-ler of Distinction." This book I have not seen and can find nothing about.

In March, 1763, there was announced in the *Gentleman's Magazine* (xxxiv, 147) another quixotic novel: *Fizigigg; or the modern Quixote*; "a tale. 6 d. Williams." What the nature of this book was I cannot say, for I have been unable to find any copy still existing or any other mention of it. Apparently, like the poetical Medley mentioned just above, it was not particularly remarked in its own day, as none of the magazines saw fit to give it a review. From the title we should judge that it would belong in the list of works influ-enced, at least in conception, by *The Female Quixote*.

In the *Town and Country Magazine* for March, 1772, appeared "A Bristol Oddity" signed "Another Oddity Hunter" in which one F-1-o is accused of being a quixotic reader of romances, preparing to hang himself for his Dulcinea. This is really a prose satire, an attack on John Fowler, Chatterton's rival, but not written by Chatterton.[56]

The next book in this category is *The Spiritual Quixote: or the summer's Ramble of Mr. Geoffrey Wildgoose.* "A comic romance. In three volumes, 12 mo. 9 s. Dodsley."

[55] Watt, *Bibliotheca Britannia*.
[56] Meyerstein E. W. H., *A Life of Thomas Chatterton* (N. Y., 1930), 90-1.

It was thus announced in the *Gentleman's Magazine* for April, 1773 (xliii, 193). Written by the Rev. Richard Graves, it is a satire on the strolling Methodists and is aimed not so much at the creed of the Wesleys and Whitefield as at their method of travelling among the people and exciting them. The Advertisement suggests that the author, though averse to the way the Methodists ramble the country, is not really against them in his heart. The novel is dedicated to Monsieur Pattypan, Pastry Cook to George III.[57] This dedication is followed by a prefatory anecdote of an old gentleman and his manuscript, "Christopher Collop, the comely curate of Cotswold", who is a lineal ancestor of Diedrich Knickerbocker and his *History of New York*.[58] From this anecdote and the various humorous prefaces we are led to expect something genially amusing; the genial tone is rather successfully kept. Considering it is ostensibly religious satire, it is remarkable for lack of bitterness and a certain vagrancy of interest from the topic in question to the acting of Garrick, the latest fashion of sending messages at Bath, Swift's memorandum on the pane of an inn, Mr. Shenstone's cascades at Leasowes, or a poor vicar's misfortune of being forced to collect tithes from his parish. The nature and the purpose of the work are both stated and explained:[59]

like a true Spiritual Quixote, to abandon his dwelling; and, in imitation of Mr. Whitfield and his associates, to use his earnest endeavours, to revive the practice of primitive piety and the doctrines of the Reformation, by turning missionary and publishing his religious notions in every part of the kingdom.

[57] *The Spiritual Quixote.* In *British Novelists* (ed. Barbauld, 1810), xxxii, 13.

[58] I have discussed Irving's debt to Graves in detail in "A Possible Ancestor of Diedrich Knickerbocker", *American Literature* (March, 1930), ii, 21-4.

[59] *Id.*, xxxii, 40, 54.

The author goes on to explain that here the reformer shares the folly of Don Quixote in that both wished to revive something out-of-date in the present state of civilization. There are a few direct borrowings from *Don Quixote*. Wildgoose takes as his squire Jeremiah Tugwell,[60] the shoemaker. His name has the various forms of Tugwell, Tagwell, or Tackwell, according to the learning of the speaker, but the author finally settles on Tugwell. This is certainly reminiscent of the forms of Don Quixote's name, whose biographers called him[61] "Quixada, or Quesada, . . . although it may be gathered by very probable conjectures, that he was called Quixana."

The plot of the novel is rambling: there are many minor adventures, loosely strung together, usually introduced for some obvious purpose and difficult to recall even immediately after reading the book. Readers would be least apt to forget Wildgoose and Jerry arrested for stealing a horse which Wildgoose has naïvely pre-empted at time of need; the scene of hysterical enthusiasm after the meeting in Monmouth; or some one of the more physical misfortunes which were prone to attend Wildgoose's attempts at speaking, misfortunes which smack of Smollett without the palliation of that boisterous vigor and rapidity of action which make even the worst of his tolerable. The continuity of these adventures is further interrupted by the long interpolated life histories so generously offered by the passing stranger in an eighteenth century novel. Miss Townshend, Mrs. Booby, Captain Johnson, Mr. Rivers,—all favor Wildgoose with the freest confidence almost upon encounter. The longest account, that of Mr. Rivers, was considered by contemporary reviewers the best part of the book; and there is much to be said for the judgment. It is Mr. Graves' own love story rather accurately told and it conveys an earnestness and depth of feeling quite at variance with the ironic tone pervading the book. A long tale told by one of the characters

---

[60] *The Spiritual Quixote*, xxxii, 31.
[61] *Don Quixote* (tr. T. Shelton, 1900), i, 2.

is in keeping with this type of novel and is to be found
both in *Don Quixote* and *The Female Quixote*, but with
this difference: in these last the tales are extravagant
romances, giving us an example of the thing satirized; the
story of Mr. Rivers and Miss Woodville being a simple
love-story of middle-class England and having nothing to
do with religion completely lacks this artistic significance.
Its effect is much more like the story of Miss Williams in
Roderick Random or of the Man of the Hill in *Tom Jones*.
In other ways *The Spiritual Quixote* suggests Fielding as a
much nearer master than Cervantes: the story is strongly
localized in the English countryside, especially the Cotswolds
and Bath with its environs, which Graves himself knew so
well; there are little essays occasionally such as an essay
upon quixotism. But as the incidents lack the vividness of
Smollett so the characters lack the robust vitality of Fielding.
Jeremiah is the most alive, the most humorous, the most
often in trouble, usually because of his fondness for ale
and cheese. Graves' debt to Mrs. Lennox is certainly no
large one—for title and for original suggestion of the
design. His execution is entirely different.

In 1785 is listed the publication of *The Country Quixote*,[62]
"A Poetical, Political, Satirical Colloquy. 4 vols. Ln.,
Keanly", where may be seen the influence in title. The book
I have been unable to locate.

The Amicable Quixote, which appeared (with no name on
the title-page) in 1788, is rather a compilation than a connected novel and is carelessly written, without construction,
and absolutely devoid of characterization. There is a wooden
hero, George Bruce, the quixote, who foolishly rates friendship higher than any other relation, and a suffering heroine,
Emily Bryant, who are happily united in the end, although
there has been no apparent obstacle to their union at any time
except Bruce's disguise as a footman in Emily's family.
Bruce's quixotism only breaks out sporadically as when he

---

[62] Ford and Lansing, *Cervantes a Tentative Bibliography* (Cambridge, 1931), 126.

becomes conspicuous at the theatre by finding Iago's betrayal of friendship far more interesting than Othello's relations with Desdemona or by ignoring the love story of *The Fair Penitent* and extravagantly admiring the friends. Occasionally, too, without warning he indulges in several pages of monologue upon the subject of friendship. The most important element of quixotism is found in the characters who are introduced mechanically one after the other through the central part of the book, each one labelled with a *humour* name indicating his idiosyncrasy, each one allowed to give evidence of his peculiarity and then dismissed completely. Thus we have Sir Stately Perfect, who counted the bows he received during a day; Valentine Wince, who pretended immediate warm friendship and broke it off as immediately; Mrs. Wince, who interpreted every remark as an insult to her; Simon Quillit, who passed all his time in writing letters or reading aloud those he had written to available victims; Mrs. Benwal, a pious lady who named the rooms and furniture of her house after parts in the Bible:[63]

—there is the Ark parlour; there is the little Canaan closet; the Red Sea room—that's where the company dine; the Moses and Aaron drawing-room, where she entertains her two rectors in town and country, with the principal managing people of the charities. There's the Shem and Japheth dressing-room, where she distributes the apparel which she gives away—

The hero's quixotism is cured by the heroine's great danger and his subsequent realization of the power of love. But the quixotism has been so artificially introduced that the reader scarcely recognizes any need of a cure—or for that matter distinguishes any character.

A moral touch is stressed with Miss Meredyth, a young woman who has passed cheerily from liaison to liaison, always discriminating against married men out of her generosity

[63] *The Amicable Quixote* (Ln., 1788), i, 124-5. [Yale]

toward the wives, until a serious illness suddenly brings to her realization that all *feminine* happiness must be founded upon virtue.

Although quixotism is the most important idea in the book, it adds nothing to the type of the quixotic novel except the original idea. A compilation of long quotations, moral statements, isolated conversations does not offer sufficient body to admit of serious comparison with *Don Quixote* or *The Female Quixote.*

In 1797 appeared *The History of Sir George Warrington; or the Political Quixote.* "By the Author of the Female Quixote. Ln., J. Bell." Encouraged by her own former success and its imitations, Mrs. Lennox made this last desperate attempt to tap again a vein that was becoming exhausted. The story is by far the most digressive of any of hers, consisting of numerous episodes loosely hung together. Several people are quixotic in idea. Sir George Warrington, the central character, gave his early days to hunting, but during an illness began to read voraciously:[64] "—the subjects that most engaged his attention were the descriptions of wars, particularly where the hero had emancipated his country from slavery and subjection. Pascal Paoli was the subject of his warmest admiration;". It is easy but perhaps not safe to conjecture that Mrs. Lennox chose Pascal Paoli not casually but because of the enthusiasm of her old friend's biographer, who by 1797 had already been for five years the well-known author of the great *Life.*

Sir George is led astray by theories of Democracy, Liberty, and Equality, especially as expounded by Thomas Paine in his *Rights of Man.* He falls under the spell of the French Revolution and finally gives up his life to go forth in pursuit of his ideals. At an inn he meets Benjamin Porter who has eloped with his master's daughter because he has heard that master, Squire Thornton, constantly expounding the idea of equality. The daughter, Charlotte Thornton, has eloped with him because, like Arabella, she has been reading

[64] *History of Sir George Warrington* (Ln., 1797), i, 30.

French romances and her head is filled with false ideas of gallantry.

Later Sir George meets Louisa Moreland, a dependent girl who had been in a convent in France, until it was broken up by Democracy and she was set adrift. We never entirely lose sight of her again, as she is loved by Sir George, but she undergoes many hardships, going into service, suffering injustice and malicious treatment before the happy solution. Our quixote next meets Mr. Goldeney and visits him in his home. Mr. Goldeney has many fine theories of philanthropy on which he waxes eloquent, but Sir George is disillusioned by his cruelty to his dependents and by his suspecting himself of a theft in connivance with the butler. Mr. Davenport, a scheming republican, then gains influence over the quixote and persuades him to live with the Wilmots whose three daughters, Myrtilla, Rosetta, Fidellia, furnish additional complications. Myrtilla, engaged to Captain Montague, has sense, but the other two are vain and make trouble for Louisa through jealousy. Sir George reaches the climax of folly when he leads a mob of common people against Annesley and is shot. He only escapes serious results through the efforts of Captain Montague. When his health and senses are restored, he returns to his home where he finds the real Louisa whose place had been taken by an impostor. The story ends with three weddings. The number fails to make up for the fact that no single love affair has awakened even a casual interest.

Certainly as far as narrative goes, it is the weakest of Mrs. Lennox's works. The story rambles, as an old person digresses, and here and there are echoes of other stories. The French convent comes from *Harriot Stuart*; the quixotism of Charlotte Thornton suggests *The Female Quixote*; the awakening of Sir George is as unconvincing as Arabella's. Like her he is brought almost to death by his folly; and he is instantly recovered of his quixotism when he discovers that republicans are atheists! There is no characterization; even Louisa and Sir George are figureheads, and all the others are merely names on which to hang an idiosyncrasy. Much of the novel is essay in form: there are treatises on the education of young women, illustrated by the story of Kitty Davis, the impostor, a young woman educated above her rank; there are frequent reflections upon rank and worldliness; throughout occur axioms of piety and rambling remarks on goodness and virtue.

It is kinder not to linger over this novel, which is but a feeble piecing together of episode and reflection, too digressive to make even the obvious point of satire on ardent republicans, too persistent in moralizing to awaken a glimmer of interest.   The most amazing thing is that, in 1797, at the age of seventy-seven, Mrs. Lennox had her finger so astutely on the pulse of her time that in *The Political Quixote* she reflected the English distrust of Paine's extreme theories and of the enthusiasm for equality, so dangerously put in practice in France.

In 1801 *The Infernal Quixote. A Tale of the Day* by Charles Lucas[65] also exposes the sad effects of the modern free philosophies on their followers.   The title of the book comes from the analogy between these modern free minds and the Infernal Spirits of Milton whose doctrine is

Better to reign in Hell than serve in Heaven.

Captain James Marauder, the epitome of Godwin's doctrine "All principle is folly", is an example of one trying to win his own advantage in all directions.   From a glorious beginning with every advantage, heralded by the great as a brilliant leader, expectant heir of the Duke of Silsbury, he sinks to an ignominious death, hurling himself over a cliff after he has been betrayed by his attorney, deserted by two fair ladies he has sought, captured and proved the guilty leader

[65] *The Infernal Quixote. A Tale of the Day.* In Four Volumes. By Charles Lucas A.M. Author of the Castle of St. Donats, &c. "Better to reign in Hell than serve in Heaven." Milton's Satan. London: Printed at the Minerva-Press, for William Lane, Leadenhall-Street. 1801. [Yale]

of rebels against the Government in Ireland. His constant foil is Wilson, son of a carpenter, honest, humble, Christian, whose fortunes rise as Marauder's descend. The author is chiefly interested in showing that the doctrines of Voltaire, "Tom Pain's *Age of Reason*", of Godwin's *Political Justice*, —the ideas that animated the French Revolution—lead to insanity, poverty, disgrace, suicide. The two latter books are often quoted from in the text or in lengthy footnotes. Opposed to these critics—skeptics, fanatics, who end in misery—are the upright who defend and believe in Christianity and who achieve success, wealth, happiness. The book has little to recommend it in conception or execution; it lacks unity, jumping from an attempted rape by Marauder to a lengthy disquisition on the Diabolists or Modern Philosophers, dividing them into nine categories, each of which is described tediously without sharpness of detail or incisive satire, from the Stoics and Peripatetics through the Naturals, Reasoners, and Nothingers. The book falls between its two aims: to tell a romantic story and to expose the dangers of revolutionary writings. Since Marauder is never convincingly a quixote, rather, completely a conventional hero, the relation of the book to the quixotic series is distant and feeble.

Two later productions resemble *The Female Quixote* only in name. These are: *The Political Quixote; or, The Adventures of the renowned Don Blackibo, Dwarfino, and his trusty 'Squire, Seditiono*: "a romance, in which are introduced many popular and celebrated political characters of the present day. Preface signed: George Buxton." (London, 1820); and a poem, *The Spiritual Quixote, Geoffrey Wildgoose, in Cheltenham; or, A Discourse on a race-course* (Cheltenham, 1827). These show that the idea which Mrs. Lennox had borrowed served as a convenient vehicle for political or farcical satire.

A literary resemblance, not of title but of content, may be traced between Arabella and Jane Austen's famous satire on the Gothic romances, *Northanger Abbey*. Miss Austen is doing what Mrs. Lennox did before her, when she points out the effect of romantic reading upon a young girl. Certainly Arabella's words and habits are echoed when, speaking of Catherine Morland's sister as her confidant, "It is remarkable, however, that she neither insisted on Catherine's writing by every post, nor exacted her promise of transmitting the character of every new acquaintance, nor a detail of every interesting conversation that Bath might produce." The circumstances surrounding Catherine Morland, however, are very different from those about Arabella, and in treatment there is little comparable. Miss Austen has as a subject for satire a type of reading which was just at the height of popularity, and has treated it with a delightful irony and without burlesque. Jane Austen's high approval of *The Female Quixote* makes it more probable that Mrs. Lennox's earlier treatment of a similar theme influenced her to attempt the same with the romantic reading which had supplanted the French romances in popularity.

Although this brief survey includes all the English imitations of *The Female Quixote* that I have been able to find, it does not include the book which most patently would not have existed without it. This is *Female Quixotism; exhibited in the Romantic Opinions and Extravagant Adventures of Dorcasina Sheldon,* "written by Tabitha Tenney," an American. The second edition was published in Newburyport, Massachusetts, in 1808[66] and it ran to several editions during the century. It is the story of a young girl situated much as Arabella was, in the country alone with a father who,[67] "attached to novels himself, as a source of amusement, from which he had received no injury, he did not foresee, or suspect the mischiefs they might produce, in a young girl like me, ignorant of the world, and of a turn of mind naturally romantic. I was therefore left to gratify my taste for this kind of reading without restraint; and this imprudent indulgence has been the cause of my ruin."

[66] I can find no record or copy of a first edition.

[67] Tenney, *Female Quixotism* (Newburyport, Mass., 1808), ii, 210. [Yale]

Dorcasina at twenty refuses the offer of Lysander, a friend of her father, because his letter was so cold and unlike the manner of lovers in novels. At thirty-four she has her first and most important adventure with O'Connor, an Irish rascal, who almost succeeds in luring her away to Philadelphia with him, but her promise to her father holds her. She refuses to be entirely undeceived until her father takes her past the square in Philadelphia, where he is being publicly whipped as a thief.

The village schoolmaster, a young scholar of nineteen from New Haven, takes her up while she is still mourning O'Connor and under the name of Philander practices all kinds of tricks upon her and her maid Betty, who suffers even more than the faithful Lucy did. He plays a hoax with a conceited barber newly come to town, kidnaps them for a night, and in general mauls them about thoroughly in a way to have enlightened anyone less obsessed than Dorcasina. After Philander's departure all is peaceful for Mr. Sheldon and his aging daughter for seven years. Then at the ripe age of forty-one Dorcasina carries on a languishing intrigue with the wounded Captain Barry, aged twenty-five, who has been forced to seek refuge in their home. His man, James, deceives her even to the extent of eloping, when the discovery that he is not his master sends her home again. The next interlude is with Mr. Cumberland, a practical widower from Philadelphia, who has come out to bargain for Dorcasina. After considerable misunderstanding because of the trickery of Scipio, the negro butler, and Betty's sudden ambitions, Mr. Cumberland retires in high dudgeon without a bride.

At this point Mr. Sheldon dies and Dorcasina is left without any protectors except the Stanleys, old friends whose daughter, Harriot, has been kept from novels because of their dire effect on Dorcasina. During her illness after her father's death Dorcasina rereads *Roderick Random* and although she is now fifty, old and wrinkled, with no teeth and given to alarming wigs, she is caught by the name of a new employee, John Brown, "an honest serving-man", and immediately translates him into a gentleman in love with her. Her obstinate folly would have led her to marriage, if the Stanleys had not connived at her removal to a farm in the country and John's departure for his home. Even under partial guard at this home Dorcasina is wooed by an old Charleston rake and only the hands of justice seizing him save her from a fatal marriage. It is by his words after he has been caught that she is finally disillusioned. He tells her she is a fool, old and ugly, and no one would dream of marrying her except for her money. Shocked back to her senses, she realizes too late that her reading has kept her from accepting an honorable marriage in her youth and has made her a ridiculous and lonely old woman. The novel closes with her letter of confession to Harriot Stanley, which with the prefatory letter addressed "to all Columbian young ladies who read novels and romances" leaves no doubt as to the didactic purpose of the novel: "—when you compare it with the most extravagant parts of the authentic history of the celebrated hero of La Mancha, the renowned Don Quixote, I presume you will no longer doubt its being a true uncoloured history of a romantic country girl, whose head had been turned by the unrestrained perusal of Novels and Romances. That, by observing their baneful effects on Miss Sheldon, who was in every other respect a sensible, judicious, and amiable girl, you may avoid the disgraces and disasters that so long rendered her despicable and miserable, is the sincere wish, (My dear young Ladies, Of your Friend and Admirer,) The Compiler."

The novels here considered so dangerous are not the old romances, but the more recent English novels. The only ones actually named are *Roderick Random* mentioned above and *Sir Charles Grandison*. When Dorcasina is being carried off on one of Philander's practical jokes, she comforts herself:[68] "The very same accident had formerly happened to Harriet Byron, though she was, to be sure, rescued in a

---

[68] Tenney, *Female Quixotism* (Newburyport, Mass., 1808), i, 167.

different manner." The only other clue we have to her favorites are such passages as:[69] " 'And, besides, it was no new thing; for I have frequently read of ladies being forcibly carried off by resolute lovers.' 'Oh! those poisonous, those fatal novels!' exclaimed Mr. Sheldon; 'how have they warped your judgment, and perverted your understanding.' "

Or again of O'Connor:[70] "He even went so far, encouraged by the imprudent step she had taken, as to propose to her, not to return again to her father's house; but to take an apartment in the inn, have the banns published the next Sunday; and to go to Philadelphia and have the nuptial knot tied, with all practicable dispatch. This business performed, he proposed to get the proper recommendations to her father, and then return, and, throwing themselves at his feet, humbly implore his forgiveness.

Dorcasina listened to him in silent pleasure. This manner of proceedings was so conformable to many instances which she had read in her favorite authors, that she was upon the point of giving her consent."

Clarissa Harlowe would certainly be included in the list of dangerous novels, as Richardson had been considered harmful by Jonathan Edwards in Northampton in earlier years. Fielding, Smollett, Ann Radcliffe—probably all of these were intended in the satire.

The book has more of realism than *The Female Quixote.* Dorcasina is not the romantic heroine with the glamour of beauty that Arabella is. She is frankly an old maid with absurd ideas of romance, making herself ridiculous when brought in contact with sensible people. Contrast is offered by the faithful Betty who suffers certainly more than she deserves from actual physical discomforts as well as from ghosts and thunder-storms. Scipio, too, is a genuine person with his negro dialect and his love of waggery. The other people scarcely count, except as conventional figures in the background: Mr. Sheldon, the Stanleys, Captain

[69] Tenney, *Female Quixotism*, i, 171.
[70] *Id.*, i, 68-9.

Barry. In general outline *Female Quixotism* is like *Don Quixote* and *The Female Quixote* in that it is chiefly concerned with one quixotic figure deluded by reading, and a faithful attendant; it differs in the natural touches of local color in connection with the Pennsylvania scene, the realism of the treatment of the heroine, left desolate at the end with no hope of a happy solution, and in the obvious didacticism which pervades. *Female Quixotism*, unquestionably an offshoot of *The Female Quixote*, has the advantages of independent execution and original atmosphere, but the style is inferior to Mrs. Lennox's.

Another book written in America which shows the influence of *Don Quixote*, though not directly that of *The Female Quixote*, is *Modern Chivalry, containing the Adventures of a Captain, and Teague O'Regan, His Servant*. It was written by H. H. Brackenridge between the years 1793 and 1805. I include it because it seems to me that through the influence in its design and the originality of its development it deserves a place in any consideration of quixotic novels during this period. The book is written frankly in lighter mood, centering in the adventures of Captain John Farrago and his Irish servant, Teague, but including all kinds of contemporary satire on elections, on the Society of Philosophers, on Congress. All bodies mentioned, including a group of Presbyterian elders, desire the services of the ignorant Teague, for anything from a Kickapoo chieftain to a witch in *Macbeth*. The Captain is chiefly occupied in rescuing his willing and unworthy servant from the claims of democracy, but he at length decides that the Irishman's rôle is politics and bends his energies toward making him a gentleman. Additional humor is brought in with Duncan Ferguson, the Scotch Covenanter who always carries with him *Satan's Invisible Kingdom Discovered* and who becomes the Captain's servant after Teague is appointed an excise-officer by the President. When the two are travelling with the Captain there are many clashes, as Duncan carries his national partiality so far as to explain why Scotch women are chosen for witches:[71] "Ane Scotch witch is worth a dozen English or American. They can loup farther, and sink a ship in half the time." Almost all the episodes are entertaining; they are usually original; the satire on some existing custom or body is obvious, but not too obvious; the Captain's bland manner of interference and reasoning is seldom ruffled beyond the point of inflicting punishment on the irrepressible Teague; and Teague himself is an unfailing source of troublesome activity. He suggests Sancho, but is more impressionable and is allowed a larger share of the action. Besides the Irish and Scotch characters some negroes are introduced, with dialect, one especially who testifies before the Society of Philosophers to the effect that the entire race was originally black. This last named society comes in for more than its share of ridicule; their last absurd act is to send the tarred-and-feathered Teague to France as a curious animal specimen from the New World.

The Captain explains, himself, why he is called a quixote:[72] "I have been called the modern Don Quixote, on account of the eccentricity of my rambles, or the singularity which they conceive themselves to discover in my conversation and manner."

The author frequently stops to chat with his readers at the beginning of the books, rather in the manner of Fielding. He comments upon the incidents in, or the fame of, a preceding volume, and threatens certain men in high places with an entrance into a succeeding volume unless they mend their ways. The entire work he contests is done, not for content but for style, as there is too little attention given to style nowadays.[73] "The English language is undoubtedly written better in America than in England, especially since the

---

[71] Brackenridge H. H., *Modern Chivalry* (Wilmington, 1825), ii, 194.

[72] *Id.*, ii, 183-4.

[73] *Id.*, i, 68.

time of that literary dunce, Sam Johnson, who was totally destitute of taste for the *vraie naturelle*, or simplicity of nature." Such a stricture does not necessarily place the author with the romantic school, as the simplicity of the French marquis who has retired to nature and the fruits of hunting is satirized with equal alacrity. None of the satire is bitter, except perhaps that upon the treaties with fake Indian chiefs. The book is like *Don Quixote* in its light spirit, its careless insouciance, its central character; it is different in that it is strictly localized in a country of elections, Presbyterian elders, and Congress, and is made to serve as a warning against popular elections and the dangers of democracy. One of the most entertaining and original of the imitations of *Don Quixote*, it shows an American author reacting several years later to the spirit that was rife in England in the middle of the century. In fact, the two American imitations deserve a place with the earlier works that have consistency and purpose: with *The Female Quixote, Launcelot Greaves*, and *The Spiritual Quixote*, rather than with the later insignificant productions which deserve attention only as they illustrate an interest of such vitality that it had not been entirely sapped by the end of the century.

Through all this series of quixotic novels, *The Female Quixote* stands quite alone as a type of imitation of *Don Quixote*. It possesses something of the spirit and tone of the original. More than any other novel that we have discussed does it maintain the gentle quaintness and distinctive fancy which characterized Cervantes. Though set against an eighteenth century background, as is *Launcelot Greaves*, the theme does not acquire an absurd unreality—probably because, in general, it overshadows the background. Though written with a purpose, as is *Female Quixotism*, it does not deteriorate into a humorous vehicle for conveying a definite teaching. It gives us, primarily, the appealing characters of Arabella and faithful Lucy. Joined to these are many amusing and ingeniously conceived incidents, knit together with a little too much quotation from the romances and imitation of their extravagances. The whole has lost much of its appeal today, because few of us are acquainted with the romances satirized and there is not matter sufficiently unusual in the novel, besides that satire, to attract many. Mrs. Lennox has made a contribution, however, not only in the simple, clear carrying out of the plot, and in the humor of the situations, but also in the creation of Arabella, who emerges as a genuine figure in eighteenth century fiction.

CHAPTER IV

Less Important Novels of Mrs. Lennox

BESIDES *The Female Quixote* and *The Political Quixote* Mrs. Lennox wrote four novels: *The Life of Harriot Stuart* (1751); *Henrietta* (1758); *Sophia* or *Harriot and Sophia*, as it is sometimes called (1762); and *Euphemia* (1790). None of these save *Henrietta* achieved any real notice. I shall therefore deal with them briefly, giving a short digest of each and indicating any important literary influences which seem to be reflected in it.

The Life of Harriot Stuart was Mrs. Lennox's first work of any length, and is best known in the literary world today through the banquet which Dr. Johnson gave the author to celebrate its publication. It is interesting biographically because many of the incidents of Harriot's life, especially those in America and upon her arrival in England, coincide with what Mrs. Lennox evidently wished believed of her early days. People have taken this novel to be autobiographical and, since they did it during Mrs. Lennox's lifetime, the probability is that she gave out that it was, at least partially, a study of her own early experiences.

Harriot Stuart is the daughter of an officer who is sent first to Ireland and then offered a good post in America, which he decides to accept. He sails with his family, three daughters and a son. Harriot is the second daughter and a literary prodigy, brilliant and beautiful, completely outshining her elder sister, for whom she has little affection. She lavishes her love upon her older brother and a younger sister, Fanny; she also reveres and loves her father, but her natural affection for her mother is constantly repelled by unjust and unsympathetic treatment. On the boat going over they meet two young men: Maynard, an officer of the ship, who is favored by Harriot's mother, and Dumont, a wealthy papist of New York, engaged to his cousin in England, a young man of great intelligence and attractiveness with the same tastes as Harriot. She writes verses to him and they become very intimate, reading Otway's *Orphan* together and charming all listeners. The Stuarts are met in New York by Governor Belmein,[1] his lady and daughters, and from there go on to Albany where Colonel Stuart has full command. In Albany Harriot has a love-affair with Governor Belmein's son, but the governor objects to the match because Harriot will have practically no dowry. The lover insists on her marrying him anyway, but her father's pride is greatly hurt and he will allow her to have nothing to do with him. Belmein leaves the fort to escape punishment after a duel, and Maynard comes up to press his suit for Harriot. Her mother insists on the marriage and even her father is about to yield, when Harriot is kidnapped by Indians and taken to the estate of Belmein's brother. There Belmein kills her love for him by his violent solicitations—for Harriot is a very proper young person—and she succeeds in escaping to the fort again, with the brother's help. Soon after her return her father dies, her brother and young Belmein go to Jamaica, Maynard is finally refused and sails away on his man-of-war, and Harriot goes to New York with her mother and sisters.

In New York she meets Dumont again and entirely wins his heart despite the throng of fair damsels who besiege him constantly. Her aunt has sent for her to come to England, but before she sails she promises Dumont not to marry for a year. Harriot leaves in the spring with her governess, Mrs. Blandon, but before they have been long on the water the ship is seized by a Spanish privateer. From this they are rescued by an English man-of-war, captained by a large, formidable, lascivious man, almost a Byronic hero, who promptly decides to win Harriot. Mrs. Blandon and her

---

[1] William Burnet was governor of New York from 1720-1728. Perhaps it is to him that Mrs. Lennox here refers (see *Civil List of the State of New York*) or it may be to his successor, General Montgomerie, governor from 1728-31.

charge would be quite helpless but for his nephew, Mr.
Campbel, an extremely kind and generous person, who also
falls in love with Harriot but who stands in great awe of his
uncle and dares take no step against his authority. The
captain is attempting the rape of Harriot when she melo-
dramatically seizes his dagger from the hangar and stabs
him. Unfortunately the ship's crew gather against her, but
she saves herself from the mob by heroically leaping to the
window from which she is going to drown herself. Mr.
Campbel saves her and the crew is won by her beauty and
daring.

Arrived in London, Harriot finds that her aunt's house is
closed.[2]

The fellow, immediately drawing near the window of
the coach, informed us that Lady L— had not been in
town the whole winter, and that the house was to be lett.
I was amazed my aunt had taken no measures to inform me
she was in the country, as well as to hear she had intirely
quitted her house, knowing that she never before had spent
a whole winter out of town. . . . . 'It must needs be, said
the landlady, that you are quite strangers in town, otherwise
you would have known that that lady has not been here this
great while; and they say that she has lost her senses, and
is confined at M— Hall, under the care of her brother-in-
law, Sir Edward L— . . . Your aunt, miss, pursued she,
lost her only son about eight months ago, who died of a
malignant fever. She was seized with it herself; and her
excessive grief, together with the effects of that fatal distemper, deprived her of her senses. I am told too, that she
has quite lost the use of her limbs, and is wheeled about
her apartment in a chair. . . . her husband's relations allow
no one to see her, but her own servants.'

Left entirely alone in London—except for her faithful
governess, who is, however, soon carried off by small-pox—
Harriot is taken under the protection of Mrs. Dormer, an
older lady who happens to have lodgings in the same house
with her. Harriot finds her aunt's relatives cold to her and

[2] *The Life of Harriot Stuart,* i, 218, 219, 222.

remains with Mrs. Dormer, at whose home she meets a man of the world who takes her to the Lady Cecilia, a lady of the court previously interested in a manuscript of her poems. This lady makes many promises which she fails to fulfill, and, though there are many at her house who might have helped Harriot, they are prevented because all think she is Lady Cecilia's protégée. At length our heroine realizes that her supposed benefactress is famous for her unfulfilled promises, and she is glad to go to live with the lady's sister in the country. There she is unfortunate enough to win away the countess' daughter's lover, and to alienate the foreign tutor, whose story is believed, and she is sent away on the charge of trying to seduce him. Forced to return to Mrs. Dormer, Harriot is rejoiced to see Dumont again. All the plans are made for their wedding when he is called to the deathbed of his cousin. Harriot, coming into town, is told by an old gentleman that her lover has married his cousin and allows herself to be taken away by him, thinking she is going to her mother and Fanny. Instead she is taken to a French convent, where she is shut up with other unfortunate ladies. Through another forced resident there her poems come to the attention of a marchioness who visits her with a count. The count, true to form, falls in love with Harriot, and by a ruse lures her to his home in St. Denis. There Harriot is rescued by a former mistress of the count who enables her to get away, but not before Dumont has seen her in the count's house and thinks that she has become his mistress. Returning to London, Harriot finds her mother and Fanny arrived from America. Mr. Campbel is also there and is about to be married to Harriot as a reward for his faithfulness when news comes of the loyalty of Dumont. He enters and learns the truth about Harriot; eventually the two lovers are joined with the remarkable and unnaturally unselfish acquiescence of the previous husband-to-be:

Not all his [Campbel's] remonstrances could prevail upon me to consent to give my hand to Dumont, till his health was perfectly restored; and I had the pleasure to see him assist at that sacred ceremony, which united me forever to my beloved Dumont, with a serenity in his countenance, which persuaded me his heart was entirely at ease.

Besides the history of Harriot there are two other stories: that of Mrs. Dormer, who suffered through yielding to love, and that of Mrs. Bellville, Harriot's friend in the convent, who suffered from her sister's lack of virtue and her own strict adherence to it, but who was at length rewarded with a husband and happiness.

The story shows a distinct narrative power; it moves along rapidly and coherently, and most of the incidents are clearly presented though they lack originality. The novel suffers from lack of characterization. All the gallants are exactly alike: Dumont, Belmein, Campbel, Clayton, differ not in the slightest degree, save that one declares his passion more fluently or more respectfully or more poetically than another. We see no possible reason why Harriot should not love Dumont, then Belmein, Dumont again, Campbel, and finally Dumont at the end; for, except for the names, they are one character,—and that the dimmest sort of character. The young ladies are likewise taken from one pattern, except the members of Harriot's family, who are rather more clearly distinguished. Mrs. Dormer is but a continuation of Mrs. Blandon, blessed with a little higher station in life. The only characters that we feel are real at all are those whom we have reason to think Mrs. Lennox took from her own experience. Harriot's father has a definite personality and a very attractive one. We can almost feel a daughter's pride and love shining through the portrayal of this gracious, dignified officer. The mother, too, while less clear, is a real person, though she has much more sympathy with her elder, practical-minded daughter than with the flighty, poetical, romantic heroine. The other two characters whom we might choose to rescue from the charge of being merely names are the Lady Cecilia, who seems to assume a certain reality, even though it is an unpleasant one, and Repeti, the French tutor. He is vain, clever, and deceitful, capable of an inexorable malice against anyone who once offends him. In the cases of the characters where she had living models Mrs. Lennox was successful in achieving a reality in portrayal; otherwise we have types acting mechanically, mere puppets drawn by the strings of a young girl's romantic fancy.

The scenes from the novel which have most interest are those in which Mrs. Lennox drops her romancing and gives simple descriptions of things which, in all probability, she witnessed herself. Such is her father's arrival in Albany.[3]

My father was received with much respect by the inhabitants of A—, who had impatiently expected us. We were saluted by all the ships in the harbour, who had their flags and streamers out; and the mayor, with the principal persons of the city, waited our landing, and conducted us to the fort, in which was a very fine house, where the commanding officer always resided.

She also gives a description of the governor's meeting with the Five Indian Nations to renew the treaty. This was an event of great pomp and seems to have made a keen impression on her mind. The meeting she refers to here was probably the one in October, 1728, when the new governor, General Montgomerie, came to confer with the Indians.[4] The one just before was in 1722, when she would have been too young to remember it, and there is no other recorded before she left for England in 1735.[5]

The five Indian nations with which we were in alliance were accustomed to come every third year to A—, and were met by the governour of N— to renew a treaty of peace with them, which was confirmed by presents to the extent of several hundred pounds, allowed by the government of

[3] *The Life of Harriot Stuart*, i, 44.

[4] *London Documents.* N. Y. State: "Documents Relative to Early Colonial History," v, 440.

[5] *Harriot Stuart*, i, 86, 7.

Britain for that purpose.   These savage people were assembled in great numbers, on the large plain behind the fort:
they had brought with them their wives and children, and
none but the aged and infirm were left behind.   We saw,
with astonishment, a new sort of city raised in the compass
of a few hours: for these people, when they travel, carry
with them the materials for building their houses, which con-
sist of the bark of trees, and two or three wooden poles, with
some bear skins to lye on: thus a square of ten feet will
serve to contain a very large family; and it being now in the
middle of summer, their hutts were decorated with the
boughs of trees on the outside, to keep out the sun, which
(on account of their different verdure) formed a new and
beautiful prospect.   I constantly spent some hours every
evening in the garden, which was at a small distance from
the fort, where I took great pleasure in viewing the Indians
at a distance; for I was too much terrified at them, to walk
out among their hutts, as several gentlemen and ladies who
were come from N— did.   The governor's intended interview with the Indians, drew great numbers of people from
all parts of the country: my father was preparing to receive
him with the usual formalities;

This description sounds like a personal reminiscence;
reading between the lines, we can distinguish the child's
keen interest in such unusual sights and occurrences, and the
impression which the gala occasion made upon Charlotte
Ramsay whose life in the tiny frontier center must have been
often monotonous.

There is some poetry included in this novel, much of
which is reprinted from Miss Ramsay's 1747 volume,
although there are a few new pieces.   These do not differ
from the other poems by her: they are in the riming closed
couplet or the quatrain form, not distinguished by any originality of thought or more than ordinary facility of verse.
All deal with the one subject which pervades the book—love.
Harriot, the sentimental heroine, is interested in this subject exclusively, and the poems are all her effusions.   She is
constantly moved to put down her emotions on paper and
then leaves these manuscripts about where they will accidentally come to view, and, of course, be admired by the finder.

The motive of surprise is never used in the novel; it is always expectation. Each event is ushered in by some such lugubrious foreboding as this: "Little did I realize what horrid experiences this step would involve me in." Or[6] "I left her so sensibly affected with this little parting, that I could not help expressing my surprise at it. Alas! I did not foresee that it would be long ere I should see her again, and that fortune was preparing the severest afflictions for me!"

The novel partakes of the sentimental nature of its heroine. Extraordinarily vain and forever conscious of the impression that her looks and speeches are going to make upon others, Harriot is also unfailingly moral and lacking in all sense of humor. In this respect there is a further similarity between her and the whole book, which does not contain one iota of legitimate humor. The modern reader may extract some from the extreme sensibility or silliness of Harriot, her pursuits by unworthy, dishonorable men, and her own conventionally virtuous romance. We tire of the theme, and the story lacks virility. There is certainly a little influence of *Clarissa Harlowe* in the sufferings of the virtuous maiden reflected here. For the most part, however, we have Mrs. Lennox experimenting. She takes a little background from her own experience,—the most natural, real parts of the novel—and lards all this over with the romantic fancy of a young, rather foolish girl somewhat spoiled by early appreciation of her literary powers and beauty. Most of the incidents which bear any stamp of originality redound to the advantage of Harriot and furnish her with an opportunity to appear as a great martyr, a great saint, a lady of remarkable virtue or remarkable courage. It is easy to believe that this is the first novel of a young lady, for there is a certain seriousness about unimportant things, an overemphasis upon what are really rather inconsequential interests of the young—especially the young of Harriot's sex—which stamps it as essentially a puerile production.

The novel was heavily scored in its own day by Lady Mary

---

[6] *The Life of Harriot Stuart*, ii, 92.

Wortley Montagu in a letter to the Countess of Bute, dated March, 1752.[7]

—but I believe you are already tired of hearing of him, as much as I was with the memoirs of Miss H. Stuart; who, being intended for an example of wit and virtue, is a jilt and a fool in every page. But while I was indolently perusing the marvellous figures she exhibits, no more resembling anything in human nature than the wooden cut in the Seven Champions, I was roused into great surprise and indignation by the monstrous abuse of one of the very few women I have a real value for; I mean Lady B. F. . . .

The *Gentleman's Magazine* makes only a brief comment:[8]

These volumes contain a series of love-affairs from 11 years of age, attended with a number of her adventures and misfortunes, which were borne with the patience, and are penn'd with the purity of a *Clarissa* . . .

The *Monthly Review* criticizes at greater length:[9]

We are persuaded that this is really the produce of a female pen; and therefore some may think it intitled to our more favourable regard. However, without a compliment to the author, we may safely venture to pronounce her work to be the best in the novel way that has been lately published. Her language is pretty good, and the manners of her persons, of nature, and agreeable to what we daily see in common life. But at the same time it must be owned that this work affords nothing great, or noble, or useful, or entertaining. Here are no striking characters, no interesting events, nor in short anything that will strongly fix the attention, or greatly improve the morals of the reader.

The reviewer emphasizes the salient point when he states that there is no weight to this novel; it is gracefully written in a simple, straightforward style, especially noticeable in

[7] *Letters of Lady Mary Wortley Montagu* (ed. Wharncliffe, 1861), ii, 221. For more from this same letter see above, p. 6.

[8] *Gentleman's Magazine* (Dec., 1750), xx, 575.

[9] *Monthly Review* (Dec., 1750), iv, 180.

the narrative portions, but, except for the interesting light
on American Colonial manners in Albany, there is little that
is not too trivial and inconsequential to be considered worth
writing.

Mrs. Lennox's next novel was the *Female Quixote* (1752),
which has already been discussed. She did not write another
until 1758, when *Henrietta* appeared.[10] It was in two volumes, and was fairly successful, for an edition also came
out in Dublin in 1758, two volumes in one with continuous
pagination, "Printed for George Faulkner, in Essex-street,
Sarah Cotter, in Skinner-row, and Hulton Bradley, at the
King's Arms and Two Bibles in Dame-street, Booksellers."
A second edition was printed for Millar in London in 1761,
which differed from the first in that it included the dedication
to the Duchess of Newcastle which we have seen her asking
permission to present in her letter of 1759 to the Duchess.
As from internal and external evidence it is probable that
here Johnson again wrote for Mrs. Lennox I shall quote the
dedication.

Dedication to the Second Edition.
To her Grace The Dutchess of Newcastle.

Madam,

The condescension and benignity with which your Grace
has hitherto favoured my performances and attempts, have
at least given me boldness enough to intreat your patronage
for a little novel.

Those to whom this book is new, will expect the name of
such a patroness to be followed by some work of deep
research and elevated dignity; but they whose nearer approaches to your Grace, have enabled them to distinguish
your private virtues, will not be disappointed when they find
it recommended only by purity and innocence. To obtain
the approbation of a judgment like yours, it is necessary to
mean well; and, to gain kindness from such benevolence, to
mean well is commonly sufficient.

---

[10] *London Evening-Post* (Feb. 2, 1758). The second edition is
advertised in the *London Chronicle* on March 19, 1761, and again on
March 7, 1769.

Had your Grace resolved only to countenance those who could have enlarged your knowledge, or refined your sentiments, few could have aspired to the honour of your notice, and far had I been removed from all hope of the favours which I have enjoyed, and the expectations which I have been permitted to indulge. But true greatness is always accessible, and pride will never be confounded with dignity by those who remember that your Grace admitted this address from,

Madam,

Your Grace's most obliged,

London,   and most devoted Servant,
Nov. 20, 1760.   Charlotte Lennox.

It seems more likely that the dedication is by Johnson in that the end of the second paragraph offers a similarity in idea and diction to part of a sentence in Johnson's "Review of A Journal of Eight Days' Journey" in the *Literary Magazine*, 1757:[11] "but, with us, to mean well is a degree of merit, which overbalances much greater errours than impurity of style."

Mrs. Lennox's play of *The Sister* (1769) was founded on this novel; therefore we find the novel readvertised in 1769.[12] In 1770 it was advertised as printed for T. Lowndes. There was an assignment of *Henrietta* on September 20, 1769; W. and J. Richardson had bought it at Millar's sale on June 13, 1769, and on September 20, they sold a third share to T. Lowndes, who promised to use his influence to get them the printing of a new edition when there should be need of one.[13] As I have found no copy of a 1770 edition of *Henrietta* I think this advertisement was simply the result of the assignment. In 1787-8 there was a new edition by Harrison and Co. for the *Novelist's Magazine* including plates, two volumes in one with continuous pagination; there

---

[11] Johnson, *Works* (1825), vi, 20. The *Literary Magazine* for April 15 to May 15, 1757, ii, 16t, no. xiii, has the clause beginning "but with us as to mean well".

[12] *London Chronicle* for March 7, 1769; for March 24, 1770.

[13] British Museum. Add. MS. 38730.

were several issues of this edition. In her letter to the Duchess of Newcastle Mrs. Lennox says that *Henrietta* has already met with considerable success and has been translated several times abroad; there were two translations of it published in French in 1760.

It has been said that the title of one chapter of *Henrietta*, "In which our heroine is in great distress", might serve as a synopsis for the whole book. We can certainly see the influence of Richardson in general conception, for the theme is the sufferings of virtue when exposed to the sins of the world and its ultimate triumph. Henrietta Courteney, our heroine, is the daughter of a love-marriage between the younger son of an earl who immediately disinherits him and the poor daughter of an officer's widow. She and her brother, Charles, are early left alone in the world, and he goes abroad as tutor to a duke's son. She endures various hardships until her father's sister, Lady Meadows, through family pride, takes her into her household and cares for her as if she were her own daughter. All would have been well had it not been for the machinations of the Catholic priest, Danvers, powerful member of Lady Meadows' household. Through his influence Henrietta is forced to choose between a convent in France and a Catholic baronet, rich, pinquid, obnoxious. In this predicament she flees from her aunt's home to London. Through a misunderstanding she there goes to a house of ill-repute, kept by a Mrs. Eccles. Mr. Bale, the kindly, generous, elderly business man who has been her guardian and adviser since her mother's death, is on the continent, but his son comes to see Henrietta and makes friendly offers to her. When she is annoyed by the attentions of a young lord at Mrs. Eccles', he helps her to go to Mrs. Willis, a kindly lady who fills the rôle of Mrs. Blandon or Mrs. Dormer in *Harriot Stuart* and who is Henrietta's staunch friend to the end. At this house Henrietta is visited by a loud-voiced shrewish woman, who proves to be young Mr. Bale's wife, come to reproach our heroine for winning her husband from her. She proceeds to insult Henrietta who, upheld by the dignity of conscious virtue, thus answers her :[14]

Go, learn from your husband who I am; and blush, if you can, for the injurious language you have given a person as much your superior by birth, as in that virtue perhaps of which you boast, and which has not withheld you from such indecent transports of jealousy as it would become a virtuous woman to suppress.

Henrietta is given to asserting her virtue thus; but she accompanies her consciousness of virtue with a frankness of speech and independence of action.[15]

'I am not used to scolding,' said Miss Courteney, calmly, retiring towards her bedchamber, 'and you, Mrs. Bale, seem to be an excellent scold.' The lady, provoked at this appellation, employed the coarsest language imaginable to express her resentment of the injury; but Miss Courteney took shelter in her bedchamber, the door of which she double-locked.

Unable any longer to accept the protection of young Mr. Bale and spurned by Lady Meadows unless she will accept the Catholic religion, Henrietta decides to earn her own living and is taken into the service of Miss Cordwain, the vulgar daughter of an enormously rich packer, who is just negotiating a marriage with the lord who had previously pursued Henrietta. They go to the castle of Lord B——, where he immediately seeks out Henrietta and converses with her in the garden. Unfortunately this interview is witnessed by Miss Cordwain who, to revenge herself, accuses Henrietta of stealing her bracelet. Mr. Cordwain, who is unconscionably stupid and ill-bred, adds his threats to his daughter's. The matter comes to the attention of the earl, the countess, and the young lord. Henrietta's birth is discovered to them by the lord and she is treated with respect. The packer unexpectedly finds the bracelet in his daughter's pocket, and at once proclaims his discovery, to her intense mortification,

---

[14] *Henrietta* (London, A. Millar, 1758), i, 238.
[15] *Id.*, i, 239.

and the disgust of the lord and his parents. They, however, conceal their feelings, and, as Mrs. Lennox phrases it:[16]

Thus did these noble persons accommodate themselves to the manners of those whom they in secret despised; and, for the sake of a few paltry thousands, shewed the utmost solicitude to associate plebean meanness in the honours of a noble ancestry, and to give title, rank, precedence, to one who would disgrace them all.

The countess is much impressed with Henrietta's dignity and beauty, giving her a letter to her sister in town, with the idea that, if she keeps some account of her position, it will be easier to guard her son till the marriage with Miss Cordwain is completed. Henrietta succeeds in obtaining a position with a Mrs. Autumn, a woman of fifty who tries to appear young and giddy. Our heroine is much disgusted with her behavior and refuses to accede to her pose by flattery or by conniving at her intrigues. She loses her place again, and is summoned by her uncle, the earl, who has been interviewed by Lord B———. Their plan is that Henrietta shall agree to her aunt's request for the sake of the fortune, and, with the dowry which her aunt promises, marry Lord B———. This young gentleman considers that he is being magnanimous and proving a great love for Henrietta by resigning his pretensions to the great fortune of Miss Cordwain and taking Henrietta instead, provided she will make this concession. She, however, is loyal to her faith and spurns the offer.

The countess asks her to come and live with her, but she refuses and instead takes service as a companion with a relative of the countess, a Miss Belmour. This young lady is indulging in a love-affair with a married man. Henrietta gives her salutary and virtuous advice as to how to test his love. It does not stand the test, and, in disgust, Miss Belmour and her companion go to Paris. While travelling they meet Melvil and Freeman, who are really the duke's son and Courteney, journeying *incognito*. The young men

[16] *Henrietta* (Ln., 1758), ii, 92-3.

follow them to Paris, where the marquis falls ill from his excessive love for Henrietta, who returns it. Courteney preserves his integrity by informing the duke of his son's weakness, but stumbles when, to induce his charge's recovery, he seeks to seduce Henrietta. Just after his attempt fails he learns that she is his sister and is overcome with remorse. Miss Belmour, meanwhile, has succumbed again to the charms of Mr. Campley and Henrietta with her virtue unsullied feels called upon to leave her. She returns to England with Mr. Bale and there her brother succeeds in discovering the perfidy of Mr. Danvers. At this psychological moment he persuades Lady Meadows to give Henrietta the once-promised dowry and the duke, with remarkable nobility of spirit and lack of calculation, allows his son to marry the beautiful and virtuous Henrietta, now acknowledged by her aunt and provided with a respectable inheritance.[17]

The charming marchioness did not make her first public appearance in town till late in the ensuing winter; when her beauty, her sufferings, her virtue, and her good fortune, were for a long time the subjects of conversation. . . . Every branch of the Courteney family made frequent advances toward a reconciliation with the marchioness and her brother: but generous as they were, they had too just a sense of the indignities they had suffered from them, to admit of it; and, in this steady resentment, they had, as it usually happens with successful persons, the world on their side.

In this novel we find Mrs. Lennox more worldly wise than in her two earlier novels. She is constantly alive to the advantages that the world gives to wealth over virtue, beauty, and even birth. Many references to this subject show bitterness and resentment on the part of the author, and a disillusioned attitude toward the eighteenth century world of fashion. The men and women of society who are introduced are represented as vain, shallow, and mercenary. Even the countess who is Henrietta's benefactress selfishly watches out for her own and her son's material welfare. The silly,

[17] *Henrietta* (London, 1758), ii, 313, 315.

hollow ideals of society are laid bare in all their sordid unpleasantness. Henrietta, whose sufferings we follow, is too much the paragon of beauty and virtue to win our whole-hearted sympathy. She is too conscious of her virtue and of the sins of others, and she never hesitates to inform her acquaintances how they might improve themselves—not infrequently, it turns out, by following her excellent example. In her character we see the influence of Richardson. Much more time is given to delineating her emotions and reactions than to the actual events of the story. We have seen that in her two earlier novels Mrs. Lennox showed a certain power in narration, in clear telling of a story. We miss that here, where the desire to present a moral heroine and her reactions under her trials has slowed the tale.

The characterization in this novel is stronger than in *Harriot Stuart*. Mr. Bale is a pleasant old gentleman and his son is rather interesting, too, in his sheepish attempt at wickedness. Miss Belmour, Miss Woodby, and Miss Cordwain are typical women of fashion who show the hollowness and futility of their lives, bounded by the petty interests of the day and governed by the dictates of a mercenary code. Their sole cause for living seems to be to fall in and out of love and to make a prosperous match. The gallants are moulded from the same pattern as those in *Harriot Stuart* with a little less sentimentality in their portrayal.

There is a rather successful attempt at burlesque in Mrs. Autumn whose ridiculous treatment of her long-suffering husband is as absurd as her pretense of giddy youth:[18]

'Yet he ought to be satisfied with me for what I did this evening, Languish indiscreetly betrayed the violence of his passion, by eagerly running (though there were two gentlemen nearer) to take up my glove which I had dropped. I took no notice of the dying air with which he presented it to me; but, as if his touch had polluted it, I received it haughtily from him and threw it aside. Sure this instance of disdain was enough to satisfy a jealous husband; yet mine, instead of looking pleased, coloured with jealousy and rage, and

[18] *Henrietta* (London, 1758), ii, 127.

gave me such furious glances: however, this will always be the case, where there is so great a disproportion in age; Mr. Autumn is not less than forty. But hey-day! is the girl asleep?' continued she, looking at Henrietta, who stood fixed in thought; for the absurd affectation of her mistress gave her matter enough for reflection.

The pseudo-learned lady of the day is satirized in the person of a caller upon the countess' sister.[19]

'Madam,' replied Mrs. ———, 'I take care that my servants shall not think me an atheist. They know my principles better: they know that I am a deist; they have heard me declare that I believe there is an intelligent cause which governs the world by physical rules. As for moral attributes, there is no such thing; it is impious and absurd to suppose it. The arbitrary constitution of things in the human system produces happiness and misery: . . . . Prayer, and such like artifices of religion, is foolish: for whatever is, is right. To talk of imitating God, is blasphemy. His Providence is extended to collective bodies only; he has no regard for individuals: nor is the soul a distinct substance from the body. There is no future state; it is all a fiction. To argue from unequal distributions is absurd and blasphemous. Whatever is, is best. The law of nature is sufficiently clear; and there is no need of supernatural revelation.'

Mrs. Lennox shows herself an ally of Johnson and Goldsmith in their attempts to stem the tide of deism, when she ridicules the doctrines of Pope, Shaftesbury, Bolingbroke as voiced by a lady who fails to practice them.[20]

'Oh,' said Lady D—, laughing, 'it would ill become one of her elevated understanding, to have natural affections: those she treats as vulgar prejudices. Her own sex are the objects of her scorn, because they are subject to such weaknesses as tenderness and pity. She reads Seneca on friendship in the morning; and exclaims, O the exalted passion! how divinely he treats it! what noble sentiments! In the afternoon she overreaches her friend and applauds her own

---

[19] *Henrietta* (London, 1758), ii, 110.
[20] *Id.*, ii, 111.

wisdom. Epictetus is studied with great care. She will preach a moral sermon out of Epictetus that will last two hours. Epictetus teaches her to regulate her passions. She reads him intently while her maid is combing her hair, and closes her book to storm at the poor trembling creature for accidentally hurting her with the comb.'

Miss Talbot must have taken offense at the "learned lady", for she writes to Mrs. Carter, December 10, 1758.[21]

Henrietta has been useful to us here, but there are many things in it that I dislike, and that tally with my opinion of the writer. That brother is execrable.—There are bits of pride and sauciness in Henrietta, and reflections in one place tending to ridicule a particular Providence, to which I object very greatly.

Mrs. Carter writes back just as disapproving in tone:

I did not think you would like Henrietta a bit more than I find you do; it was not a book to please you.

It is illuminating that the "blues" disapprove of the traits in Henrietta that keep her from being the typical sentimental heroine as well as of the criticism of deism.

Mrs. Lennox does not omit to confer praise upon the work of the novelist who had been so generous in his treatment of *The Female Quixote*. Henrietta is talking with Mrs. Eccles, the milliner with whom she first lodges by mistake.[22]

'—you chose very well when you chose this; it is one of the most exquisite pieces of humour in our language.'
'But what have you got?—O! the Adventures of Joseph Andrews—Yes, that is a very pretty book, to be sure!—but there is Mrs. Haywood's Novels, did you ever read them? Oh! they are the finest love-sick, passionate stories; I assure you, you'll like them vastly: pray, take a volume of Haywood upon my recommendation.'

[21] *Letters of Mrs. Carter and Miss Talbot* (ed. Pennington), ii, 271, 278.
[22] *Henrietta* (Ln., 1758), i, 36.

'Excuse me,' said Henrietta, 'I am very well satisfied with what I have; I have read this book three times already, and yet I assure you, I shall begin it again with as much eagerness and delight as I did at first.'

In relegating Mrs. Haywood to an inferior position Mrs. Lennox was following the example of the intellectual readers of her day, who condescended to this extremely "popular" writer. The praise of Fielding is interesting to note inasmuch as Johnson was offended by the coarseness of his novels and, in general, censured him. Mrs. Lennox had other literary relations and opinions than those she experienced as Johnson's protégée.

Henrietta met with general favor in the reviews and was commended for its gentility. The *Monthly Review* is most lavish in its praise, though the review is short.[23]

We look upon this to be the best novel that has appeared since *Pompey the Little* [by Frank Coventry, 1751]. The incidents are probable and interesting; the characters duly varied and well supported; the dialogue and conversation-scenes, spirited and natural, both in genteel and low life; the satire generally just; and the moral exemplary and important.

This is higher praise than this magazine accords to any other of Mrs. Lennox's novels. *The Critical Review* also commends it, especially in its treatment of religious subjects. It gives some lengthy quotations and continues:[24]

Mrs. Lennox has forfeited no part of her reputation by this publication; which we warmly recommend as one of the best and most pleasing novels that has appeared for some years. The story is simple, uniform and interesting; the stile is equal, easy, and well kept up, sinking nowhere below the level of genteel life, a compliment which cannot be paid to one of the most celebrated novel-writers we have.[25] The characters are natural and properly supported.—Tho' the

[23] *Monthly Review* (March, 1758), 1st series, xviii, 273.
[24] *Critical Review* (Feb., 1758), ii, 122-130.
[25] This reference is probably to Fielding.

reputation of Henrietta is chiefly founded on her steady adherence to the principles of the Protestant religion; that preference is given with a delicacy, that not the most bigotted Roman catholic could be offended at; the heroine nowhere betrays the rudeness of party, or the malevolence of religious attachment. The whole is interspersed with some short and spirited reflections aptly introduced, and here and there are some light sketches of humour very entertaining.

It is interesting that both these reviews cite *Henrietta* as the best novel in some years. There is a certain dignity about the work which won it respect. Not silly as was *Harriot Stuart*, lacking the ingenuity of *The Female Quixote*, it yet possesses an economy of style, a clearness of plot, and a sensible criticism of eighteenth century fashionable life which entitle it to second place among the novels of Mrs. Lennox. Though Henrietta does the conventional things— faints, blushes, is easily alarmed, and enlarges upon her virtue—she has courage and initiative. Her unquestionable intellectual powers and her independence of others' opinions where principle is concerned, combined with swiftness and lack of hesitation in action, give her strength. The novel acquires further distinction from the unusual or amusing minor characters and from the ease with which Mrs. Lennox writes. The experience of many translations besides her own creative work has given her familiarity with the language and a wide vocabulary which she employs with skill and often with grace. She never indulges in great scenes of emotion; these are passed over rapidly or told about in a few words. She doubtless realized her limitations and did not attempt heights which she had not the power to attain. For this, credit should be given her. The general note of the novel is restraint and economy both of incident and of moral reflection.

Mrs. Lennox's next novel was *Sophia* or *Harriot and Sophia*. It appeared in Mrs. Lennox's periodical publication, *The Lady's Museum* (1760-1), and in book form in 1762. The main part of the story has to do with the love affair of Sophia and Sir Charles Stanley. Sophia and

Harriot Darnley are daughters of a selfish, imprudent, society-loving widow of small means. Sophia is virtuous and pious, Harriot gay, beautiful, shallow, worldly, and her mother's favorite. Sir Charles Stanley, Harriot's wealthiest and most generous admirer, prefers Sophia after he once sees her, and attempts to seduce her. With the help of Mr. Herbert, a kindly old gentleman and her *deus ex machina*, she flees to the country to live at the home of Mr. Lawson, a country parson. There she becomes entangled in the affair of Dolly Lawson and William Gibbon, a neighboring youth whose wealthy eccentric old aunt has been highly offended by Mrs. Lawson's ridicule of her misuse of words and refuses to allow the marriage. Sir Charles mistakes William for Sophia's lover and hastily withdraws his recently-made offer of marriage. Sophia eventually goes out to service with a Mrs. Howard, an unpleasant lady, philanthropic of speech and niggardly of action, but leaves after several distressful happenings brought about by Mrs. Howard's malice and young Mr. Howard's love for her. After reconciling Mrs. Gibbon to the marriage of Dolly and William, she returns to town to take care of her mother who has been deserted by Harriot, now living handsomely in sin with a young lord. The contrast between impecunious virtue sewing patiently for her mother in a quiet cottage and the wicked Harriot with her gaudy chariot is heavily stressed. At length Sir Charles returns, having discovered from Mr. Howard that Sophia was guiltless. The two are happily married, with a flat mercenary morality in the union of rich young rake and innocent impoverished heroine that suggests *Pamela*; Mrs. Darnley conveniently dies; and Harriot marries a poor young captain and goes off to America. Thus is virtue rewarded and vice punished.

Sophia was translated into French and the translation published in London and Paris in 1770. In the preface the translator, after paying high honor to the art of novel-writing in England under Richardson and Fielding, exonerates this novel from being merely an imitation of these two great novelists as most succeeding English novels have been, and makes great claims for the charm of its heroine. She need not rely upon the fame of her creator, Mrs. Lennox, well known though she be in the world of letters, since "il suffit de la connoître pour l'aimer, et d'être vertueux pour chercher à l'imiter."

To a twentieth century eye Sophia's charm is less obvious, even though by her[26] "unwearied application to reading, her mind became a beautiful store-house of ideas: hence she derived the power and the habit of constant reflection, which at once enlarged her understanding, and confirmed her in the principles of piety and virtue."

Sir Charles Stanley, the debonair young hero, however,[27] "instantly saw something in her looks and person which inspired him with more respect than he had been used to feel for Mrs. Darnley and Harriot, a dignity which she derived from innate virtue, and exalted understanding. Struck with that inexplicable charm in her countenance which made it impossible to look on her with indifference, he began to consider her with an attention which greatly disgusted Harriot, who could not conceive that where she was present any other object was worthy notice."

We hear much of the wit and charm of Sophia but we seldom experience them. Her great learning and piety bore us as she buoys herself up through her hardships by the "modest approbation" of her own virtues. It is difficult to take a scene like the following seriously:[28]

The wretched fallen Harriot was proud! the diamonds that glittered in her hair, the gilt chariot, and the luxurious table; these monuments of her disgrace contributed to keep up the insolence of a woman, who by the loss of her honour was lower than the meanest of her servants, who could boast of an uncorrupted virtue.

[26] *Sophia* (Ln., 1762), i, 6.
[27] *Id.*, i, 24.
[28] *Id.*, ii, 112.

Sophia received her with the modest dignity of conscious virtue, and Harriot, tho' incapable of much reflection, yet soon perceived the miserable figure she made, in the presence of such a character, and stood silent and abashed, while Sophia contemplated her finery with an eye of pity and anguish.

The Man of Feeling is anticipated in the excessive sensibility of our hero:[29]

'Angelick creature!' exclaimed Sir Charles, with his eyes swimming in tears,; (or) —while her surprise kept her motionless, he threw himself at her feet, and taking one of her hands, pressed it respectfully to his lips, tears at the same time falling from his eyes.

Sophia is the least successful of all Mrs. Lennox's heroines. She has little of the sweet natural charm which Arabella possessed, and she lacks the independence and occasional pertness of Henrietta. The mother is like Harriot's mother in *Harriot Stuart*. Mr. Herbert is the Mr. Bale of *Henrietta* more distinctly drawn and given more opportunity to exploit his kindliness and moralistic views. Mrs. Howard reminds us of the Lady Cecilia in *Harriot Stuart* save that the more detailed picture given here shows her as a more actively unpleasant and despicable character. Mrs. Lennox must have known and hated the prototype of such ladies, for she draws them with a vigor and energy which argue personal resentment. Mrs. Gibbon rides a hobby as did Mrs. Autumn in *Henrietta*; her attempt to use long words and her subsequent mistakes put her in the class which includes such delightful figures as Mistress Quickly and Mrs. Slipslop earlier, Tabitha Bramble later, and which reaches its apotheosis in Mrs. Malaprop.[30]

'—she declared she would never more have any *collection* with such vulgar creatures . . from that moment she broke

[29] *Sophia* (Ln., 1762), ii, 207.
[30] *Id.*, i, 213-4, 220; ii, 258.

off any *treatise* of marriage between her nephew and me.' . . . 'and to *felicitate* your success, I will let her know that I am willing to receive the honour of a visit from her.' . . . 'You see, Madam,' said she, 'what *affluence* your commands have over me:'

In condemning the book for lack of characterization, we should have to except Mrs. Howard, Mrs. Gibbon, and the more slightly sketched figures of the Lawsons. *Sophia* belongs in the same class with *Henrietta*, but it is greatly inferior in style, characterization, and narrative. There is something in the situation of the two daughters and the mother which reminds one dimly of Mrs. Dashwood and her two daughters, Elinor and Marianne, in *Sense and Sensibility*. Jane Austen suggests the same general relation, but she has humanized them all and made the folly of Marianne romantic rather than vicious, to say nothing of the charm which she has bestowed upon the affectionate but weak mother and the generous, sensible Elinor. If she knew *The Female Quixote* so well, it is possible that she had read other novels of Mrs. Lennox and found something that appealed to her in the situation depicted in *Sophia*.

The criticism in the *Monthly Review* is by William Kenrick, and is a just one:[31]

It is a common error, with such adventures as meet with any degree of success, either in brandishing the goose-quill or the truncheon to push their good-luck too far, and risk a reverse of fortune by keeping the field too long. Next to the difficulty of making an honorable retreat, after a battle is lost, is that of knowing how far to pursue the good fortune of conquest, and where to retire securely to enjoy the spoils of victory. . . . . Hence it is expected of a writer, who hath acquired any portion of literary fame, that every new work he produces should be superior to the last; . . . . Mrs. Lenox, therefore, should not be disappointed if her *Sophia* does not meet with so warm a reception as the *Female Quixote*, *Henrietta*, and some other of her pieces, have been honoured with. Indeed, we must confess, that this perfor-

---

[31] *Monthly Review* (July, 1762), xxvii, 73-4.

mance, consisting of a love-story, not uninteresting in point of incident, nor inelegantly written, wants nevertheless, much of that spirit and variety which this species of composition peculiarly requires, and which are more conspicuous in some of her former works.

The review in the *Gentleman's Magazine* is not so discerning as this, but is interesting from the light it sheds upon the reputation Mrs. Lennox enjoyed among her contemporaries.[32]

It would, perhaps, be a sufficient recommendation of this work to say that it is written by Mrs. Charlotte Len-nox, the celebrated authoress of the Female Quixote; it is, however, but justice to add, that this novel is natural, elegant, and interesting; that it contains many observations which shew a perfect knowledge of the human heart, and a delicate sense of sublime virtue; To retail the story would be to injure the writer, in whose words alone it ought to be read, and at the same time to preclude a pleasure which we wish all our readers to partake, and which can only be found in the work itself.

Sophia even more than *Henrietta* places Mrs. Lennox in the class of the novelists who write for the "propagation of virtue". In *Humphry Clinker* Smollett says of contemporary novelists:[33]

Tim had made shift to live for many years by writing novels at the rate of five pounds a volume; but that branch of business is now engrossed by female authors, who publish merely for the propagation of virtue, with so much ease, and spirit, and delicacy, and knowledge of the human heart, and all in the serene tranquillity of high life, that the reader is not only enchanted by their genius, but reformed by their morality.

Smollett's recipe for success, substituting sentimental morality for literary value, is carried out better in *Sophia* than in any other of Mrs. Lennox's novels.

Mrs. Lennox's later novel, *Euphemia*, comes toward the

---

[32] *Gentleman's Magazine* (June, 1762), xxxii, 243.
[33] Smollett T., *Humphry Clinker* (ed. Saintsbury), 198.

close of her literary career, in 1790.[34] Much had been achieved in the history of the novel between 1762 and 1790. The vogue of the sentimental heroine introduced by Richardson had had its period of prosperity and was passing. Henry Mackenzie had written, between 1770 and 1780, three of his distinctively sentimental novels which had won wide audiences. It was popular for a time to imitate the man of feeling. People were also beginning to be interested in social problems and the didactic novel was taking shape. Fanny Burney had achieved success with *Evelina* and *Cecilia*, and Horace Walpole made the Gothic romance a popular type with *The Castle of Otranto*. Finally, in 1789, with *The Castles of Athlin and Dunbayne* Mrs. Ann Radcliffe gave to the world her first Gothic romance (at least it is of that type, though geographically speaking it is a Scottish romance), inaugurating the romantic appreciation of nature and combining it with a tale of horror and a setting of gloom. Thus tendencies and influences had changed, and when Mrs. Lennox began writing her next novel she found herself in a different literary setting from that of her earlier work, when people were just being roused to enthusiasm by *Clarissa Harlowe*, *Tom Jones*, or *Roderick Random*. It is significant that, forty years after her first novel, Mrs. Lennox was able to write one which met with a fair amount of favor, at least in the reviews.

Mrs. Lennox chose this time to attempt the novel of letters. *Euphemia* is composed of the letters between Euphemia Lumley, later Neville, and Maria Harley. Each tells her own story, though Maria's is entirely conventional and of no especial interest. Living with her uncle, who is extremely

---

[34] *London Chronicle* (June, 1790), "this Day was published, In Four Volumes Twelves Price 12 s. sewed, *Euphemia*. A Novel. By Mrs. Charlotte Lennox, Author of the Female Quixote, Henrietta, the Sisters, and Sophia; Novels. Printed for T. Cadell, in the Strand; and T. and J. Evans, Paternoster row." Another advertisement appeared in *St. James's Chronicle* (May 31, June 1, 5, 1790); on June 9 an apology was inserted "for heretofore calling *The Sister* a novel, when it is well-known that it is a play."

fond of her, she falls in love with a distant relative against
whose father her uncle has an eternal grudge because of an
early love-affair in which he was double-crossed. After
many adventures her uncle becomes reconciled to her lover
and she is happily married.

Euphemia's story is more interesting. Early left an
orphan, on her mother's death she marries Lieutenant Neville
because her mother has especially requested it, thinking that
in this way her daughter will be well cared for. There is
never much sympathy between them. He is an arrogant,
egotistical man, ambitious, extravagant, and haughty. That
there is little actual friction is due to Euphemia's restraint
and patience, for she submits to his wishes unless they are
too unreasonable. If she does persist in some little thing, he
takes pleasure in nagging her about it and will never admit
that he is wrong. He is most disagreeably represented in
such little scenes as when Euphemia is caring for a boy on
the boat who is desperately ill with small-pox and Lt.
Neville gives aid by telling her that her treatment will surely
kill him and that she has employed the wrong remedies all
the way through; or when Euphemia is in bed after the
birth of her child he comes in and finds a Dutch woman wash-
ing the floor, and, in a fit of wrath that she should thus
cool the room, he kicks over the pail and bursts into a volley
of abuse of the woman, who comprehends nothing of his
talk. He takes his wife to America in the hope that there
he will be able to save enough money to pay his debts and
provide for the future. They come over with the Bellendens.
Colonel Bellenden is to be the lieutenant-governor of New
York and Neville is his first officer. Colonel Bellenden has,
besides his wife, three daughters: Miss Bellenden, a haughty
beauty, vain and silly; Clara, another prodigy in beauty and
learning, who closely resembles Harriot Stuart; and Louisa,
a quiet, dignified young lady. The Nevilles accompany the
Colonel and his family first to New York and then to Albany,
where they all live in the fort. Two children are born to

Mrs. Neville, Edward and Maria. Soon after, Mr. Neville, regardless of her wishes, takes them to Schenectady where he has command. Little Edward is lost by his father in the woods and disappears. About two years later the colonel dies and Mr. Neville goes to Albany to be in charge of the fort there. Just as Euphemia is about to return to England she falls ill. During her illness her son appears to her in a dream and begs her not to leave without him. She goes up toward Schenectady to convalesce, and one day in the woods Edward and William, an old servant, appear, both dressed in Indian garb. Soon after, Mr. Neville's wealthy uncle summons him home, and they return to England, but not before the "young Huron" as Edward is called, has been much admired in New York. Arrived in London, Euphemia wins the uncle's heart, so that at his death he leaves her an independent fortune, much to her husband's disgust. He has fallen into his old extravagant habits and seeks to lead Edward into them, flouting Euphemia's authority in her son's face, to her infinite distress. The book ends with Mrs. Neville happy in her son and daughter and looking forward to seeing Maria.

There is little consistent story here. The book is made up of pictures of life or of tiny incidents almost as though it were a book of reminiscences. As most of the story is laid in America, and as those are the scenes most simply and faithfully presented, it is easy to surmise that we here have Mrs. Lennox going back in spirit to the scenes of her childhood and recreating them with an old person's exact memory of the early part of his life. The renewed interest in strange lands and peoples and the theme of the "noble savage" may have suggested to her that a presentation of what she had actually seen would be acceptable. Besides this biographical element in the settings, one cannot help feeling that Mr. Neville is Mr. Lennox. There is an intimacy about the way his character is presented that makes us feel that the writer certainly knew such a person and knew him in the relation here presented. The fact that there is nothing inconsistent

with the little we know about Mr. Lennox in this portrayal—
on the other hand, that he is just what we should imagine
him, especially in his relation with his son—substantiates this
surmise.

The family at the fort in Albany is the same as the one in
Harriot Stuart: Colonel Bellenden is as gracious and beloved
as Colonel Stuart, Mrs. Bellenden is pictured less, and the
elder daughter more, distinctly than the corresponding
characters in the earlier work, but they share the same general outlines.   Clara is Harriot over again, sharing the same
literary and poetic propensities and repeating her love-affairs
almost identically.   For instance, the governor's son falls
in love with her, but is discouraged from marrying her by
his father's pride.   She is finally won by a new character,
Mr. Euston, a visiting Englishman, who is interested in the
Indians and has spent years among them.   Another new
character, a young man of rank from England who is apt
to be rather unbalanced and do strange things, even before
his soldiers, woos Clara and then more successfully her
sister, Louisa.   One incident of his peculiar behavior during
a military review sounds too much like a reminiscence not
to believe that Mrs. Lennox is here presenting an unusual
circumstance which was a subject of conversation when she
was a child at the fort.[35]   Mrs. Benson is Mrs. Blandon or
Mrs. Willis, from *Harriot Stuart* or *Henrietta*, as you wish.
Euphemia is inclined to moralizing and is pictured as a
woman of great piety, but she holds our sympathy.   We
never feel any youth about her; she is essentially old, mature,
and experienced.   We pity her sufferings and her position,
and like her for her uncomplaining fortitude.

Much of this novel of little incident is taken up with
moral axiom; both Euphemia and Mrs. Benson are prone
to reflect upon the imminence of death and the wages of sin.
Many of the short reflections have a Johnsonian flavor; some
are briefly and effectively phrased.   For example :[36]

[35] *Euphemia*, iii, 141-2.
[36] *Id.*, iv, 49, 194-5.

The life of a good man is a continual prayer.

Conversation, said she, has been properly stiled the air of the soul; they who value the health and ease of the mind, ought to chuse an element pure and serene for it to breathe in.

Especially in the last two volumes occurs more and more of this tendency to philosophize and pause to reflect upon general truths. It gives the work rather the effect of an essay than a novel.

There are many scenes in America which are authentically and simply described. That Mrs. Lennox is calling upon her memory is evident for two reasons: many of the descriptions are practically the same as those in *Harriot Stuart*; all the background is early Colonial and not contemporary with the time Mrs. Lennox was writing, when, of course, everything was quite changed. There is an anachronism here, for Clara is reading *Cecilia*, upon which Euphemia makes this comment:[37]

This was a novel, newly published in your world; and because it has uncommon merit, I suppose you have read it. Mr. Euston presented it to Clara; and told us, that Cecilia is the performance of a young lady, whose elegant genius is generally admired.

As *Cecilia* did not appear until July, 1782, it fits oddly with New York before the Revolution.

Mrs. Lennox's reference to Fanny Burney is generous compared to that lady's attitude toward her, which, as we have seen, was not of the pleasantest. It seems probable that they had little to do with each other, so little that Mrs. Lennox may not have known of Miss Burney's diffidence, may have had no opportunity to form an independent judgment of her, and may simply be reflecting the well-known admiration of her friend, Dr. Johnson. At any rate, we have no reason to suppose that this is included as a com-

[37] *Euphemia*, iii, 107.

pliment to a personal friend as were similar references to Richardson, Johnson, and Fielding.

There are a few signs of Mrs. Lennox's being alive to the tendencies of her own time. One is shown in the description of nature; here is a picture of the Hudson and its banks.[38]

> but in the morning we were again becalmed, and as we moved slowly along the liquid plain, which was as smooth as glass, we were at leisure to admire the magnificent scene that presented itself to our eyes.—The river here being very narrow, running between a ridge of mountains on each side, whose tops covered with groves of lofty trees, seemed to hide their heads in the clouds, while their sloping sides were adorned with the most beautiful verdure, and trees of many species unknown to us. The awful gloom from the surrounding shades, the solemn stillness, inspired a soft and pleasing melancholy, which we enjoyed in silence, being, as the poet says, 'rapt in pensive musing'.

Such words as "groves", "verdures", "gloom", and "melancholy" remind us of Mrs. Ann Radcliffe and the sort of nature which she presents. Only one of her novels, *The Castles of Athlin and Dunbayne*, had appeared as yet, and this came out the year before *Euphemia*, in September, 1789. Besides the similarity noted, in the nature description, there are two other analogies between these two novels. In both there is a son who is stolen and brought up among people who live more simply than his parents do; he is found to possess not only native graces but also all the virtues. Alleyn, in Mrs. Radcliffe's book, is brought up, like Douglas, by a simple shepherd; Edward is trained by the Indians and later by a Jesuit priest in Canada. Cross writes of the didactic novel from 1790 on:[39] "Another procedure of the novelist was to place in the plot a young negro, or an English boy born and bred in the West Indies, and to let him comment on English customs in the light of nature."

[38] *Euphemia*, iii, 8.
[39] Cross Wilbur L., *Development of the English Novel* (N. Y., 1923), 91.

This is exactly what Edward does when he is taken to New York. He amazes people with his extraordinary knowledge on some points and naïveté on others. In the "Young Huron", as he is called, we see the noble savage, who had caught the imagination of the eighteenth century. Echoes of this are to be found in such lines as the following:[40] "In a word, the savage is subject to none but natural evils," or the description of the Indians who showed great sympathy at the death of Colonel Bellenden:[41] "The request they (the Mohawks) made, to be permitted to pay their compliments of condolence to the widow and daughters of the Great Chief, as they stile him, show that these untutored savages, have in their minds those natural principles of humanity, which is the foundation of true politeness." These ill accord with the truer, less sentimentalized picture of the Indians Mrs. Lennox gives more frequently and which bears the mark of personal knowledge; they are interesting, however, as a sign that she did conform to the changing taste of the time.

The other similarity between the two books is in the recognition scenes of the two young men. In *The Castles of Athlin and Dunbayne* the Baroness thus recognizes her son:[42]

'It is,—it is my Philip!' said she, with strong emotion; 'I have, indeed, found my long lost child; that strawberry on his arm confirms the decision.'

In *Euphemia* Mrs. Lennox is more original, and the mark by which Euphemia recognizes her son is the print of a bow and arrow on his breast, caused by a fright she received from an Indian before Edward was born. This method of certain recognition is by no means new: the strawberry mark at once reminds us of *Joseph Andrews* and the general device may be traced in English fiction to the mark of a

[40] *Euphemia*, iii, 31.
[41] *Id.*, iv, 70.
[42] Radcliffe Ann, *The Castles of Athlin and Dunbayne* (The Second Edition, Ln., 1793), 275.

lion's paw on the neck of a character in Sidney's *Arcadia*
and to the bright cross on Havelok's back in *The Lay of
Havelok the Dane.*

In taking over the letter form, Mrs. Lennox may have
been encouraged by the success of such books as *Evelina*
(1788) and *Julia de Roubigné* (1777). Thus in many
respects we see Mrs. Lennox reflecting tendencies of the
closing decades of the eighteenth century. She reminds us
a little of Mrs. Radcliffe in her nature descriptions. She
shows the influence of the belief in the natural goodness of
the savage, a theory which had begun early in the century
but had received especial impetus from Rousseau's *Emile*
(1762). She adheres still to the earlier sentimentality
but tinges it with didacticism as the fashion is. Finally,
she uses the letter form, which is just on the verge of
decline. Mingled with all these contemporary fashions is
a large element of biographical detail, both of Mrs. Lennox's life as a child in Albany, and of some of her
experiences as a wife and mother. There is a mellowness
about the flavor of the whole, a rather gentle detach-
ment, as of one now losing interest in life except through
the halo of reminiscence, which lends the book a distinctive
charm.

Euphemia interested the readers of the time, if we may
judge by the lengthy reviews it received in many magazines.
The European Magazine and London Review (Aug., 1790)
praises it in general, citing for especial commendation the
character of Mr. Neville,—which seems to the reviewer to
be drawn from life,—and the picturesque representations
of scenes from upper New York. *The General Magazine
and Impartial Review* (July, 1790) also praises it at considerable length and is pleased with the large number of
profitable maxims, from which several quotations are included. *The Monthly Review* is less enthusiastic about
Euphemia, though the moral tone and general refinement are
commended. The article closes (2nd series, iii, 89), however, with an encomium of Mrs. Lennox, which I shall quote.

We always imagined, with respect to the literary abilities of this Lady, (whose productions are nearly coeval with the existence of our Review) that it was impossible for a writer endowed with so much genius, to offer any performance to the public, that would prove unworthy the perusal of readers who have any pretensions to the praise of discernment and taste; and we are still of the same opinion.

The Critical Review grants it the longest and most detailed account of any magazine. I shall quote parts of it (July, 1790, lxx, 81-3).

If we enlarge in our account of this pleasing novel, it is chiefly because we think it uncommon in construction, and interesting from some of its descriptions; accounts of a country which, though long in our possession, has scarcely ever been described in a picturesque narrative. Euphemia does not appear, at first, the most striking personage of the history. It begins where most novels usually end, by her marriage; a marriage dictated by duty and convenience rather than affection. The character of Mr. Neville, her husband, is drawn only in the little incidents of Euphemia's correspondence; and it seems to be copied from nature, where similar inconsistencies are sometimes found . . . . .—his failings are the source of Euphemia's distresses, and afford her not only an opportunity of establishing her own character, but of giving a striking example to wives in similar situations: yet the conclusion does not leave the mind wholly at rest: the trials of our heroine are not at an end: and, though in possession of many sources of happiness, the whole may be tainted by the inconsiderate, hasty conduct of such a husband . . . . The characters, however, though drawn without any splendid traits, are sufficiently distinct, and very ably supported: indeed, in every part of these volumes, we see characters delineated with so much apparent fidelity, and preserved with such strict consistency, that we almost forget we are reading a novel. This last work of Mrs. Charlotte Lennox, if it should prove her last, will not sully her fame. If she does not shine with meridian splendor, she sets with a mild radiance, more pleasing and more attractive.

The recognition of an attempt to portray characters quietly and really here suggests that the thing we find in Jane

Austen a few years later was not so different from the method employed in this later work as from the technique of *Harriot Stuart* or of Richardson's *Clarissa Harlowe.* Did Mrs. Lennox, with the true-to-life unromantic characters in *Euphemia,* set an example for Jane Austen, as she did with the heroine led astray by her reading in *The Female Quixote,* and with the relations between a mother and her two daughters in *Sophia*?

Mrs. Lennox's last novel, *The History of Sir George Warrington; or, The Political Quixote* (1798), has been discussed with *The Female Quixote* and the succeeding series of quixotic novels.

The contributions which Mrs. Lennox made to the advancement of the novel are not many, chiefly because she followed so closely the tendencies of the period in which she was writing. Even *The Female Quixote,* the plot of which is original with her, is in general character suggested by a noticeable bent in eighteenth century writers to copy from Cervantes and the quixotic character. In her other novels we have instances of the sentimental heroine: in *Henrietta* done with considerable success; in *Sophia* with little to distinguish it from the ordinary novel of the time. It is in the American scenes of *Harriot Stuart* and *Euphemia* that we find something original with Mrs. Lennox and interesting historically and biographically. The accurate simple accounts of a passage up the Hudson and of life in the fort at Albany with occasional excursions into the surrounding country are the most valuable and unusual portions of these novels. Mrs. Lennox is most successful, both in scenes and characters, when she is drawing upon her personal experience. She possesses little originality and is easily influenced by prevailing fashions of writing. She has, however, a natural ease in telling a story, and her narratives are, in general, good. In *Euphemia,* which contains more philosophizing than any other novel of hers, there is dignity and succinctness in the expression of the aphorisms. Her early heroines have an independence of mind and action which sets them off from many of their prototypes and gives them charm, even today. In addition—and what mattered especially to an eighteenth century critic—all her novels pay strict attention to the rules of decorum and are characterized by excessive gentility. This acts to the detriment of humor, of which, comparatively speaking, her novels contain little. They seek rather to instruct than to amuse, except in the case of *The Female Quixote*, and of separate minor characters in the other novels. On the whole, it is this tendency to instruct which detracts from the vitality of the works and relegates them to obscurity. The parts which have freshness today are a few characters like Colonel Stuart, Henrietta, Mrs. Howard, and Mr. Neville, and the Colonial scenes drawn from Mrs. Lennox's childhood experience.

CHAPTER V

Mrs. Lennox's Poetic Attempts

ALTHOUGH Charlotte Ramsay began her literary career as a writer of verse and although she later attempted a pastoral drama in verse our interest in her poetry today is more in the attention it received in its own day as shown by a reprinting in the *Gentleman's Magazine*, the appearance of a new poem by her there, the poems written to her in praise of her poems or in reply to them, than in the poems themselves. The complete conventionality of subject, phraseology, and form makes them little deserving of attention for their own sake. On the other hand, the revision in the poem she chooses most often to reprint and slight alterations in other poems reprinted connect with Baretti's ode to her on writing poetry in which he blames Johnson for her changing interest, and lend a biographical interest.

It is through two unique works of the period that these revisions and their connection with Johnson appear. The first is *Proposals* for printing her poems by subscription with a printing of her poem, "On Reading Hutchinson on the Passions", dated November 4, 1752, of which the only known copy is in the Yale Library and of which I am presenting a facsimile here. The second is an ode to Charlotte Lennox by Baretti in his hand, one of nineteen poems in a manuscript book found at Casale, Italy, with a letter by Baretti accompanying the book in which he conveys it to "mio carissimo Don Rimigio", dated at London, May 30, 1754. The book and letter belong to Captain Frank Lester Pleadwell to whose generosity I owe my copy of the ode. It has never before been printed.

In the *Proposals* the printing of "On Reading Hutchinson on the Passions" has many changes in text which arouse interest. I am therefore giving below the text of the poem as originally published by S. Paterson in 1747.

November 4, 1752.

PROPOSALS

For PRINTING by SUBSCRIPTION,

POEMS

O N

SEVERAL OCCASIONS.

BY THE
AUTHOR of the FEMALE QUIXOTE.

SUBSCRIPTIONS are taken in by
Mr. MILLAR, in the Strand; and Mr. DODSLEY, in Pall-mall.

CONDITIONS.

I. THE Work fhall be printed in a neat Quarto Volume, on the fame Paper and Letter with the Specimen annexed.

II. The Work is ready for the Prefs, and will be delivered to the Subfcribers towards the latter End of March 1753.

III. Thofe who are willing to encourage this Undertaking, by their Subfcriptions, are defired to pay Half a Crown at the Time of Subfcribing, and another Half Crown on the Delivery of the Book fewed in Blue Paper.

REceived of
being the firft Payment for
of the above Book, which I promife to deliver agreeable to the Terms of thefe Propofals.

Charlotte Lennox

HUTCHINSON on the PASSIONS.

THOU who thro' Nature's various maze canſt rove,
⠀⠀And ſhew what ſprings the rapid paſſions move;
Teach us to combat anger, grief and fear,
Recall the ſigh, and check the ſtarting tear.
Why was thy ſoft philoſophy addreſt,
All to the vacant ear, and ~~quiet breaſt~~
With eaſe may peaceful apathy be taught
To theſe who ſtagnate in a calm of thought:
Whoſe hearts by love or hate were ne'er poſſeſt,
Who ne'er were wretched, and who ne'er were bleſt:
Who one dull ſlumber through their lives maintain,
And only dream of pleaſure and of pain;
Serenely ſtupid.⠀⠀So ſome gentle ſtream
Steals thro' the winding valleys ſtill the ſame;
So ſilent down the muddy channel creeps;
While the ſoft zephyr on its boſom ſleeps.

My fervent foul a nobler art requires,
Not to fupprefs, but regulate her fires:
Some better guides, who temperately wife
Allow to feel, yet teach us to defpife.
To Rèafon's fway fubject the Soul's domain,
And not fubdue the paffions, but reftrain.

On reading HUTCHISON on the PASSIONS.

Thou who thro' Nature's various Faults can rove,
And shew what Springs the eager Passions move;
Teach us to combat Anger, Grief and Fear,
Recal the Sigh, and stop the falling Tear.
5 Oh be thy soft Philosophy addrest,
To the untroubled Ear and tranquil Breast:
To these be all thy peaceful Notions taught,
Who idly rove amidst a Calm of Thought:
Whose Soul by Love or Hate were ne'er possest,
10 Who ne'er were wretched, and who ne'er were blest:
Whose fainter Wishes, Pleasures, Fears remain,
Dreams but of Bliss, and Shadows of a Pain:
Serenely stupid: so some shallow Stream
Flows thro' the winding Valleys still the same:
15 Whom no rude Wind can ever discompose,
Who fears no Winter Rain, or falling Snows;
But slowly down its flow'ry Borders creeps,
And the soft Zephyr on its Bosom sleeps.
Oh couldst thou teach the tortur'd Soul to know,
20 With Patience, each Extream of human Woe;
To bear with Ills, and unrepining prove
The Frowns of Fortune, and the Racks of Love:
Still should my Breast some quiet Moments share,
Still rise superior to each threatning Care:
25 Nor fear approaching Ills, or distant Woes,
But in *Philander's* Absence find Repose.

This poem was apparently Mrs. Lennox's favorite of her own creation as she reprints it three times after the initial printing. She uses it in *Harriot Stuart* (ii, 146, 147) in almost the same form. The only changes are: the correction of "Hutchison" to "Hutchinson" in the title; "maxims" for "Notions" in l. 7; "but of pain" for "of a Pain" in l. 12; a plural for the singular "Soul" in l. 9 and a singular for the plural "Borders" in l. 17; the first letters of nouns are reduced to lower case and five exclamation points are introduced. But the version in the *Proposals* almost two years later contains significant alterations; the same version is retained in the *Lady's Museum* (ii, 667) about ten years later with one or two slight changes in spelling or punctuation. In this altered version the opening idea is greatly clarified by the change to the question "Why was" in l. 5 and by the complete change of ll. 7 and 8. The changes of words in ll. 1, 2, 4, 6 also make for accuracy and clarity. The altered ll. 11 and 12 build a more unified picture than the scattering, elaborate, figurative lines in the 1747 version. The more concise apposite effect continues through the word changes and the omission of two lines (15, 16) in the figure. The greatest change comes in the last six lines introduced instead of the eight in the original; here the conventional pastoral note of personal lament and emotional suffering because of "Philander's Absence" disappears entirely and is replaced by calm reasoning testifying to the power of "Reason's sway" and enthroning restraint and regulation of the passions as a "nobler art".

Of the three other poems of Mrs. Lennox that she uses more than once none appears but twice. Of these a lyric from *Philander* is reprinted in the *Lady's Museum* (i, 45) without change save that the first stanza is set to music. The irregular ode "To Death" from *Harriot Stuart* (ii, 9) is used in the *Lady's Museum* (i, 48) with the third from the last line changed from the personal

> Enough of life's distress I've seen:

to

> Do grief and sickness waste the frame in vain?,

a question more parallel with the preceding line "Are my days lengthen'd [*Lady's Museum*, length'ned] to prolong my pain?", but rendering meaningless the succeeding lines which are vivified by the personal expression of the earlier version. The last poem in *Poems* (86) "Shallum to Hilpah, an Epistle from the Spectator", a rewriting in verse of the letter from Shalum to Hilpa in the *Spectator* No. 584, is reprinted in the *Lady's Museum* (ii, 668) as "Shalum, Master of Mount Tirzah, to Hilpa, Mistress of the Valleys. An Antediluvian Love Letter. By a Young Lady." with the reference to the *Spectator* omitted. Immediately following it in the *Lady's*

Museum (ii, 669) is "Hilpa Mistress of the Valleys, to Shalum, Master of Mount Tirzah. By the same.", a rewriting of Hilpa's answer in "The Sequel of the Story of Shalum and Hilpa", *Spectator* No. 585, a work which Mrs. Lennox apparently added to her previous poetic productions to fill the pages of her magazine in 1761.

Besides the changes of capitalization, spelling, punctuation in the reprinting of the first poem there are minor changes of wording as in the figure "Like a tall Oak" (*Poems*, 88) to "So the fair cedar" (*Lady's Museum*, ii, 669). The prose of the *Spectator* has both: "It flourishes as a mountain oak, or as a cedar on the top of Tirzah,". Several lines are shifted with an occasional omission, resulting in greater coherence; and the rewording of the lines

> Remember, fair One, that the Age of Man
> Is but a thousand Years, and quickly gone:
> Beauty, tho' much admir'd, yet soon is past,
> Its transient Glories but some Centuries last: (*Poems*, 87)

to read

> Daughter of Zilpah, think on life's short date;
> To a poor thousand years 'tis fix'd by fate,
> How soon are beauty's transient glories past;
> Its fading bloom will scarce four centuries last.

gives an effect of greater dignity and restraint. The changes in the poems of Mrs. Lennox used more than once, then, are slight save in the *Proposals*, but, as there, are in the direction of more restraint and balance.

Since Johnson had notably influenced and aided Mrs. Lennox in her literary ventures during 1752 and 3 and since these changes, especially those in the *Proposals*, are of the sort he would approve most highly, with his known interest in dedications, prefaces, and proposals the question of his influence here naturally rises. The likelihood of a Johnsonian touch is heightened by Baretti's ode to Mrs. Lennox, a translation of which I am presenting here.[1] The original is in verses of seven syllables, *settinari,* arranged in twenty-six six-line stanzas with a rime scheme abcabc.

Ode to Charlotte Lennox

Now that you have nearly reached the Aonian summit, do you think of turning back? How do such cowardly thoughts arise in so sublime a mind, Charlotte?

Now that only a few steps remain to be taken up the difficult hill, shall we see a woman like you change her mind and turn back with despondent face?

Now that Clio herself comes to meet you and wishes to change lyres with you; now that the shining God opens to you his sweet schools, Charlotte, will you turn back your step?

Alas, what fatal powers, envious of the glories of British soil, suggest these thoughts to you, make you rebel against Phoebus and Love?

Bestir, bestir yourself, return and tread with light step the first pathways. You fearful? You downcast on a way now so short? Ah no, that must never be true!

Return to sing of love on the calm waters of your native river; return to the nymphs to fill your heart with sweetness.

But do you not yield attention to my honest advice, do you neither speak nor reply? Rather, with blushing cheek, and downcast, troubled eye, are you perturbed at my words?

And this silent, strange behaviour, what does it mean, Charlotte? Why close your mind to him who wishes to encourage you to the lofty goal?

What? But I already divine the secret cause of all this waywardness. I know who it is would dissuade you from the beautiful road. I know, I know, who is opposed to me.

Johnson, inflexible Englishman, who thinks a graceful nothing a sin and a vice; who weighs for a month in the balance of his judgment every one of his own lines.

---

[1] I give the ode in the original Italian in Appendix IV. This translation I owe to Captain Pleadwell, Lacy Collison-Morley, and Jeannette Byington.

Johnson, whose heart is full of austerities, whose head is filled with serious philosophy; who fears that an innocent feeling can only be the key to the temple of Priapus;

Johnson, Johnson, it is he who has been at you with his terrible words, and I myself feel his austere voice lording it over my own mind and senses.

But (pardon me, my sage and inflexible follower of the Greek husband) But (don't be offended my loquacious Muse now dares to contradict you).

But it is not true that the Apollonian art must be consecrated wholly to virtue. Let not Virtue, naked and thin, inhabit a royal palace built by Love alone;

Or, if it wishes to have a comfortable room up there under the Heliconian roof, it must drop its austere demeanour and be a companion to him who was the architect.

Truly, it must not always disdain and fly from the gentle son of the lame Sicilian; and through excessive wrath, vainly preaching to us, bring about its own destruction.

In lofty style let Homer paint the virtuous Nestor and Ulysses, but then singing of the fierce Pelides, let him dream and feign that love transfixes him.

Let the pious Aeneas erect an altar to Diana on the inhospitable shore; but let him first drink the tears from the eyes of the dear afflicted Dido.

Let Charles and Godfrey brandish their stout swords against the barbarian and infidel nations; but the Orlandos and the Rinaldos may not withstand the meeting with Angelica and Armida.

What am I saying? Rather, on the lonely banks of the Sorga, let a friend of Plato tell how many tears overflowed from his loving eyes for the modest Laura.

Let him tell of the curling tresses disordered by the wind or flowing in it; and beneath a beech or oak let the French Shepherd enjoy the foreign words.

And while he softly soothes the breezes round with his divine lyre and at his sweet song in his woodland retreat everything feels and breathes love;

Let even Johnson hear, admire, and praise his tender lays in silence; nor let virtue attribute to him as a crime his anything but lascivious lays.

Now banish from you that idle fear which forbids your speaking of love; follow, Charlotte, follow the Tuscan poet boldly and fearlessly.

And if you have no more love drama for that Shepherd, who leaves you betrayed, swiftly create another flame and complain at all hours of an imagined pain.

Yes, yes, let a feigned sorrow, if not a real one, never be extinguished in you, and let your talent make your language equal to the language of Italy.

At the close of the ninth stanza Baretti announces he knows who is opposed to him and who is dissuading Charlotte "from the beautiful road". With Baretti's well-known enthusiasm for the pastoral form it seems likely that here he is objecting to Johnson's influence that has removed "Dreams but of Bliss", "Shadows of a Pain", "Flow'ry Borders", and "Philander's Absence" from Charlotte's poetry, and is urging her against weighing each word in the balance with the consequent loss of so many words, and against turning a "graceful nothing" into something "austere" and "filled with serious philosophy". At the very end he exhorts her not to renounce "love drama for that Shepherd", as she has by omitting "Philander's Absence".

The likelihood that Baretti refers to Johnson's restricting influence on Charlotte as shown in these revisions of her poems is heightened by the fact that the only other poetic work of Mrs. Lennox is her pastoral drama, *Philander*. The production of this piece may derive from Baretti's counsel to return to the poetic muse, as her imitation, here acknowledged, of the Italian pastoral poet, Guarini, may result from their earlier intercourse as well as from the poem written her by her Italian master in 1754.

Baretti's enthusiasm for Charlotte's earlier conventional poetry of the pastoral type is difficult to share. One can only conjecture whether the "native river" of stanza six is the Thames or the Hudson. Had Mrs. Lennox accepted the suggestion and put "nymphs" on the "calm waters" of the Hudson before Goldsmith conveyed the victims of land-enclosures to the "wild Oswego" or Gray sang of "savage Youth" in "Chili's boundless forests" she might have touched one fresh note of romantic poetry instead of clinging to a convention that was beginning to be outworn by 1711.

On December 1-3, 1757, in the *London Chronicle* was announced: "Philander. A Dramatic Pastoral. By the author of the Female Quixote. London: Printed for A. Millar, in the Strand. MDCCLVIII. Price One Shilling." *Philander* was a small pamphlet, only forty-eight pages long, consisting of three short acts with no scene divisions. It was dedicated to Lord Charlemont. In the dedication Mrs. Lennox gives credit to outside influence and assistance:

The merit of this poem is but small in my own opinion, and yet, of the little praise which it may receive, I must resign a part, by confessing that the first hint was taken from the *Pastor Fido* and that the two songs marked with asterisks*, were written by another hand. (See pp. 11 and 14.)

Whatever praise this confession may detract from my abilities, it will add to my sincerity; and I should discover little knowledge of your Lordship, if I should endeavour to recommend myself rather by elevation of genius than by purity of manners.

I am, with great respect,
My Lord,
Your Lordship's
Most obliged
Humble servant,

London,
Nov. 20, 1757.   Charlotte Lennox.

The ease and effectiveness with which the heavy formal constructions in these sentences are brought to a conclusion, particularly the dignity of the apology, point to Johnson as author, as do the other sentences of the dedication. As I have suggested above, since there is no external evidence against his authorship and the internal evidence is strong for it this is another of Mrs. Lennox's dedications probably written by Johnson.

The plot of *Philander* is slight.   Sylvia has been betrothed in her infancy to Philander, son of Menander, priest of Apollo, but she is now a huntress and wishes to follow Diana. Nerina, her friend, Thirsis, Philander's friend, and Philander pursue her in vain, for she refuses to fulfill her early promise. At length Philander saves her from the satyr who comes upon her sleeping alone in a wood, but even then she spurns him.   Montano tells her that unless she marries Philander as she promised, Apollo has decreed that she be sacrificed. She is about to be offered up on the altar, still cold and unrelenting, when Philander rushes in and tries to slay himself.   Thirsis prevents it, but this attempt means that Apollo demands Philander as sacrifice instead of Sylvia. Struck by this noble deed, Sylvia finds that she loves him and asks to die in his place; but Apollo appears in person and allows both to live.

The scene is laid in Arcadia, and companies of nymphs and satyrs are several times introduced.   It is written in a blank verse easy and natural.   A fair example follows:

> Oh! bend not thus thy drooping head to earth,
> Like tender plants beneath the beating storm;
> This day thy father, by thy griefs impell'd,
> With grateful off'rings seeks his patron god;
> Prostrate before his altar now he lies,
> And all his pious prayers ascend for thee.

Almost half of the very slim content is taken up with songs in couplet or in quatrain.   As we have seen in the dedication above, Mrs. Lennox gives the credit for two of the longest to another author, perhaps to Baretti, if she wrote this in reply to his ode.   They are all filled with pastoral settings, nymphs, and love.   The verse is not original or imaginative, but it is correct and usually graceful.   The general impression is that *Philander* is flimsy and light, neither very poetic nor convincing, but as a sample of imitation of an artificial type it is fairly satisfactory.

The piece, slight as it was, received some notices in its own day.   The *Critical Review* (Nov., 1757, iv, 468) accords it fairly long mention, praising it, in general, for "its uncommon elegance and purity. The sentiments are proper, soft and delicate: the versification is varied, spirited and correct; and the songs are well-turned, poetical and harmonious." The reviewer takes exception, however, to the introduction of the *deus ex machina* in which respect Mrs. Lennox differed from the original. The same objection is found in Baker and Reed's *Biographia Dramatica*.[2] "It is not intended, nor indeed of merit sufficient, for the stage. The hint of this piece is taken from the *Pastor Fido* of Guarini, and the catastrophe would have been more interesting had it been formed on the Italian poet. It would at least have rendered unnecessary the introduction of a personage whose appearance ought to be seldom or never introduced, except in masques and allegorical pieces; we mean a deity *in propria persona*." The *Monthly Review* (1st series, xvii, 568) in a brief mention of its nature decides that "it is altogether worthy the Authour of the Female Quixote." Certainly it is not in a class with the work just mentioned, even allowing for the difference in type. Chiefly interesting as showing Mrs. Lennox trying her hand again at poetry, this time in dramatic form, it harks back to the poetic-pastoral suggestion of Baretti and marks her versatility.

[2] Baker and Reed, *Biographia Dramatica* (London, 1812), iii, 142.

CHAPTER VI

Dramatic Works of Mrs. Lennox

THE only play written to be acted and entirely Mrs. Lennox's own work is *The Sister*. The prologue was by Colman and the epilogue by Goldsmith. It was given at the Covent Garden Theatre on Saturday, February 18, 1759, and was withdrawn after the first night's performance, which was a very unfortunate one.[1] The play is founded upon incidents in the last part of Mrs. Lennox's own novel of *Henrietta*, which had appeared and met with some success eleven years before. From the letter Mrs. Lennox wrote Garrick about this play we may infer that he at some time told her that she might make part of this novel into a drama. Apparently he was unwilling to produce it, because it was given a year after Mrs. Lennox wrote him about it at the rival theatre of Covent Garden.

Colman's prologue calls attention to Mrs. Lennox's successful novel and begs indulgence for her new venture:

> Boast not your gallant deeds, romantic man!
> To-night a Female Quixote draws her pen.
> Arm'd by the Comic Muse, these lists she enters,
> And sallies forth—in quest of strange adventures!
> . . . .
> Smile on our fair knight-errantry to-day,
> And raise no spells to blast a female play.
> Oft has our Author, upon other ground,
> Courted your smiles, and oft indulgence found.
> Read in the closet, you approv'd her page;
> Yet still she dreads the perils of the stage.

The play belongs essentially to the school of sentimental comedy. Harriot Courteney, the Henrietta of the novel, has left her aunt because of her Roman Catholic prejudices, and at the time the play opens has been for some time with Miss

---

[1] Genest John, *History of the English Stage* (Bath, 1832), v, 241.

Autumn, a fashionable coquette who lives with her step-mother, Lady Autumn. The latter lady belongs to the well-established line of character old ladies who fancy themselves still young and beautiful, irresistible charmers of the other sex. Lord Clairville, son of Lord Belmont, is travelling with his tutor, Mr. Courteney, Harriot's brother, but they come over secretly from Paris under the names of Belmour and Freeman to see the lady whom the Earl has chosen for his son. She meets with his disapproval, but he falls in love with Harriot, while Courteney and Miss Autumn are mutually attracted, though her coquetry keeps them from acknowledging it. Courteney seeks to persuade Harriot to accept illicit favors from Lord Clairville, lest the latter's passion lead him to offer his hand to her. Courteney feels that he must do this to maintain his trust as guardian of the young man. Just after Harriot has repulsed him in offended rage he discovers that she is his sister. He plans to keep this a secret, fearing that if Clairville finds it out he will then seek more than ever to marry Harriot, since her birth is equal to his. He plans to take her away in secret the next day. The intention is discovered and makes trouble as Miss Autumn suspects Harriot of taking her lover, and Clairville becomes madly jealous, insults Courteney, and challenges him to a duel. The latter feels in honor bound to accept the challenge, but fires into the air, while Clairville purposely misses his friend. At this juncture Harriot has thought best to reveal the relationship and Lady Autumn has already given her consent to Courteney's marrying Miss Autumn under the delusion that she is accepting him for herself. The Earl of Belmont enters in the fifth act, brought by a letter from his son in which Lord Clairville had an-nounced his arrival and expressed dissatisfaction with the lady intended as his bride. The Earl at first blames Courteney, but the latter is exonerated through the testimony of his charge and his sister, both of whom defend his integrity and loyalty to his duty. The Earl threatens his son to no avail, and then amazes him by presenting him with

Harriot as his bride. Miss Autumn and Courteney have also come to an understanding so that the outcome is satisfactory to all but Lady Autumn, who recovers from her bewilderment at the turn affairs have taken and allows matters to go on uninterruptedly. The play closes with a long moral speech by Courteney in which he thus instructs Lord Clairville and the audience:

As for me, tho' perhaps I have proved myself rather too young to be your governor, I am yet old enough to be your friend, and shall ever be proud of that distinction, not from the consideration of your wealth and honour; but because I am convinced that you want neither example nor precept to instruct you, that there are no characters so truly noble, as that of a woman of virtue, and a man of real honour.

Harriot is as sententious as her brother, for she draws this lesson from their recognition:

Oh! that my brother may be taught by this adventure, never more to insult distress and innocence; and to consider every virtuous, unprotected young woman as a sister.

The character of Courteney is far more important in the play than it was in the novel. Here all the action centers in him as the dominating figure. On the whole, Miss Autumn is more real and attractive than Harriot, the colorless heroine. The following excerpts from their conversation serve to illustrate the difference between them:

Miss Courteney: Ha! Ha! Ha! and yet you despise him, my dear.
Miss Autumn: Despise him—why yes—and yet I do not despise him neither.—I only mean that I do not like him.
Miss C. Why should you not like him? is he not handsome? has he not wit, learning, elegance?
Miss A. Pooh! to convince you that I do not like him, observe how ill I will treat him the next time we meet.

. . . .

Miss A. I protest I tremble at the idea, of being one day, what my step-mother is at present. Oh heavens! in the midst of wrinkles and grey hairs, to dream of gentle languishments, vows, ardors!—but there is some comfort yet, fifty and I are at an immense distance.

Miss C. Do not cheat yourself, my dear, with that thought; young though you are, you will be old: whatever advances with such rapidity cannot be accounted far distant—

Miss A. Well, I am determined to grow grave in time: dear Harriot, give me a lesson every day till you have compleated my reformation:—but is not that Freeman and Belmour yonder? they are certainly come in search of us. . . . . . Well, my sage mistress of eighteen, will you pretend to assert that he is not thinking of me? Now can I not for my life resist the inclination to teaze him a little.—

Miss Autumn has life and occasionally sparkles, while, though a coquette, she displays real feeling at the close when she thinks Courteney is lost to her. Lady Autumn furnishes the only real attempt at a humorous character in the play. She is taken from the Mrs. Autumn whom Henrietta served for some time in the novel *Henrietta*. She belongs to the line of coy old ladies whose most famous early representative is Lady Wishfort in Congreve's *The Way of the World* (1700), and who were to find an equally famous kinswoman a few years later in the person of Mrs. Malaprop in Sheridan's *The Rivals*. She suffers under the delusion that Freeman is in love with her and constantly discusses the matter with her maid Simple. The following is a fair sample of their conversation:

Lady Autumn. The snake!—O, I was mistaken: it was only a caterpillar, which my fears had magnified into a snake. Mr. Freeman then offered me his hand, to lead me home; but it was with such a timid aspect!—Since that day, his friend Belmour and he have been constant visitors at my house; and although his passion has been continually increasing, yet he has concealed it so carefully, that no person in the family has discovered it but myself.

Simple. I'll answer for it, Madam, nobody dreams of any such thing.—But I wonder the gentleman has not broke his mind to your Ladyship!—

Lady A. No, he has been silent, awfully silent, as to that point—such is his extreme timidity!—Timidity, Simple, ever accompanies a violent passion; for flames, as the poet says, burn highest, when they tremble most.

The Earl and his son are hopelessly wooden, especially the former, who acts only as a kind of *deus ex machina* and inconsistently changes his mind about his son's bride at the end in order to allow virtue to be rewarded and youth to be made happy.

Lord Belmont.   Take her, Clairville; the best, the worthiest girl a father can bestow, a truly virtuous woman! She who could sacrifice her fortune to her conscience, and subject her inclinations to her duty; who could despise riches, and triumph over love; she brings you in herself a treasure more valuable than both the Indies.   Take her, my son, and endeavour to deserve her.

Though lacking in characterization and humor and conventionally sentimental in tone, the play has some merit. The action is clear and well-defined, the speeches are short and advance the plot, and the whole moves with some swiftness.   Although one is painfully conscious of a slimness of content and a flimsiness about *The Sister*, the play is neatly presented.

In spite of its failure on the stage the play was printed very shortly afterwards, being announced in the *London Chronicle* for March 4, 1769, about two weeks after the performance.   In less than two weeks this edition was exhausted, for in the *London Chronicle* for March 21, 1769, we find the following notice:

This day was published Price 1s. 6d.   The Second Edition, of The Sister, A Comedy. by Mrs. Charlotte Lennox, Pr. for J. Dodsley, at Pall Mall; and T. Davies in Russell street, Covent Garden.

The explanation of the sudden popularity of this comedy in published form comes in all probability from the peculiar circumstances of its first and only performance and its subsequent notoriety in the periodicals.   There seems to have been a general impression that there was a malicious tendency among some of the audience to make the play a failure, regardless of its merit.   The newspapers, in commenting upon it, tend to sympathize with Mrs. Lennox and find the reception unjust. The account in *Lloyd's Evening Post* (Feb. 20, 1769, p. 178-9) tells of what must have been an unpleasant evening for actors and author: "It met with a good deal of opposition from part of the audience, who indeed, appeared to come prejudiced against the performance, as they began their attack upon it even in the first Act." The account (see above, p. 37) tells of such a riot in the fifth act that Mr. Powell, who took the part of Courteney, had to come out and beg the audience to be quiet until the play was concluded. After this the trouble-makers quieted down, but left no doubt as to their judgment at the end of the performance.

The *St. James's Chronicle* (Feb. 21, 1769) also testifies to a stormy evening.

On Saturday last was *half-acted* at this Theatre, a new Comedy called *The Sister*, written by the truly ingenious Author of the Female Quixote, and partly founded on another of her Productions, called Henrietta. In an Age so favourable to Sentimental Comedy, and Novels in Dialogue, we cannot help thinking the censure passed on the fair Author rather severe. As far as we are capable of judging from so interrupted an Exhibition, the Piece is neither deficient in Interest, Sentiment, or Diction. We shall, however, defer a further Examination of its Merits, till it appears in Print, in which form we hope the Author will again submit it to the Public.

So generous an account of the evening's catastrophe may have done something toward soothing poor Mrs. Lennox's sorely wounded feelings.

The Gazetteer and Daily Advertiser (Feb. 20, 1769) is even more outspoken in condemning the offenders. After a thorough digest of the play, the reviewer writes:

I cannot help condemning the ill-nature of a part of the audience, who, to gratify a bad disposition, considered not the anxiety they occasioned to one who may have spent many tedious days in producing for them a few hours rational entertainment; nor the quiet of another who has devoted herself to their service[2] . . . . .; nor regarded how much they disturbed the entertainment of the far greater part of the audience; but doubt not it will be more indulgently received at future representations.

The magazines do not take Mrs. Lennox's part so generally as the newspapers. The *Critical Review* (March, 1769, xxvii, 223-4) blames her for lack of humor and originality, but is not severe. The *Town and Country Magazine* acknowledges its failure, but offers this balm (Feb., 1769, i, 94):

Notwithstanding the audience would not suffer the piece to be given out for a second representation, this cannot be ascribed so much to want of abilities in the author, as to her inexperience in the *jeu de théâtre*; for the lady possesses great merit in many other departments of polite literature.

The *Gentleman's Magazine* (April, 1769, xxxix, 199) comes to her defense along the same lines.

This is the performance of Mrs. Charlotte Lenox, an ingenious lady, well known in the literary world by her excellent writings, particularly the Female Quixote, and Shakespeare illustrated . . . . It wants the intermixture of light scenes, such as familiar acquaintance with the stage might have furnished without the abilities of Mrs. Lenox, and which, if her abilities had been still greater, could not, perhaps, have been furnished without a familiar acquaintance with the stage. The audience expressed their disapprobation of it with so much clamour and appearance of prejudice, that she would not suffer an attempt to exhibit it a second time.
She has published it without either remonstrance or complaint, and those who read it in the closet will probably wonder at its treatment on the stage, especially considering the merit and sex of the writer.

It is in the *Monthly Review*, however, that we find an exhaustive treatment of *The Sister* (xi, 245-9). Much of

---

[2] The reference here is probably to Mrs. Bulkeley, who took the part of Miss Autumn.

it seems foolish to us today: such is the lengthy attempt to prove that it is morally wholesome, since Courteney does not really intend to seduce Harriot for Clairville, but is only sounding her; such also is the objection "that the daughter of an Earl calls her mother *Mamma* . . . . The word *Mamma* is never used among people of fashion, at least out of the nursery." The reviewer finds much to condemn in lack of characterization and dramatic technique, but he praises Mrs. Lennox's judgment and imagination and laments that the play "should have been driven with violence from the stage, and not suffered either to perish by desertion, or to be exhibited the usual time, if it would bring an audience."

The general tendency to believe that there was a party against the play is substantiated by Langton's anecdote told by Boswell (see above, p. 37) in which Goldsmith told Johnson that he had been advised to go and hiss Mrs. Lennox's play because she had attacked Shakespeare in her book *Shakespear Illustrated.* It is curious that Goldsmith should have been asked to hiss a play for which he wrote the epilogue. The only ground upon which he would be thought to be sympathetic toward such a proceeding is his reaction against sentimental drama. On January 29, 1768, *The Good-Natured Man* had been given at Covent Garden and had enjoyed a moderate run of nine consecutive nights, at the same time that Kelly's *False Delicacy*, the apotheosis of sentimental drama, was being performed at the Drury Lane. The papers[3] of the time had commented upon the contrast between them and recognized the re-introduction of a differ-

---

[3] *Whitehall Evening Post* (Feb. 2-4, 1768). Goldsmith's epilogue not only Forster but also Prior approved, saying it was "an excellent epilogue, the best perhaps he has written." See Prior, *Life of Goldsmith* (Ln., 1837), ii, 197. There is a manuscript copy in the possession of J. A. Spoor of Chicago, which, he informs me, is not in Goldsmith's handwriting or in Bishop Percy's. He knows nothing of the history of the manuscript or by whom it was copied. The copy differs in no way from the version in the 1769 copy of *The Sister*, except that in the former the "ed" ending is used and in the latter it is elided to " 'd".

ent type of comedy with Goldsmith. He was therefore known as an opponent of the sentimental drama, and it was perhaps in this capacity that he was called upon to join the party against *The Sister*. His attitude toward moral plays is shown in the first few lines of the epilogue in question.

> What? five long acts—and all to make us wiser!
> Our authoress sure has wanted an adviser.
> Had she consulted me, she should have made
> Her moral play a speaking masquerade;
> Warmed up each bustling scene, and in her rage
> Have emptied all the green-room on the stage.
> My life on't, this had kept her play from sinking;
> Have pleased our eyes, and saved the pain of thinking.
> Well, since she thus has shown her want of skill,
> What if I give a masquerade?—I will.

That Mrs. Lennox suspected some particular person of trying to ruin her play is apparent from the letter written by Johnson to Mrs. Thrale on October 28, 1779, quoted above (see p. 54). The person accused by Mrs. Lennox challenges the imagination. One thinks of Richard Cumberland, who was inclined to be jealous of other writers, so much so that Fanny Burney writes thus of him:[4] "For Mr. Cumberland, though in all other respects an agreeable and good man, is so notorious for hating and envying and spiting all authors in the dramatic line, that he is hardly decent in his behavior towards them." That Sheridan had the same opinion of him is shown by the character of Sir Fretful Plagiary in *The Critic*. Cumberland was vitally interested in the stage at the time of Mrs. Lennox's production, for on December 2, 1769, his play of *The Brothers*[5] was given at Covent Garden where it met with success. That Mrs. Lennox was included in the school of which he was the acknowledged head is shown by this account of the fate of writers of sentimental comedy after the performance of *She Stoops to Conquer* had caused the illness of their heroine, Miss Sententia Hornbook.[6]

> Mr. C——d, Mr. K——y, Mrs. G——ths, Mrs. L——x, Mr. O——n, are sending hourly to inquire after her; because when she dies, as the proverb says, they may quake with fear.

Mrs. Lennox's being in the same field of writing with Cumberland would increase the rivalry, and might tend to make him more anxious to wish her ill-luck. The only evidence we have against its being Cumberland is that he did not meet Goldsmith until 1771-2,[7] and the offender here was an acquaintance of Goldsmith's. It seems impossible, therefore, to fasten the ill-natured act upon any one person, and we can only conjecture that it may have been an opponent of the sentimental drama, a strong admirer of Shakespeare who resented Mrs. Lennox's strictures upon him in her book, *Shakespear Illustrated*, or Richard Cumberland. It must have been some satisfaction to her in this dismal failure to know that there was an active attempt to make the play unsuccessful and that such a sad outcome was not due entirely to a lack of merit in the play itself. The rallying to her defense in the contemporary periodicals should also have offered a balm to her discouraged spirits.

Despite its failure in London *The Sister* was chosen by Herr J. C. Bock as worthy of being translated into German for the theatre in Hamburg in 1776. It is not listed as one of the plays performed from April, 1775, to March, 1776, but as a cast is printed it must have been performed at some time. Except for the fact that the translation has a more

[6] Williams S. T., *Richard Cumberland* (Yale University Press, 1917), 124-5. The names supplied are Cumberland, Kelly, Griffiths, Lennox, and O'Brien.

[7] Cumberland tells us that he did not meet Goldsmith until the latter was so nearly through writing *She Stoops to Conquer* that they discussed possible titles for it. As the play was written during 1771, it is unlikely that they knew each other in 1769. See *Memoirs of Richard Cumberland* (ed. Henry Flanders, Philadelphia, 1856), 185.

frequent division into scenes in the first two acts,—a new scene every time there is a change of personnel on the stage—the only change is a brief attempt at humor in the very beginning.   In Mrs. Lennox's play the third speech is Courteney's:

I come now to bring you unwelcome news—the Earl of Belmont is in town.
Clairville.   My father in town!

The German has:

Courteney.   Der Graf von Bellmont—
Clairville.   Mein Vater?
Co.   Ist — —
Cl. (ershrocken) Todt?
Co.   Nicht—aber in der Stadt.

This flicker exhausted the translator's attempts at brightening the dialogue of *The Sister*.

That *The Sister* is not without dramatic possibilities is proved by the fact that Lieutenant-General John Burgoyne borrowed heavily from it for his successful play of *The Heiress*.   In the Preface to the published version of the play he acknowledges a general indebtedness to novels and defends the custom of building upon another man's ground as well as upon one's own.   He does not, however, make any mention of *The Sister*.   The *Monthly Review* (March, 1786, lxxiv, 209) scores Burgoyne heavily for his borrowings and mentions among other sources the novels of Mrs. Lennox.   No published recognition of *The Heiress's* relation to *The Sister* occurs until 1823, when an article on General Burgoyne appearing in *The Morning Herald* for September 25 notes the connection.

Of his dramatic works, incomparably the most valuable is the comedy of *The Heiress*—which may, indeed, be called the last real comedy produced on the English stage—and it had the singular good fortune that the source from which it is almost wholly derived escaped entirely the research, or the animadversions of the critics of the day.   It is, in fact, little more than a judicious alteration of a former obscure, but by no means despicable comedy, *The Sister*; and its principal claim to originality must be rested upon the character of Miss Alscrip—certainly a very advantageous substitute for the *Miss Autumn* of the original. . . . . . one should not depreciate the merit of that intellectual alchemy which transmutes the dross, or the *baser* metal of inferior writers into sterling ore, and sends it forth again with the current stamp and polish of the more valuable metals. And the praise of this achievement no one who shall compare *The Heiress* with *The Sister* will deny to General Burgoyne. All that he is really censurable for, is the disingenuousness of a Preface, in which he apologetically alludes to previous examples of taking 'instead of small and detached parts, the complete plots of plays from a novel,' but evades all allusion to the comedy above-mentioned; from which not only the complete plot, but the general incidents and several of the characters of his play are most palpably derived.

Besides this article we have a letter from Miss Warburton to Caroline Burgoyne, written just after the above had appeared in the *Morning Herald*, in which she says:[8]

I happen to *know* that your father took the idea of The Heiress from Mrs. Lennox's novel of *Henrietta*, which he reckoned one of the cleverest works of its class that had appeared; and I think what he says in his preface about acknowledging obligations to novelists was aimed at Sheridan, who could never bear to be told (what was, however, perfectly true) that his Sir Oliver Surface and his two nephews were borrowed from his mother's beautiful novel of *Sidney Biddulph*.

The Heiress achieved such noticeable popularity in its own day that it is curious that no mention of its debt to *The Sister* came until almost forty years later. Mrs. Lennox, who was, of course, still alive in 1786, made no attempt to claim any credit for it and apparently felt no resentment at Burgoyne's alteration of her play. Genest in his comment upon *The Sister* gives Mrs. Lennox credit for three characters in *The Heiress*.

[8] De Fonblanqué E. B., *Political and Military Episodes from the Life and Correspondence of Rt. Hon. John Burgoyne* (London, 1876), 406.

This comedy was so ill-treated by the audience on the first night, that the authoress, Mrs. Lennox, had spirit enough to withdraw it from the theatre—it is certainly deficient in comic force—but it is well-written and deserved a better fate—Gen. Burgoyne in The Heiress is completely indebted to this play for the characters of Lord Gayville, Clifford, and Miss Alton.

There is no doubt that *The Sister* afforded Burgoyne a source for several of his characters in *The Heiress* and that he failed to acknowledge that indebtedness publicly at the time of its presentation.

The Sister is most significant in thus furnishing a source for a play which was popular a decade later. It is not important in its own right, for it is simply one in a vast group of sentimental dramas. It is interesting, however, because of the rather unusual circumstances connected with its performance. The antipathy thus shown Mrs. Lennox is illuminating from both a literary and biographical point of view. It adds to Mrs. Lennox's wide-spreading literary relations that the prologue was written by a successful theatrical man of the day, George Colman, and the epilogue by a well-known essayist, poet, and novelist, Dr. Goldsmith, one of the members of the Literary Club. The respect accorded Mrs. Lennox by contemporary periodicals at this time, in spite of the demonstration against her play, speaks well for the solidity of her reputation as a writer.

That Mrs. Lennox did not soon recover from the discouragement of this first actual dramatic attempt is shown by her letter to Garrick when she is considering revising a play for his use. She refers to her diffidence in again attempting a field of literature in which she has met with such ill-fortune. In 1774, however, she is writing to Garrick about an alteration of Racine's *Bajazet* especially for Mrs. Yates. This did not appear either on the stage or in print, but Mrs. Lennox must have kept in touch with Garrick and theatrical ventures, for in August, 1775, we find her again writing Garrick, this time apparently in answer to a reproach from him for neglecting to present material at the proper time. The outcome of this correspondence is *Old City Manners*, which was given at Drury Lane on November 9, 1775. The situation would seem to be that Mrs. Lennox sought to have Garrick present her intended alteration of *Bajazet*, but that he, being unable to take her play in the autumn of 1774, suggested to her another alteration to be done under his guidance. Mrs. Lennox evidently accepted his advice and dropped *Bajazet*, for there is no mention of such a play in Genest at this time, and none of the magazines or papers during that autumn carried any notice of its publication. Mrs. Lennox puts in after the title-page of *Old City Manners* that the alteration was suggested to her by Garrick and that he assisted "throughout this Comedy". It was printed and published on November 28, 1775, with the following title-page:

Old City Manners. A Comedy. Altered from the Original Eastward Hoe, written by Ben Jonson, Chapman, and Marston. By Mrs. Lennox. As it is performed at the Theatre-Royal, in Drury-Lane, London: Printed for T. Becket, the Corner of the Adelphi, in the Strand. 1775. (Price One Shilling.)

The prologue, like that of *The Sister*, was written by George Colman. In it he compares the cuckoldry of Charles the Second's time and that of his own day. His only reference to Mrs. Lennox is the following:

> Artists, like these (old Ben the chief!) tonight,
> Bring idleness, and industry to light;
> Their sketch by time, perhaps, impair'd too much,
> A female hand has ventur'd to retouch;

The *Biographia Dramatica* (iii, 95) briefly remarks of *Old City Manners*: "This is an alteration of *Eastward Hoe*, and was favourably received." *The Public Advertiser* for November 10, 1775, bears the same testimony:

Last night was performed (for the first time) a Comedy called, Old City Manners, altered from Ben Johnson and others, and received with the greatest Applause: it will be repeated Tomorrow-night: To which will be added, for the first Time, the revived Pantomime of Queen Mab, with Additions.

Old City Manners was given first on Thursday night, November 9, 1775, and repeated on Saturday, November 11. According to the same paper, *The Public Advertiser*, the third performance was on Monday, November 13, the fourth on Wednesday, November 15, and the fifth on Friday, November 17. The sixth performance recorded was on Monday, November 27, and was "for the benefit of the Author of the Alterations". This benefit performance for Mrs. Lennox had been advertised as early as November 17, and was probably set for the 27th because it was on that day "at Twelve" that the comedy was to be published. It did not finally appear, however, until the next day, Tuesday, November 28. The last performance of the play that we have notice of was January 8, 1776.[9] The mild success of this play was, no doubt, gratifying to Mrs. Lennox after the earlier failure; and it is pleasant to think that from this, one of her last ventures in writing, she received some financial reward as well as the less substantial favor of praise in the reviews. In the latter Mrs. Lennox's share in *Old City Manners* is but little noticed, save for a passing word of commendation. The most elaborate comment upon her skill is found in the *London Chronicle* (November 9-11, 463).

This alteration from the *Eastward Hoe* of Ben Jonson, Chapman, etc. is said to be the work of Mrs. Lenox, a lady well known as a favorite attendant in the train of the muses, and considering the grounds she had to work upon she has much improved it. . . . . Some of the Lady's additions are characteristic; and a good imitation of the original style; in others she has introduced some modern patches which are not so fortunate in their effect: though she has judiciously cut many parts, there still remain some scenes that want a similar trimming; . . . . . However, upon the whole, it was very favourably received, the audience expressing their approbation at different times by the warmest applause.

[9] Genest, *History of the English Stage*, v, 484.

Genest in his comment is diametrically opposed to this review as to the question of more changes.[10]

This is an alteration of Eastward Hoe, and everything considered, it does Mrs. Lennox credit; she might however have retained a little more of the original play—the principal change which she has made in the plot is, that the marriage of Sir Petronel and Girtred is set aside, he having a former wife living—he does not appear in the 5th act—Security is not made a cuckold—

If we turn to the play, *Old City Manners*, and compare it with *Eastward Hoe* we find that Mrs. Lennox's version is much shorter and that all the coarser scenes and balder statements are omitted. The plot of the original is briefly this: Touchstone, a goldsmith, has two daughters, Gertrude, who desires only to be a lady, and Mildred, who is sensible and gentle. Mrs. Touchstone sympathizes with the folly of the elder daughter. Touchstone also has two apprentices, Francis Quicksilver, all for fashion and folly, and Golding, the hardworking, industrious fellow. Quicksilver arranges a marriage between Gertrude and Sir Petronel Flash, and at the same time Touchstone gives Mildred to Golding. Quicksilver takes Flash to Security, who promises to advance him money on his wife's fortune. Gertrude is eager to depart in her coach for Sir Petronel's castle, and drives off with her mother, leaving him to follow. Meanwhile he and Quicksilver arrange with Winifred, Security's young wife, to go with them on board their ship for the Indies. Security helps in the deception, believing he is making Bramble, the lawyer, a cuckold. Flash, Quicksilver, and Winifred are wrecked and cast ashore separately. Flash and Quicksilver are taken to prison and Winifred meets Security, who takes her back, but she is soon hustled off to prison too. Gertrude discovers her deception and returns home, becoming reconciled with her father through her mother and sister. Golding is made a deputy and sits in judgment on the culprits.

---

[10] Genest, *History of the English Stage*, v, 481.

Touchstone's heart is finally softened by the pathetic sight of Quicksilver repenting in sackcloth and ashes and all three, Flash, Quicksilver, and Security, are set free.

Mrs. Lennox has made a few additions in her version. Mr. Fig, an honest grocer, appears in the first act and is scorned by Gertrude; he also appears later to taunt her. Sir Petronel is here discovered to be a common thief with a wife living; therefore he is not set free with Quicksilver, but disappears after the fourth act. Mildred comes to see her sister instead of Gertrude's seeking her out. The incident of Sir Petronel Flash's suggesting that they stay to kiss the king's hand before leaving for the country and Gertrude's ready acquiescence, with its accompanying dilemma, is original with Mrs. Lennox. She has made several omissions, principally connected with Winifred and the cuckolding. Much of the discussion of what is to be done with Winifred is not included; also Security is not made a cuckold here. Security's wandering about Cuckold's Haven and eventually finding Winifred there is left out entirely. Some of the short scenes in the prison are omitted from the last act of *Old City Manners,* which is much shorter than the last act of *Eastward Hoe.* Less attention is paid by Mrs. Lennox to Syndefie, Quicksilver's wench, who lives at Security's house. In the original play, Security is made to promise her a dowry as a condition of his release from prison; this detail is not attended to by Mrs. Lennox. Some of the coarser remarks of Gertrude to her mother are omitted, and several rather moral statements are substituted for them at the end. Thus in *Eastward Hoe,* v, 4, when Touchstone's family is appealing to him to be merciful to Quicksilver, Gertrude's word is merely this:

Father, it is I, father; my Lady Flash. My sister and I am friends.

In *Old City Manners* Gertrude is more sentimental:

Let me not be the only one that shall rejoice in your clemency—my offence was greater than that of your 'prentice; I sinn'd against a father, yet you forgave me.

More emphasis is placed upon the moral in the repentance of Quicksilver. In *Eastward Hoe* when Quicksilver is preparing to sing his song of repentance, he makes these remarks:

I writ it when my spirits were opprest.
It is in imitation of Maningtons, he that was hanged at Cambridge, that cut off the horse's head at a blow.

His comment in *Old City Manners* is this:

I am no poet, Sir, as the simplicity of these poor verse will show; but to those, for whose use they are design'd, they will be good enough, if they paint my vices, and the fatal consequences of them.

Mrs. Lennox takes advantage of the wish of Quicksilver to go home in his prison clothes as a lesson to the children of the streets, to make this addition and put it in the mouth of Golding:

Let your penitence, friend Quicksilver, appear in your actions, resulting from inward conviction, and not from external appearance—a foul heart may be cover'd with tatter'd cloaths, and a decent out-side is the best garment for a reclaim'd prodigal—he who endeavours to shew too much, may be suspected of repenting too little.

This moral tendency is not, however, carried to such an extent as to impair seriously the force and vigor of any of the figures. To be sure, Quicksilver is less charming as the penitent here, perhaps because we are led to take the repentance more seriously, and because he lacks a little of the gay insouciance, which in the early play accompanies even his prison scenes. In general, however, Mrs. Lennox has preserved the mood of the play. Less of the moral note intrudes than her usual style might lead us to expect.

Mrs. Lennox's position as a dramatic writer is not important. First of all, her productions in that field are very slight, consisting of one poetic pastoral drama not intended for the stage, one sentimental comedy taken from her novel

Henrietta, and one alteration of a seventeenth century comedy. We may consider the first as a sally into a new field, certainly experimental and savoring somewhat of hackwork, probably undertaken at the suggestion of her Italian master, Baretti. The second, *The Sister*, was undertaken partly as a financial venture, we may judge, and, considering the evidence in her letter to Garrick, was encouraged by friends of literary acumen who thought it likely to succeed. The last was done under Garrick's own supervision and to meet an occasional need, since at that season of the year it was customary to give a play of this type, usually *London Cuckolds*. In 1751 Garrick had substituted *Eastward Hoe*; in 1775 he substituted Mrs. Lennox's alteration of *Eastward Hoe*. In no case do we feel that Mrs. Lennox is turning naturally to this form of letters. The two legitimate plays come very near the end of her writing: *The Sister* in 1769, when she must have been almost fifty and had behind her all her works except one translation and two novels; and *Old City Manners*, coming in 1775, last but two of her efforts. In *The Sister*, the dramatic work of Mrs. Lennox's which best justifies literary criticism, we find her following, as she did in her novels, the taste of the time. Here she offered a sentimental comedy which the paucity of her knowledge of stagecraft kept from succeeding. The plot against *The Sister* caused it to suffer a harder fate than would otherwise have been accorded so conventional a drama. There is too little humor, originality, or vigor in it, however, to allow of its achieving any real success, even at a time when Cumberland and Kelly stirred large audiences to tears with their sentimental comedies. Doubtless Mrs. Lennox was handicapped by the method used in her novels, and found it especially hard to achieve dramatic force when dealing with something which she had herself used in narrative. The lack of body and the slimness of content which we feel in *The Sister* are probably due also to the fact that she was here using only a part of a larger work and was unable to enlarge her characters and action in proportion.

The lasting interest in Mrs. Lennox's plays is largely extraneous. Goldsmith's connection with *The Sister* and the circumstances of its performance lend it significance in determining Mrs. Lennox's literary reputation at this time. Garrick's slight relation to *The Sister* and important position in regard to *Old City Manners* make him form another in the circle of prominent eighteenth century figures who advised and aided Mrs. Lennox because of their esteem for her worth and abilities.

CHAPTER VII

Miscellaneous Works of Mrs. Lennox:
Shakespear Illustrated, Translations, and
The Lady's Museum

MRS. LENNOX has been presented as a novelist, a poetess, and a dramatist. Her work as a novelist is much greater, both in amount and quality, than are her attempts in poetry or the drama. Her poems were negligible even in her own day; her plays contain little originality and interest us chiefly today because of the light they throw upon her literary relations. Of her novels *The Female Quixote* stands out as an unusual and distinctively original imitation of *Don Quixote*; the importance of her other novels rests upon occasional creations of character, skilful narrative, the reflection of current tendencies in fiction, autobiographical interest, or the freshness and faithfulness of the depiction of early Colonial scenes in America. In considering these works, we have not regarded half of the actual body of Mrs. Lennox's productions, a large part of which consists of translations from the Italian or French; in addition there is her work as editor of a monthly periodical. To her translations from the Italian Mrs. Lennox added some critical remarks, and thus placed herself in the long and diverse line of Shakespearean commentators. Her translations from the Italian are all contained in the three volumes of *Shakespear Illustrated*, which is her contribution to the study of Shakespeare.

Shakespear Illustrated appeared in two parts: the first two volumes came out early in 1753, being reviewed in the *Gentleman's Magazine* for May, 1753 (xxiii, 250); volume three followed in the first part of 1754 and was reviewed in the same magazine in February of 1754 (xxiv, 99). In preparation for this work Mrs. Lennox had been learning Italian from Giuseppe Baretti for about a year; it was through her that Baretti had met Johnson and had come in contact with the literary circle of the day. Johnson had other connections, more direct than this, with *Shakespear Illustrated*. It was in the spring of 1752 that he had given Mrs. Lennox a banquet in honor of *Harriot Stuart*; in the same year he had written for her the dedication and one chapter of *The Female Quixote*. Johnson and Mrs. Lennox, then, were on friendly terms in these years. If we are inclined to wonder why Mrs. Lennox should turn to Shakespeare at this juncture, Johnson's influence at once suggests itself.[1] In 1745 Johnson had issued *Proposals* for an edition of Shakespeare published by Cave, which had not materialized because of Tonson's letter to Cave stating that he had a "title" not only to "the original copy" but also "to all the emendations to this time". In 1751 two articles in *The Rambler* indicated Johnson's continued attention to Shakespeare. In 1756 the second *Proposals* appeared, showing that Johnson had not abandoned his idea of an edition of Shakespeare during these years but was simply awaiting time and opportunity for its production. That in these second *Proposals* he presumed to declare that he would compare each play with its original is a fact not unrelated to Mrs. Lennox's book. There was an obvious need for such a work as Mrs. Lennox was attempting and it is but natural to suppose that a friend like Johnson, interested in the state of Shakespearean scholarship, was the one who made the suggestion to her, especially as it would substantially help him, if he should continue with his intended edition. In addition to this, Mrs. Lennox was sorely in need of money at the time and was perhaps casting about for some method of earning it. A work on Shakespeare was sure to rouse interest and obtain some sale. There seems to be every reason to suppose that Mrs. Lennox would seize upon

---

[1] This subject of Johnson's relation to *Shakespear Illustrated* is conclusively treated in Karl Young's "Samuel Johnson on Shakespeare: One Aspect," *University of Wisconsin Studies in Language and Literature*, 1924, no. 18, 147-227.

such a suggestion of Johnson's eagerly, especially since we can trace no signs of constitutional laziness in her. The fact that she did not know Italian did not deter her, but she set about learning it immediately and, curiously enough, chanced to find a teacher in Baretti; she was translating for publication in less than a year. It seems fair to suppose that the presentation of the sources of Shakespeare's plays was the suggestion of Johnson; whether he also is to be blamed for the critical remarks with which Mrs. Lennox accompanied her presentation of the sources is dubious. Whatever his opinion of her genius—and that it was high we have every indication—he may not have deemed her suited to do more than present the sources themselves, leaving to older, more mature, and more judicial minds to consider what use Shakespeare had made of them. Such an attitude would appear but natural, and seems more probable in that Johnson has paid so little attention to Mrs. Lennox's work in his own edition of Shakespeare, actually mentioning her book only three times.[2] In his criticism of *The Winter's Tale*, he writes:

The story is taken from the novel of *Dorastus and Faunia*, which may be read in *Shakespear Illustrated*.

Not only the source but also Mrs. Lennox's criticism he mentions in his discussion of *All's Well That Ends Well* and *Measure For Measure*.

The story is copied from a novel of Boccace, which may be read in *Shakespear Illustrated*, with remarks not more favourable to *Bertram* than my own.

The novel of *Cynthio Giraldi*, from which *Shakespear* is supposed to have borrowed this fable, may be read in *Shakespear illustrated*, elegantly translated, with remarks which will assist the enquirer to discover how much absurdity *Shakespear* has admitted or avoided.

No large amount of notice to be given a book, if it was

[2] The *Plays of William Shakespeare* (ed. Johnson. London, Tonson, 1765), ii, 349; iii, 399; i, 382.

undertaken at his suggestion! Young, in *Samuel Johnson on Shakespeare: One Aspect,* shows that Johnson has used the information and sources Mrs. Lennox provided without making any acknowledgment in several other cases, noticeably with *Richard II* and *Romeo and Juliet.* These facts influence the conclusion that Johnson was not impressed by Mrs. Lennox's critical abilities and did not care to connect himself with her expressed opinions of Shakespeare. Also, if we are to judge from his own edition of Shakespeare, he was not engrossed in a dry study of sources; he was far more interested in the characters and dramatic qualities of the plays. Although he could make the suggestion to Mrs. Lennox that such a treatment needed to be attempted and could act as her guardian to the extent of writing an illuminating dedication for her book, he could neither agree with her strictures nor fix his attention for any length of time on a scholarly comparison with sources, even though they were thus conveniently served up to him.

The dedication by Johnson is inscribed to the Earl of Orrery, as Boswell tells us: "He this year favoured Mrs. Lennox with a Dedication to the Earl of Orrery, of her *Shakespeare Illustrated.*" It seeks to protect the author from the charge of trying to lessen Shakespeare's fame; it also contains a eulogy of Shakespeare's supreme power in the representation of human life and of actual living people. Here Johnson has seen fit to elevate the Fable to first importance, although he is not consistent in this point of view either in this dedication or in the famous Preface to his own edition of Shakespeare. His dedicatory letter presages a much fairer and broader treatment of Shakespeare than we actually find in the work itself.

The nature of Mrs. Lennox's work is indicated on the title-page: "Shakespear Illustrated: or the Novels and Histories, on which the Plays of Shakespear are founded, Collected and Translated from the Original Authors. With Critical Remarks. In Two Volumes. By the Author of the Female Quixote. London: Printed for A. Millar in the

Strand. MDCCLIII." The first volume must have taken
the most time and industry on Mrs. Lennox's part, for of
the seven plays there treated six of them have an Italian
source, which Mrs. Lennox presents to her readers in English. These six plays are: *Measure for Measure, Romeo
and Juliet, Othello, Cymbeline, All's Well that Ends Well,
Twelfth Night.* The other play considered is *Macbeth*,
which has its source in Holinshed's *Chronicles of England,
Ireland, and Scotland.* In the second volume we find only
one translation done by Mrs. Lennox; this is from the
French and is the source for *The Comedy of Errors.* Mrs.
Lennox tells us that Shakespeare himself used an English
translation, which appeared in London in 1593 under the title
Menaechus. For this information she quotes Gerald Lang-
baine, the first critic to attempt to locate sources for Shakespeare's plays; he lists sources for twenty-seven in his
Account of English Dramatick Poets (Oxford, 1691, 455-
66). Mrs. Lennox herself explains:[3]

From this Translation of *Plautus's Menaechmi, Shakespear* certainly borrowed his *Comedy of Errors*; but not
being able to procure a Copy of it, and being wholly unac-
quainted with the *Latin* Tongue, I have turned Monsieur
Gueudiville's French Translation of the Menaechmi into
English, which although, as I am informed, it be not very
literal as to the Dialogue, yet the Plot, the Incidents, and
Characters, being exactly the same with the Latin Poet's it
will serve to shew how much of the Plot *Shakespear* has
borrowed in his *Comedy of Errors.*

The first source given in this second volume is that for
the *Winter's Tale* and involved no great labor on Mrs.
Lennox's part, since it is Greene's story of *Dorastus and
Fawnia.* The only other one (there being but three in this
volume) is that for *Hamlet.* To quote again from Mrs.
Lennox:[4]

The Translation of the Story of *Amleth* from the *Danish*
History of *Saxo-Grammaticus*, I was favoured with by a

[3] *Shakespear Illustrated*, ii, 219.
[4] *Id.*, ii, 267.

Friend; the Story itself is full of ridiculous Fancies, wild and improbable Circumstances, and as it is conducted, has more the appearance of a Romance than an Historical Fact.

In the first two volumes Mrs. Lennox's method of procedure is to give first of all the source and then a separate section consisting of "observations" on the use Shakespeare has made of the source in his play. This latter section usually opens with a complete digest of the plot of Shakespeare's play; thus we are able to see the two stories side by side. After the "Fable" of the play is completed Mrs. Lennox indulges in a few remarks which point out the absurdity Shakespeare has exhibited in his alteration from the original; the length of these remarks is somewhat determined by how deeply Mrs. Lennox has been stirred by Shakespeare's manifest crudities and want of judgment.

This method is continued with three plays in the third volume. The sources of *Troilus and Cressida* are found in Chaucer's poem by that name and "partly from an old Story Book, called *The three Destructions of Troy*". Mrs. Lennox gives an abstract of the story as found in Chaucer and adds her own observations. For the source of *Much Ado About Nothing* Mrs. Lennox has again had recourse to the original Italian; here she presents a translation of the *Tale of Geneura* from the fifth book of Ariosto's *Orlando Furioso*. For *King Lear* she has given the story as told in Holinshed first and in the section containing her remarks has added the old ballad and the story from Sidney's *Arcadia*. With these three Mrs. Lennox has maintained the method used entirely in the first two volumes. With *Two Gentlemen of Verona* she has confined herself to one division entitled *The Fable of the Two Gentlemen of Verona*: in this, however, she has included the story of Felix and Felismena taken from the English translation of the Spanish *Diana* by Montemayor.

Mrs. Lennox's treatment of the history plays is different and much more brief. She allows each only one chapter, wherein she usually notes that the tale is taken from Holinshed's *Chronicle* with greater or less fidelity to the facts of history, as the case may be. The "fable" of Shakespeare's play is presented at some length and if there is any especial similarity to or divergence from the source it is noted. This is exceptionally well executed by Mrs. Lennox in *Richard II* where she compares the text of the Bishop of Carlisle's speech in Shakespeare with the same passage in Holinshed to illustrate how closely Shakespeare has followed his source. She has taken up only certain ones of the history plays and in some instances has dealt with them summarily. Only four pages, for example, are devoted to *The Plan of the First Part of Henry the Fourth,* and only two to the *Third Part of King Henry the Sixth.*

In these volumes Mrs. Lennox has presented the actual stories for fourteen of Shakespeare's plays: of these, seven are translated from the Italian, one from the French, the rest are retold from English originals or translations. In addition, she has compared eight history plays with the facts recorded in Holinshed's *Chronicles*: these are *Richard II, Henry IV, Henry V,* all three parts of *Henry VI, Richard III,* and *Henry VIII.* In all, she has considered twenty-two plays of Shakespeare, though the history plays are much less carefully done than the others. Even though she did actual translating for only eight sources, she had accomplished a real task to produce two volumes in about a year after the *Female Quixote,* and the third eight months later. I call attention to this detail to emphasize the fact that whatever critical work Mrs. Lennox added must have been hastily conceived and not the result of mature deliberation and careful study. Having finished the drudgery of finding and presenting the sources, the lady unfortunately wished to express her own opinions, and profited by her hours of toil to display all the erudition of which she could make herself mistress. Having concentrated upon the plots almost entirely, she naturally tended to regard only the plots of Shakespeare's plays. Therefore, arming herself with the pseudo-classical standards of Probability, Decorum, and

Poetical Justice, Mrs. Lennox advanced upon the plays of Shakespeare. Dire were the results of her invasion to her reputation as a Shakespearean critic and a judge of true values.

As an example of Mrs. Lennox's treatment of a play I shall give rather fully her remarks on Shakespeare's alterations in *Measure for Measure*.[5] First of all,

It is to be wished . . . that he had left the Fable simple and entire as it was without loading it with useless Incidents, unnecessary Characters, and absurd and improbable Intrigue.

Shakespeare has offended against the unities by complicating the action and has thus lowered the tone of the novel.

There are a greater Diversity of Characters, and more Intrigues in the Fable of the Play, than the novel of Cinthio yet I think, wherever Shakespear has invented, he is greatly below the Novelist; since the Incidents he has added, are neither necessary nor probable.

Mrs. Lennox expresses her disapproval of tragi-comedy in the following:

That Shakespear made a wrong choice of his Subject, since he was resolved to torture it into a Comedy, appears by the low Contrivance, absurd Intrigue, and improbable Incidents, he was obliged to introduce, in order to bring about three or four Weddings, instead of one good Beheading, which was the Consequence naturally expected.

Shakespeare has been lax in the application of "poetical Justice".

Shakespear . . . yet has not mended the Moral: for he also shews Vice not only pardoned; but left in Tranquility.

At this point Mrs. Lennox goes more out of the way than usual to suggest how Shakespeare might have concluded the play satisfactorily according to the rule of justice. Isabella she would send into the cloister, and Angelo "falling into an Excess of Grief, for her Loss (since the Practice is

[5] *Shakespear Illustrated*, i, 24-37.

allowed by Christian Authors) stabs himself in Despair."
Such a conclusion would insure unity of action and a proper
moral.

The humorous parts certainly did not find a sympathetic
reader in Mrs. Lennox:

The rest is all Episode, made up of the extravagant
Behaviour of a wild Rake, the Blunders of a drunken
Clown, and the Absurdities of an ignorant Constable.

She applies Horace's doctrine of "Characters", therefore
finds much in the play inconsistent with decorum. The
Duke does things unsuited to the character of a prince.
Angelo also is troublesome, for he performs some deeds
which are the part of a good man while in other respects he
is wicked. Finally she accuses Isabella of having the manners of an "affected Prude", and concludes:

This Play therefore being absolutely defective in a due
Distribution of Rewards and Punishments: *Measure for
Measure* ought not to be the title, since Justice is not the
Virtue it inculcates; nor can Shakespear's Invention in the
Fable be praised; for what he has altered from *Cinthio*, is
altered greatly for the worse.

Having assumed this literal-minded attitude in her criticism, Mrs. Lennox proceeds to run a stormy course through
the comedies in Shakespeare. None fails to be improbable,
to lack unity, decorum, and an instructive moral. Various
things in the different comedies especially call forth her
wrath. In the *Winter's Tale* it is scarcely necessary to mention that she balks at the statue.[6]

To bring about this Scene, ridiculous as it is, Shakespear
has been guilty of many Absurdities, which would be too
tedious to mention, and which are too glaring to escape the
Observation of the most careless Reader.

The Novel has nothing in it half so low and improbable as
this Contrivance of the Statue; and indeed wherever Shakespear has altered or invented, his *Winter's Tale* is greatly
inferior to the old paltry Story that furnished him with the
Subject of it.

[6] *Shakespear Illustrated*, ii, 86.

In the romantic comedies she is always running into practical difficulties as in the *Two Gentlemen of Verona*:[7]

To make all this probable 't is necessary that the Spies and Guards set over their Princess, must be all blind, otherwise she and Sir Eglamour must unavoidably be seen by them.

Similarly, in *Cymbeline* she worries about such details as the physical impossibility of Iachimo's gaining access to a Princess, or of a Princess's being able to slip away and ride to Milford-Haven. She will admit nothing and take nothing for granted. Imogen's going into the woods and dressing as a page shock her. Even more lamentable is the fact that a princess should know how to cook. With real short-sightedness and narrowness of vision she fails to recognize the beauty and depth of Imogen. Not so did the heroines of eighteenth century fiction comport themselves:[8]

One could imagine, that full of a just Disdain for so vile and scandalous a Suspicion, the Pride of injured Virtue, affronted Dignity, and Rage of ill-requited Love, would have carried her back to the Court, there by disclaiming all future Faith and Tenderness for the unworthy Posthumous, restore herself to the Affection of her Father, and all the Rights of her Royal Birth.

In the *Comedy of Errors* Shakespeare has once again unnecessarily complicated things, to the detriment of the plot. Mrs. Lennox seriously suggests that it would have been most sensible to have fastened the two Antipholuses, the father, and the mother together at the time of the shipwreck.

Mrs. Lennox is usually ungenerous with romantic heroines. In *All's Well That Ends Well* she finds not only that Bertram is mean and cruel but also that both the main characters are degraded and that the only way of knowing that Helena is good is because the Countess says so. She finds Viola guilty of a lack of "the Modesty and Reservedness of

[7] *Shakespear Illustrated*, iii, 31.
[8] *Id.*, i, 162.

her Sex" in being so ready to adopt a masculine disguise and "mix among men". She considers the plot on the score of its "Decency" instead of employing a more artistic criterion. The humorous characters in *Twelfth Night* she disposes of in a sentence, but a more commendatory sentence than that allowed the comic part of *Measure for Measure*.[9]

There is a great deal of true comic Humour in the inferior Characters of this Play, which are entirely of the Poet's Invention.

She is also sensible of the humor in *Much Ado About Nothing* :[10]

There is a great Deal of true Wit and Humour in the Comic Scenes of this Play; the Characters of Benedict and Beatrice are properly marked, and beautifully distinguished.

This appreciation comes, however, after several pages of severe abuse. As if to make up for the comparative gentleness with which she had been discussing the history plays, Mrs. Lennox descends upon *Much Ado* with an almost vengeful ire. The "Fable" she finds "by Shakespear mangled and defaced, full of Inconsistencies, Contradictions, and Blunders." She spends pages trying to show that Margaret would never have done the thing she did without more inducement, and that she should have warned her mistress of the danger before the scene in the church or provided an explanation there. Here, as in the *Two Gentlemen of Verona*, Mrs. Lennox brings up a minor point and overemphasizes it in its relation to the rest of the story. Another instance of this, in *King Lear*, is especially striking: her insistence that the King of France should have been present to hear Cordelia's reply to her father. For three pages she discusses how important it is that this circumstance should have been attended to. In thus running off on a tangent, Mrs. Lennox vitiates the general dignity of her work.

[9] *Shakespear Illustrated*, i, 245.
[10] *Id.*, iii, 271.

She is kinder in her treatment of the tragedies than the comedies. *Romeo and Juliet* and *Hamlet* suffer most under her hand. In the former she takes exception to Romeo's interest in the Apothecary's shop[11] "—a Description, however beautiful in itself, here so ill-timed, and so inconsistent with the Condition of the Speaker, that we cannot help being shocked at the Absurdity, though we admire the Beauty of the Imagination." She considers that nothing is gained by the invention of Paris' death. In connection with this play she takes occasion to display information which, we cannot doubt, was obtained first-hand from Baretti:[12] "—the Friar fearing to be discovered by a Watch, but there is no such Establishment in any of the Cities of Italy." Again in *Othello* she shows a knowledge obtained from her instructor:[13]

Cinthio calls her Cittadina, which Mr. Rymer translates a simple Citizen; but the Italians by that Phrase mean a Woman of Quality . . . . If they were, for Example, to speak of a Woman of the middle Rank in Rome, they would say, Una Romana; if of a noble Lady, Una Cittadina Romana.

One can almost hear Baretti, with the knowledge of experience, making this distinction clear to Mrs. Lennox.

In her treatment of *Othello* Mrs. Lennox shows some penetration; she praises the creation of Othello's character, which she realizes is one of the great improvements made by Shakespeare. She takes issue with Rymer[14] for the narrowness and absurdity of his criticisms upon *Othello*. Perhaps the short-sightedness of Rymer shows her how unfruitful such criticism is, for in dealing with this play she is less rigid with her touchstones of Probability, Decorum, and Justice and betrays more understanding of Shakespeare's

---

[11] *Shakespear Illustrated*, i, 94-5.

[12] *Id.*, i, 97.

[13] *Id.*, i, 132.

[14] Rymer Thomas, *A Short View of Tragedy*, ... *with some Reflections on Shakespear* (Ln., 1693).

actual achievement. With *Macbeth*, too, she is more sympathetic, but a reason is shown by this remark :[15]

> The machinary Part of this Play is so beautifully defended and illustrated by the ingenious Mr. Johnson, in the above-mentioned Pamphlet, that I think I cannot confer greater Obligation on the Reader than by transcribing those Passages here.

She then quotes from Johnson's observations on *Macbeth* at some length. Although she finds fault with minor errors, she concludes that "this Play has fewer Faults of this Kind than any other of Shakespear's, and is deservedly allowed to be a most beautiful piece."

This is the highest praise that she accords anywhere in her three volumes. The first part of *Henry IV* is generally commended both for the humor and for Shakespeare's improvements of the characters of the prince and of Hotspur, a criticism that would be acceptable today. She finds more things to commend in the history plays than elsewhere and is less apt to strike off on strange tangents when discussing them. She does, however, feel that there are many absurdities committed by Shakespeare in crowding events to the detriment of the unities, especially that of time. Nor does she value these standards of pseudo-classicism lightly; we have her own word for it. She is commenting upon the crowding of events in *Richard III* :[16]

> Absurdities like these are such a gross Abuse of the Understanding, that all the Beauties we find scattered throughout this Play, can hardly atone for them.

With these set rules magnified grotesquely out of all proportion, it is little wonder that Mrs. Lennox is not a successful critic of Shakespeare. It would be unjust not to admit that, according to the light granted her, she has done her work faithfully and conscientiously. She has remained

---

[15] *Shakespear Illustrated*, i, 280, 292.
[16] *Id.*, iii, 169.

rigidly true to the principles with which she embarked upon her criticism and has not once let herself be swayed from her course by the beauty of Shakespeare's poetry, the human reality of his characters, or the power of his passion. That she was utterly impervious to all these is not necessarily the conclusion. Once or twice we have seen that she realizes the beauty or the humor contained in a play, but her business is to point out Shakespeare's treatment of the fable which he used as a starting point and to this she has adhered, with the sad result that she has found the great poet lacking in judgment, poetical justice, morality, invention, consistency, and true gentility. In these conclusions she accords more with the critics of the early part of the century than with the awakening appreciation of her own day, indicated in such writers as Johnson and Joseph Warton. Once again we find Mrs. Lennox a follower and not an originator. She accepted unquestioningly the rules which had been handed down to her and took advantage of her own industry to apply them severely and ruthlessly, making up in vigor what she lacked in insight and critical acumen.

In his discussion of *Shakespear Illustrated* in *Shakespeare As a Dramatic Artist* Lounsbury makes this just comment upon Mrs. Lennox and her connection with her era.

The publication of her work furnishes another exemplification of a melancholy fact which, the longer we live, forces itself more persistently upon our observation. There is nothing more to be deplored in the fortunes of individuals than the hard lot that befalls some in having been born at the wrong time or in the wrong country . . . . Such was the unhappy fate of Mrs. Lennox in regard to Shakespeare. She missed her century. Had she flourished in the period immediately following the Restoration, she would have found herself in a far more congenial atmosphere. She would have been enrolled as a distinguished figure in a set which would have sympathized with her opinions and exalted her uncommon learning and critical acumen. Had she in addition become Mrs. Rymer, the conjunction of these two stars, shooting madly from their spheres in the Shakespearean firmament, would have attracted the attention of observers for all time.

The tendencies of these late seventeenth century critics linger on into the eighteenth century and appear sporadically even in the beginning of the nineteenth. They are not common, but the fact that they do exist is shown by various appreciations of Mrs. Lennox's book. It was never generally commended, but there are a few manifestations of approval, the last occurring as late as 1809 and in America.

At the time of its publication *Shakespear Illustrated* was not reviewed at any length or with much favor anywhere except in the *Gentleman's Magazine*. It was announced in the May number with a brief notice of its nature; in the June publication the entire section dealing with Shakespeare's use of Bandello's novel in *Romeo and Juliet* is reprinted and given a place of prominence as the first number in the magazine (xxiii, 250-6). The selection closes with this comment:

> We have selected *Romeo and Juliet* for a specimen of what has been done by this writer to illustrate Shakespear, because it is one of his most regular pieces, and at present more generally known than any other. But whoever would make a just estimate of his merit should see the whole work, in which his resources are display'd, his faults detected, and many beautes of which he was supposed to be the inventor, restored to those from whom they were borrowed.

The laconic mention in the *Monthly Review* (August, 1753, ix, 145) is slightly equivocal:

> Her remarks, which are very judicious, and truly critical, are chiefly intended to prove, that Shakespear has generally spoiled every story on which the above plays are founded, by torturing them into low contrivances, absurd intrigue, and improbable incidents.

No one seems inclined to give this work notice until the year 1801. Then the following letter appeared in the *Gentleman's Magazine* (Feb., 1801, lxxi, 128-9).

Mr. Urban,   Jan. 22.

> We have had innumerable editions of Shakespeare, ... but there is, in my opinion, another publication on this sub-

ject, which would be highly useful and acceptable to a numerous class of readers; that is, a plain and concise account of the novels, tales, and histories, on which Shakespeare's plays are founded, ... Three volumes of this kind, intituled, *Shakespear Illustrated*, were published by Mrs. Lenox in 1754; and they are, I think, admirable productions, extremely entertaining and instructive, abounding with judicious remarks on the excellencies and defects of our great poet. The public would undoubtedly have been highly gratified by a new edition, with a Continuation of this excellent work; but as almost half a century is now elapsed since its publication, I am afraid it is too late to expect it from that ingenious lady. I sincerely declare, Mr. Urban, that I have no motive in writing this article, besides that of promoting the rational entertainment and advantage of the literary world; for I have not the pleasure of being acquainted with Mrs. Lennox.

Yours, etc.
J. R——n.

This letter was further substantiated by one in July of the same year (lxxii, 610).

Mr. Urban,   Close of Sarum, July 3.

I perfectly coincide with the opinion of your correspondent J. R. p. 128, in your Magazine for February last, that after all the comments, notes and criticisms on the works of Shakespeare, there is still wanting a farther illustration of him by exploring the sources from whence he derived the subjects of his wonderful dramas. . . . . Mrs. Lenox hath, it is true, led the way but she hath left many a 'wondrous tale untold.' . . . .

James Wickins.

One can only hope that Mrs. Lennox in her penury and distress was not too ill to derive some comfort from this belated appreciation of one of her earliest literary ventures.

The last lease of life which this book of Shakespearean sources enjoyed was in America. In 1809 there appeared: "Shakspeare Illustrated: or, the Novels and Histories on which the Plays of Shakspeare are founded. Collected and Translated from the Originals. By Mrs. Lennox, Author of the Female Quixote, etc. With critical Remarks and Biographical Sketches of the Writers, By Mordecai Manuel Noah. In two Volumes. Published by Bradford and Inskeep, Philadelphia; Inskeep and Bradford, N. Y.; etc. Printed by G. Palmer, Philadelphia. 1809." Only one volume of this work was compiled, as may be seen from the following letter enclosed in manuscript in a copy of *Shakspeare Illustrated* in the Boston Public Library. It is addressed to Thos. P. Barton, 318 Chestnut Street, Philadelphia.

Sir   N. Y. 28 Dec. 1842.

It would afford me great pleasure to send you a copy of the work referred to in your favour of the 25' the only copy I had was stolen within a few months past. It was entitled Shakespeare illustrated or the Novels and Histories on which the plays of Shakespeare were founded collected and translated by Mrs. Lennox Do. with critical remarks and biographical of the writters Published in Philad by James Palmer 1809 I only published one volume not being able to collect the materials for the other. It was dedicated to the Rev. Dr. Abercrombie and a copy will be found in his collection or in the old bookstores I have long cherished a wish to complete the work but have been prevented by the pressure of other occupations.

I am Sir

Very respectfully

Your obedient Servant

M. M. Noah

This effort at criticism dated from the early period of Mr. Noah's life when he was interested in the theatre and wrote several plays for production. It is no wonder he never had time to finish the work because he went into politics, became consul at Tunis, and after his dismissal from that post, became the leader of the first Zionist movement in America, in connection with which he wrote in 1837 his "Discourse on the evidences of the American Indians being the descendants of the lost tribes of Israel". It is not even surprising, considering the range of his interests, that after thirty-three years he had forgotten almost everything but the title of his straying into Shakespearean scholarship.

It is certainly no loss to the world of scholarship that the work was not completed. The Biblical gentleman who, in 1809, took it upon himself to give the world a revised and improved copy of Mrs. Lennox's work suffered a graver lack of insight and judgment than did she; what was excusable in 1753 seems strangely out of date in 1809. Johnson's dedicatory letter is replaced by a preface written by Noah, explaining the nature of his work. Part of it I shall quote here.

In all the editions of Shakspeare's plays that appeared previous to the publication of the following collection in 1753, we find the novels and histories to which Shakspeare was indebted for the fables of his plays are but slightly mentioned, and no reference is given to where they are to be found. It was this circumstance which induced Mrs. Lennox to collect and translate them.

. . . In a few instances, I have adopted the remarks of Mrs. Lenox, simply because they were appropriate, and to avoid that zeal for originality, which prompts us to convey the same meaning in different words. In addition to her collection, I have given the story on which Shakspeare has founded his *Merchant of Venice,* from the *Gesta Romanorum.*

I am fearful that the admirers of Shakspeare may think him injured by the following illustrations of his plays, and contend that, whilst innumerable beauties present themselves in quick succession to the delighted fancy, we never should pause to dwell on a solitary defect, or root out the few weeds which deform so fair a garden. But it must be recollected, that an impartial commentator, whilst analyzing the beauties, should never be insensible to the defects; and where scenes and characters are pointed out that delight the imagination, some attention should be paid to those that shock the judgment.

Philadelphia, Sept. 20, 1809.

The additional source here referred to was never added as it is not in the first volume, which contains sources for the same plays as did Mrs. Lennox's first volume, with the exception of *Measure for Measure*. Mordecai Noah has, as he states in his preface, kept many of her comments and in his own criticisms is just as severe as she is. When he departs from her in any particular it is always for the worse. One instance will suffice. In treating *Othello* where we have seen that Mrs. Lennox was gentler than her custom was, the later critic descends with heavy hand and ventures to censure points which he evidently thought Mrs. Lennox had allowed to pass too lightly, for he feels the American prejudice of color.[17]

As if it were possible that all the inestimable treasures of which the mind can boast would atone for the mortification a beautiful woman knows she must endure, in being the partner of a man of such colour as Othello. The absurdity of this incident, which is great in the novel, is considerably augmented in the play.

Most of the additional faults which Noah feels called upon to notice are in connection with the morality of Shakespeare. He is criticising Shakespeare from a religious point of view and he finds that *Cymbeline* is founded upon "indelicate and offensive principles" which Shakespeare has betrayed no desire to "expunge".

The rarity of Noah's volume even in his own day testifies to the lack of interest felt in the book. It is doubtful if, even in "backward America", where, however, Shakespeare's plays had already begun the overwhelming domination of the stage which was to continue for the next fifty years, such remarks found willing listeners, and this revised edition of Mrs. Lennox's book dropped into obscurity—if it can be said ever to have emerged.

The favorable comment which *Shakespear Illustrated* stirred is not therefore of any size or enthusiasm. On the other hand, it did not arouse much antagonism. Unfortunately for it, most of the eminent Shakespearean scholars of

[17] *Shakspeare Illustrated* (ed. Noah), i, 78.

the day saw fit to ignore it. Edward Capell in his 1767 edition of Shakespeare does not once mention it. George Steevens in his 1773 edition brings in Mrs. Lennox's name only where Johnson has done so, and in only two cases there, for he omits the reference to *Shakespear Illustrated* which Johnson included in his notes on *All's Well That Ends Well*. The example thus set by Steevens is closely adhered to by Isaac Reed, Malone, and Boswell. Save that Mrs. Lennox's book is given in the list of eighteenth century criticisms on Shakespeare, first printed in Malone (1790) and reprinted in the Boswell-Malone edition (1821), the only one of the fluent and wordy Shakespearean scholars who flourished in the last two decades of the eighteenth century to mention Mrs. Lennox is Dr. Farmer in his *Essay on the Learning of Shakespeare*. He disagrees with Mrs. Lennox about the source of *Measure for Measure*.[18] He also cites "the ingenious Mrs. Lennox" as an authority in discussing a passage in *Troilus and Cressida*.

Some opposition to Mrs. Lennox's attitude occurred in the magazines. In the *Gentleman's Magazine* for May, 1754 (xxiv, 233-4), is published a letter incited by it.

Mr. Urban.

Of all the criticisms upon Shakespear, that of a lady in a late work, intitled, *Shakespear Illustrated*, is the most bold and comprehensive; she has not only remarked inaccurate expressions, mixed metaphors, broken scenes, or violated unities, but has attacked those powers for which his negligence has been overlooked, his invention and his judgment; she has displayed the poverty of his invention, by showing that he has borrowed, and the weakness of his judgment, by distinguishing the defects and incongruity of what he has added and changed.

It has been generally taken for granted, that *Shakespear* improved every story which he made the foundation of a play, except where he was restrained by his regard for his-

---

[18] Farmer Dr. Richard, *Essay on the Learning of Shakespeare* (1767) in *The Dramatic Works of Shakespeare* (ed. Boswell-Malone, London, 1821), i, 310, 314.

torical truth; but it will appear from this work, that he has degraded Italian novels by distorting natural characters, and substituting whimsical improbabilities for natural events.

I should, indeed, greatly rejoice to see my favourite author defended against this formidable *Thalestris*, and perhaps little more than the publication of the combat is necessary to bring innumerable champions into the field in his behalf. [He then gives a detailed account of Mrs. Lennox's discussion of Shakespeare's use of his source in *Much Ado About Nothing*.]

These, Mr. Urban, among many others in the same play, are brought as instances, that Shakespear has not deserved the veneration that has been paid to him. If he can be defended, I hope some of your correspondents will attempt his defence, for which I confess myself to be unqualified.

Yours, etc.

Cambridge,   T. B.
   May 12, 1754.

This provocative letter failed in its evident attempt to start a magazine attack upon Mrs. Lennox, for we find no "defence" in the periodicals of that year. On the contrary, in this same *Gentleman's Magazine* for July, 1754 (xxiv, 311), is a pleasant reference to the work under discussion, in a letter concerning the source of Shylock in *Merchant of Venice*.

And, secondly, he supposes, that Shakespeare took all his Italian stories from their English translations, as it may be fairly proved that this was his common practice, from the perusal of a late entertaining work, entitled *Shakespear Illustrated*.

Yours, etc.

Paleophilus.

The next attack upon Mrs. Lennox came in connection with her play of *The Sister* given in February, 1769, a play which Goldsmith was asked to make one of a party to hiss because she had attacked Shakespeare in *Shakespear Illustrated*. Feeling was running high on the subject of Shakespeare in those years because of the attacks of Voltaire. In his edition of Shakespeare (1765) Johnson had referred to Voltaire as "petty". Voltaire had retaliated by an attack upon Shakespeare in his *Essay on Dramatic Art*. That this reply was known in England is shown by Mrs. Montagu's defence and the tremendous popularity it immediately achieved. This defence, *An Essay on the Writings and Genius of Shakespeare*, appeared in 1769 and through misguided patriotism which blinded literary judgment was immediately hailed as great. The force of the feeling for Shakespeare can be measured by this popularity so out of proportion to the actual value of the production. To appreciate Shakespeare and praise him had become a matter of national pride. It is therefore not strange that some of these enthusiasts should feel justified in punishing a lady who had dared to cast aspersions upon the judgment and powers of Shakespeare.

Two critics in the early nineteenth century animadvert upon *Shakespear Illustrated*. By far the most bitter of these is Francis Douce. From the evidence in his work, *Illustrations of Shakspeare and of Ancient Manners with Dissertations*, he is opposed to all the school of critics who had followed Johnson and is constantly carping at them, especially at Malone and at Johnson himself. His ill-natured remarks betoken an egotistical, jealous nature. He attacks Mrs. Lennox several times,[19] usually on minor points in her criticism. In speaking of *Measure for Measure*, he says:

Shakspeare has likewise been hastily censured by a female writer of great ingenuity, for almost every supposed deviation from the plot of Cinthio's novel, ... The female critic has likewise observed that Measure for Measure ought not to be the title, since justice is not the virtue it inculcates. But surely, if Angelo had died, it would have been *out-measuring measure*; . . .

[19] Douce Francis, *Illustrations of Shakspeare, and of Ancient Manners*: with dissertations on the Clowns and Fools of Shakspeare. A new edition. (London, 1839.) This work was first published in London in 1807, 2 vols. 97, 97n., 379, 110.

In a note on this passage the author comments upon Johnson's sentiments in his dedicatory letter as opposed to the type of criticism Mrs. Lennox has admitted.

> How much at variance is all this with the sentiments that follow on our play, and how it serves to mark the folly and absurdity of hireling dedications!

Douce gets in another thrust at Johnson in connection with his holding up to ridicule some of Mrs. Lennox's remarks on *Cymbeline,*

> not one word of which is to be found in Shakspeare. So much for the criticism and accuracy of a work to which Dr. Johnson condescended to write a dedication. He has likewise too often confided in its opinions in the course of several of his remarks on Shakspeare's plays.

The last insinuation is obviously untrue, as it has been previously shown that Johnson, in his edition of Shakespeare, omitted to echo or applaud the opinions of Mrs. Lennox.

He criticizes Mrs. Lennox again for inaccuracy in her treatment of *Much Ado About Nothing.*

> Mrs. Lenox, assuming, with the same inaccuracy as had been manifested in her critique on *Measure for Measure,* that Shakspeare borrowed his plot from Ariosto, proceeds to censure him for 'poverty of invention, want of Judgment, and wild conceits', deducing all her reasoning from false premises. This is certainly but a bad method of *illustrating* Shakspeare.

Mrs. Lennox finds a champion against these strictures in George Hardinge, that strange facetious enemy of Malone, who reproaches Douce for his lack of chivalry. After telling him that he is "the best Critick Shakspeare has yet found", he goes on to say:[20]

[20] Hardinge George, *Miscellaneous Works, in Prose and Verse* (London, 1818), Letter vi, iii, 84. Hardinge published a book called *The Essence of Malone* (Ln., 1800), in which he held up to ridicule the scholarly procedure of the editor.

I am, however, so gallant, that I am half angry with you
for your want of gallantry to Mrs. Lennox, whose book I
have not read for half a century, but which entertained me
very much when I did read it, though I have no Doubt that
she was a dashing Critick, and a superficial Historian. But
the idea was new, and the picture amusing.

This defence on the score of her sex and that she is a
"dashing Critick" and "amusing" Mrs. Lennox would probably have resented more than the abuse, which at least takes
her work seriously.

The attitude of the romantic critics appears in Nathan
Drake's prefatory essay to his *Memorials of Shakspeare*.
He is speaking of a recent work on the sources of
Shakespeare.[21]

—Ground, indeed, which had been partially preoccupied
by Mrs. Lennox, who, ... published . . . . *Shakespear
Illustrated*. Her task, however, was but very imperfectly
performed, for, of more than one half of the plays of her
author the sources remain unexplored; and her notes were
rather censures on the liberties which the bard had taken with
the incidents to which she had traced him, than elucidatory
of the exquisite manner in which he had occasionally moulded
them to his purpose, and yet more frequently enbalmed
them for immortality, by blending with their outline the
richest creations of his own fancy.

Mrs. Lennox was unfortunate in the time of writing
Shakespear Illustrated: her critical standards belong to the
previous century when her judgments would have met with
favor; and her publication comes just before the work of
the great editors of Shakespeare, beginning with Johnson in
1765. After his edition comes the rapid succession of variorum editions: the Johnson-Steevens (10 vols.) in 1773;
a second edition of this under Isaac Reed in 1778; Malone's
work, culminating in his edition (10 vols.) in 1790; a new
Johnson-Steevens by Steevens alone (15 vols.) in 1793;

---

[21] Drake Nathan, *Memorials of Shakspeare*; or, Sketches of his
Character and Genius, by various writers, now first collected. (Ln.,
1828), 63.

Reed's publication of the Johnson-Steevens (11 vols.) in 1803, fifth edition; finally the Boswell-Malone complete variorum (21 vols.) in 1821. Mrs. Lennox's paltry little volumes are at once obscured by these impressive and extĕnsive commentaries on Shakespeare. To be sure, she did something original and distinct in actually presenting the sources for the plays, but this real contribution was certainly lost sight of in her own day. More credit than she received was assuredly due her for her painstaking and careful work in translating from the Italian. Her equipment for Shakespearean scholarship was admittedly slight and she had not time for elaborate and careful study of what had been done in criticism and what needed to be done. Consequently her judgments are false and admitted as such, even by contemporaries. There are, however, fidelity and industry in this critical work of Mrs. Lennox's which command respect, if not admiration. She has done what she promised to do in presenting the sources and she has compared the plots of these tales with Shakespeare's plots. For the most part, she has concentrated upon this particular thing. Though often ill-advised and hasty in judgment, she is almost always accurate in her facts. Led astray by literal-mindedness and a bigoted array of criteria, she has rendered most of her critical remarks void today, but she has advanced a step in method of criticism, and for this she deserves a place as a Shakespearean commentator.

We have seen that in *Shakespear Illustrated* Mrs. Lennox did considerable translation from the Italian; she also executed one translation from the French. This last is but one of many which she produced in the years immediately following *Shakespear Illustrated*, the last volume of which appeared in 1754. Each of the three succeeding years saw the publication of a work "taken from the French by the Author of the Female Quixote". In November, 1755 (*London Evening-Post*, November 1, though the date on the title-page is 1756), appeared *Memoirs of Maximilian de Bethune, Duke of Sully* in three large volumes quarto. This was

followed in April, 1756 (*London Evening-Post*, April 6),
by *Memoirs of the Countess of Berci* in two volumes.
Exactly one year later in April, 1757 (*London Chronicle*,
December 1, 1757, 535, and *London Evening-Post*, February 2, 1758), came *Memoirs for the History of Madame de
Maintenon* in five volumes. There succeeded an interim of
three years in which Mrs. Lennox did some creative work,
Philander and *Henrietta*, and then in February, 1760 (*London Chronicle*, February 19, 1760, though the date on the
title-page is 1759), *The Greek Theatre of Father Brumoy*
was published with Mrs. Lennox's name on the title-page,
in which she had such distinguished collaborators as Johnson
and the Earl of Orrery. This was in three large volumes
quarto, and it marks the close of Mrs. Lennox's ambitious
attempts at translating. The next year in connection with
her periodical, *The Lady's Museum*, she executed some short
translations, the longest of which was the *History of the
Count de Comminge*, issued in book form in 1764 as the
History of the Marquis of Lussan and Isabella. In 1774
was brought out her last translation, *Meditations and Penitential Prayers of the Dutchess de la Vallière*. These works
of Mrs. Lennox I shall deal with briefly, noting any important facts about their publication, editions, or reception and
attempting to form an estimate of her abilities as a translator.

There is little of importance in connection with the
Memoirs of the Countess of Berci and *Meditations and Penitential Prayers of the Dutchess de la Vallière*. They aroused
little comment and have no especial significance. The *Critical Review* (May, 1756, i, 312) saw fit to censure the choice
of subject in the former case.

Since the ingenious lady who has favoured the world
with this translation, was about to plunder from the *French*,
we could wish she had taken from them something of more
importance. A woman of her reading surely could not be
ignorant that this was an old romance newly vamped up;
and the names changed from Alcidion, Calista, and others,
which became it well enough, into Count de Berci, etc. . . .
It would however be doing injustice to the translator, if we

did not observe that she has performed her part extremely well: the language is in general lively and spirited; and we are only sorry that it is expended upon a work so antient and romantic.

The old romance from which these memoirs can be traced is *A Tragi-Comicall History of Our Times, under the borrowed Names of Lisander and Calista.* By V. d'Audiguier. This was first translated into English in 1621.[22] The French original was evidently retold with different names inserted and Mrs. Lennox translated this. The outline of events in the *History of Lisander and Calista* and the *Memoirs of the Countess of Berci* is the same, but the relating of the incidents is much elaborated in the latter, an elaboration which justifies the objections of the reviewer. In connection with this translation the *Monthly Review* (June, 1756, xiv, 516-520) offers the following encomium on Mrs. Lennox:

The language, however, is very passable; and, it must be confessed that the Lady to whom it owes its present appearance, is a much better writer than most of her contemporary Novelists.

The subject of the *Meditations and Penitential Prayers* was also censured,[23] on the ground that the prayers of a woman who was forced to cease from her sin by circumstances rather than conviction would be neither helpful nor instructive.

More attention was given to the *Memoirs of Sully* than to any other work of Mrs. Lennox. It appeared first in an

[22] d. Audiguier V., *A Tragi-Comicall History of Our Times, under the Borrowed Names of Lisander and Calista.* (Ln., Printed by R. Y. for G. Latham, at the Bishop's head in Paules Churchyard. Anno Domini. 1635.) See Esdaile Arundell, *A List of English Tales and Romances Printed Before 1740* (Ln., for Bibliographical Society, Dec., 1912), Pt. 1, 13. There was an edition in 1621, followed by others in 1627 and 1652. The 1635 edition is the only one I have been able to consult.

[23] *Monthly Review* (Dec., 1774), li, 485 and *Critical Review* (Feb., 1775), xxxix, 186.

elegant edition of three quarto volumes and passed to six-
teen editions, eight English, three Scotch, three both Edinburgh and London, one American, and the last the Bohn
French classics series edition. *Sully's Memoirs* was one of
the standard works which A. Donaldson of Edinburgh seized
upon to produce in a cheap pirated edition, printing it in
1760 in five volumes duodecimo after Millar and Dodsley
had put out the first in three volumes in 1756 and a second
less costly in five volumes octavo in 1757. In 1761, the
year after Donaldson's much cheaper edition, they issued a
third edition in three volumes quarto again, but in 1763 they
changed the format to six volumes duodecimo the better to
compete with the Scotch editor. The advertisement in the
London Chronicle (July 19, 1763, p. 71) explains the change:

The Proprietors of Mrs. Lenox's Translation of the
Memoirs of the Duke of Sully, having been invaded in their
Property by a pirated Edition printed in Scotland, under a
pretence of its being a different Translation, when, in Effect,
it is the same (excepting where mutilated by the Scotch
Editor, as it is in many Places, which will be restored in the
present Edition) in order to do themselves Justice for so
flagrant an Injury, they propose to print an elegant and
cheap Edition of this Work in Six Volumes, in Twelves,
containing a greater Quantity than usual in that Size, at the
very easy Price of Half a Crown for every Volume sewed
in blue Paper. . . . And as the Proprietors are determined in
every Respect to make this Edition worthy of Approbation,
they flatter themselves it will be encouraged by the Public,
not only as being preferable in itself, but as being published
by those alone who were at the Expence of the Translation.

Despite Millar and Dodsley's cheaper format there were
two publications of the *Memoirs* in 1773 in Edinburgh, probably two issues of the same edition. Both are in five volumes duodecimo and are identical save for title-pages and
the inclusion of a dedication in volume one of one edition.
The names of the printers of one, A. Kincaid and W. Creech,
appear on the title-page of volume five of the other, the other
volumes of the latter being printed and sold by John Robert-

son. It seems likely that Kincaid and Creech took over the edition, making it up with their names on the title-pages and omitting the dedication to the memory of Sir Joseph Yates. This 1773 Scotch edition made no mention of Mrs. Lennox as translator and pretended only to slight changes in the text. The preface to the French edition was shortened, omitting the account of previous editions of Sully's memoirs in France as affording "very little instruction or entertainment to any reader". The text of the preface contains frequent variants in reading, such as "perceived" for "shew", but these slight changes are rarer in the work itself. When the change amounts to a shift in order, Mrs. Lennox's translation is far preferable, as at the end of Book IX where the Scotch edition by inverting the sentence sacrifices an effective climactic ending. From the rapid disappearance even of verbal changes after the preface and first chapter of the first book it is obvious that the claim to its being a different translation is spurious.

The two English editions of 1778 by Rivington and Dodsley would seem to have been issued in connection with Mrs. Lennox's claiming of her literary property after fourteen years and her objection to their preparation of a new edition without treating with her. (See her letter to Johnson, above, p. 51.) Apparently the edition with her name on the title-page is the result of Johnson's intervention and an amicable arrangement between Mrs. Lennox and Dodsley. There was no other issue until after her death in 1804, but the English editions of 1810 and 1817 and the Bohn classics edition give her the credit for the translation and admit only such changes as she would herself wish since the appearance of French material correcting M. de L'Ecluse's edition. A brief historical introduction, later attributed to Sir Walter Scott, was included in the 1810 and also in the 1817 and 1856 editions. As may be readily seen from the number of editions and from the fact that it was twice pirated in Scotland this work at once became a classic and Mrs. Lennox chose wisely when she translated it from the French.

The dedication to the Duke of Newcastle is probably by Johnson (see above, p. 20). Here as in the dedication he had written a few years before for *Shakespear Illustrated* an apology is made for the author's "sex and manner of life". Much space is given to showing the usefulness of such a publication at the present juncture of affairs in England. The review of *Sully's Memoirs* in the *Literary Magazine* (September, 1756, i, 281-2) is, according to Boswell (i, 309), also by Johnson. Part of it I shall quote, as it serves to account somewhat for the popularity of the work in England.

This translation has already been so well received by the public that we can add little to its reputation by the addition of our suffrage in its favour. But as the copies are about to be multiplied by a cheaper edition; it is not yet too late to remark, that those memoirs contain an account of that time in which France just began to assume her superiority in Europe; . . . There can be no age or people to which such a history may not be useful or pleasing, but it must more particularly invite the attention of those who like us are now labouring with the same distress, and whose duty it is to endeavour at the same relief.

. . . The style of the translation is easy, spritely, and elegant, equally remote from the turgid and the mean.

A long quotation is then given to illustrate the style and nature of the work. An equally favorable and much longer review appeared in the *Monthly Review* (xiv, 561-573; xv, 209-216). A great part of this is also made up of quotation, and whole incidents are reproduced. Much interest is shown in the contents of the work itself, and the mention of the translator is only casual.

Mrs. Lennox's next translation was *Memoirs for the History of Madame de Maintenon*, which appeared in five volumes the year after *Sully's Memoirs*, in 1757. Though it did not pass to a second edition it was as favorably reviewed as the previous translation. In choosing both Mrs. Lennox was following the accepted literary judgment of the day, for, as Miss Talbot had expressed approval of the French

Mémoires of Sully (see above, p. 21), she likewise mentions Maintenon:[24]

> Did I ever tell you I was reading Mme. de Maintenon's Letters. . . . She seems to have been both a great and a good woman.

The review of the book in the *Monthly Review* (xvii, 80-1) was written by Goldsmith (see above, p. 22); he does not mention Mrs. Lennox at all except to praise her for translating only five volumes whereas Monsieur de la Beaumelle has foisted upon the French public a fifteen volume work. The *Critical Review* (April, 1757, iii, 347-361) in the course of a long article cites Monsieur de la Beaumelle's work and compares it with the part Mrs. Lennox has chosen to present.[25] A digest of the work is given and a passing notice of several errors in the printing. Mrs. Lennox is also advised, before the next edition comes out, to correct several Gallicisms which annoy the reviewer.

The most favorable mention is found in the *Literary Magazine* (ii, 427-31, 469-73). The general plan of the *Memoirs* is given in great detail, and this commendation is then accorded the translator:

> It is with great satisfaction we take this opportunity to inform our readers that in the translation we find few or none of those prettinesses which deform the original. The author of the Female *Quixote* has a juster knowledge of nature, than to think of *elevating and surprizing*, where the human heart is to be unfolded, and portraits to be given of men and manners with a regularity of design, and with true and bold touches of the pencil. She has here given the world an incontrovertible proof of a sound taste, which could not be debauched by the *French* author's *Dolce Piquante*, but

---

[24] *A Series of Letters Between Mrs. Elizabeth Carter and Miss Catherine Talbot*, etc. (London, 1809), ii, 103-4.

[25] The actual work which Mrs. Lennox translated I have discovered from a comparison with her translation to be: *Mémoires pour servir à l'histoire de Mme. de Maintenon, et à celle du siècle passé.* Par L'Angliviel de la Beaumelle. A Amsterdam. Aux depens de l'auteur. M.DCC.LV. 6 vols.

has preferred the more solid entertainment of truth and nature. We shall conclude with recommending the translation, in preference to the original, to all who have anything of a manly relish in their reading; and as a specimen of Mrs. Lennox's stile which is equally sustained throughout the work, we shall here insert the description of Mme. de Maintenon in her last moments.

The *Memoirs for the History of Mme. de Maintenon* is dedicated to the Countess of Northumberland. All but the last sentence and signature of the dedication is on a leaf which is a cancel. This probably indicates a change from another patron to the Countess of Northumberland, as, although this is a period when Johnson was writing many dedications and reviews for Mrs. Lennox, the internal evidence, save for the first sentence of the second paragraph, would lead one to judge it were rather Mrs. Lennox's attempt to imitate Johnson's dedicatory style than his own writing. The opening sentence argues strongly against Johnson's authorship. Since the work is scarce and the dedication brief, I shall quote it here.

To the right honourable The Countess of Northumberland.

Madam,

The lady whose history I take the liberty to offer you, was a striking example of the power of fortune, when, for a long series of years, that power was exerted in her favour, till it raised her at last to a throne. This happy influence of her star extends to her memory and name; and in no single instance is it more to be envied, than that to this translation of her memoirs is prefixed the name of the Countess of Northumberland.

An exalted understanding, superiority of genius, universal benevolence, and unfeigned piety; such were the qualities by which Madame de Maintenon was distinguished: such are the qualities, which, in you, madam, adorn the most eminent rank, add lustre to the noblest line of ancestors, and give dignity to wealth. To whom, therefore, can I with so great propriety dedicate these memoirs as to your ladyship?

You have, madam, expressly forbid me to praise you why was I not enjoined to forbear flattery only? I might then have expatiated freely on a character, where the highest panegyrick would have been but an offering to truth: but, although you have suppressed praise, madam, permit me to declare, that the protection you have been pleased to afford this work, will be always considered as an honour by her, who is, with all imaginable respect, Madam,

Your Ladyship's Most Obliged
And Most Obedient Servant,

Charlotte Lennox.

A book of assignments[26] gives accounts for printing one thousand copies of this work, let out to two printers.   There were six sets for the translator.

The last translation to be discussed is that in which Mrs. Lennox had distinguished collaborators.   In February, 1760, appeared *The Greek Theatre of Father Brumoy* in three volumes quarto.   The dedication, besides the external evidence for Johnson's authorship (see above, p. 26), bears strong internal evidence of being written by him.   As the work is rare today, I shall give the dedication here:

To His Royal Highness George, Prince of Wales.
Sir,

On the day which fills every inhabitant of Britain with expectations of continued and uniform prosperity, may it be permitted me to acknowledge, with the greatest respect, my obligations to your Royal Highness, for suffering me to introduce this translation to the public under the protection of your illustrious name.

The arts of the drama, for which I have presumed to solicit your Royal Highness's patronage, have been always honoured with the protection of princes, as the arts which add grace to precept, and teach virtue by multiplying delights.

Of the employments which engage the labours and studies of mankind, some are incited by the power of necessity, and some dictated by the love of pleasure; to works of necessity, we are driven by nature; in pursuit of pleasure, we are influenced by example.   Nations may receive plenty from the cultivation of the soil, but they must owe their politeness to the refinements of the court; and the encouragement which

[26] BM Add. Mss. 38730.

your Royal Highness has given to the endeavours of genius,
has already kindled new ardors of emulation, and brightened
the prospects of the learned and the studious, who consider
the birth of your Royal Highness as the birth of science, and
promise to themselves and to prosperity, that from this day
shall be reckoned a more illustrious period of letters and of
patronage.

I am, with the profoundest respect,
Sir,

Your Royal Highness's
Most obedient, and
Most humble Servant,

June 4.
1759.   Charlotte Lennox.

Volume one contains, after the dedication, a preface written by the Earl of Cork and Orrery in which he considers
the state of the theatre in all ages, winding up with a
comment upon the rather destitute condition of the English
stage at the time. He includes in this preface praise of
Johnson's style, as he concludes a comparison of the French
and English languages with[27]

Mr. Johnson has shewn us the line of beauty ; . . . . Under
all our disadvantages, which will be fully seen in Mr. Johnson's letter to the earl of Chesterfield, and in the preface to
the English dictionary, we have no reason to doubt, that
English purity might equal Attic eloquence.

He also offers a pretty compliment to Mrs. Lennox in
comparing French novels with English which

wandering from nature and probability, attempt only to
represent persons who never existed even in imagination,
faultless monsters, or aukward fine gentlemen. . . . . If
particulars may claim an exception to this general remark,
The Female Quixote and *Henrietta*, I hope may lay some
claim to that exception.

Besides this preface the Earl of Cork and Orrery has pro-

---

[27] *The Greek Theatre of Father Brumoy* (Ln., 1759), i, pp. iii, iv, v.
In the first quotation the catchword on p. iii gives "eloquence", the
first word on p. iv "elegance".

vided the translation of the first three essays by Father Brumoy. After this come translations of several plays, all of which are done by Mrs. Lennox. Volume two consists entirely of plays and comments upon them, or accounts which are partially synopses of plots and partially criticisms; all of this volume is executed by Mrs. Lennox. It is in volume three that she receives most aid; the advertisement states exactly what pieces have been done by other hands and by whom done. Johnson has provided two essays; the comedies, *The Birds*, and *Peace* are translated "by a young gentleman"—there is no clue to what his name might have been—*The Frogs* is done by the hand of Dr. Gregory Sharpe, *The Cyclops* by Dr. Grainger, "author of the translation of Tibullus", and the *Discourse on the Cyclops* by John Bourryau.

The *Monthly Review* (xxiii, 287-302, 452-467) comments upon the inequality of the style in the translation. After giving a long account of the substance contained in the three volumes, the reviewer falls upon the Earl of Orrery and gives illustrations of some of the awkward passages he is responsible for. His only other comment upon style is brief:

As to that part of the version performed by Mrs. Lenox, we need only observe, that a Lady who has power to engage such noble and able Coadjutors, cannot be supposed deficient in merit herself.

The *Critical Review* (February, 1760, ix, 116-127), on the other hand, bestows high encomiums upon the shape this work has taken in English. It is "A work valuable in the original, but rendered more valuable by the translation." The reviewer criticizes the tediousness of Brumoy as a writer and notes other faults.

Several of these faults are obviated in the translation. The work as it stands in English is, with respect to stile, almost faultless; the language is strong, clear, and melodious: those embarrassed periods complained of above are not seen; and though in the preliminary discourses the metaphors and forced allusions are necessarily preserved, they assume an air of gentility, if we may so express it, in the translation, which looked somehow like pedantry in the original.

Mrs. Lennox, whose name is prefixed to this translation, can receive

no addition to her fame from the praises of a journalist. It is sufficient therefore to say, that the same intimate acquaintance with nature and her own language appears in this performance, for which her other works are so particularly esteemed.

The preface of the Earl of Orrery is here praised, and the writer again lavishes commendation upon the translators.

We turn with reluctance from the preface of the translator to that of the author: nor can we help indulging one reflection by the way. We are sorry to see such abilities laid out in translating which might have been so much more adequately employed in producing something excellent; for, what is the greatest applause that can be given to the ingenious persons we refer to, but that of having excellently translated a book, a better than which any one of them could probably have written.

As regards the style of Mrs. Lennox's translations, it varies materially in her different works. The pieces in *Shakespear Illustrated* are carefully and naturally presented. Perhaps Baretti helped her by explaining the meaning and allowing her to put it in easy English. At any rate, we find little that is awkward in this work. We cannot say as much for some of her translations from the French. Especially in the longer works does she sometimes lapse. Sully's *Memoirs* seems, on the whole, to be the most carefully done and the piece in which her style is most clear, idiomatic, and sustained. In *Memoirs for the History of Mme. de Maintenon* and *The Greek Theatre of Father Brumoy*, we find numerous examples of careless work. Take a sentence like this from the former:[28]

[28] *Memoirs for the History of Mme. de Maintenon* (London, 1757), i, 56.

But he altered this resolution, when he had formed those great designs, which the duke of Sully has preserved to us, which he confided to d'Aubigné, and which we now treat as chimeras.

Similarly awkward is this translation from *The Greek Theatre*:[29]

—Il témoigne qu'il voudrait fort se dispenser de voir Ajax.
—He gives plain indications that he would rather dispense with from seeing Ajax.

The "Gallicisms" for which Mrs. Lennox was censured in the *Memoirs de Maintenon* are even more noticeable in *The Greek Theatre*.[30]

Euripides, dit Aristote, quoique d'ailleurs peu exact, peu châtié dans la conduite et la disposition de ses Sujets, paroît pourtant le plus tragique de tous les Poètes.
Euripides, says Aristotle, although not very exact nor chastized in the subject of his plays, has yet more of the tragic passion than any other poet.

Even more unpleasantly literal is the following:[31]

Ajax ne put dévorer cet affront.
This was an affront which Ajax could not digest.

Such errors are not frequent enough to render the general style awkward in any of the translations. When we consider that Mrs. Lennox produced all these translations in rapid succession, and apparently under financial pressure, it is remarkable that they are as finished as they are. The general impression in reading them is of great naturalness and ease. The apparent carelessness in *The Greek Theatre of Father Brumoy*, where, having had so much experience in this sort of work, Mrs. Lennox would be expected to

---

[29] Brumoy R. P., *Le Théâtre des Grecs* (Paris, 1730), ii, 232. [Yale] *The Greek Theatre of Father Brumoy* (London, 1759), ii, 199.

[30] *Id.*, French original, ii, 230. *Id.*, tr. Mrs. Lennox, ii, 198.

[31] *Id.*, French original, ii, 230. *Id.*, tr. Mrs. Lennox, ii, 198.

be most graceful, may be accounted for by the fact that, as she states in her letter to the Duchess of Newcastle, she was suffering from ill-health during the years of its execution.

The only work of Mrs. Lennox which has not yet been considered is *The Lady's Museum*, a periodical which appeared monthly for eleven numbers, from March, 1760, through January, 1761. It was advertised in the *London Chronicle* for February 19, 1760, in this way.

By the King's Authority. On the first of March 1760, will be published, Price 1s. embellished with copper-plates. (To be published the first of every month with the Magazines) Number 1 of The Lady's Museum. Consisting of a Course of Female Education, and Variety of other Particulars for the Information and Amusement of the Ladies. By Mrs. Charlotte Lennox. Author of the Female Quixote, Henrietta, etc. Printed for J. Newbery, at the Bible and Sun in St. Paul's Church yard; J. Coote, at the King's Arms in Pater Noster row; and sold by the Booksellers, in Great Britain and Ireland.

Mrs. Lennox was falling in with a popular tendency when she undertook to bring out a periodical. Forster thus writes of the periodicals at that time :[32]

The booksellers were never more active than at the close of 1759. . . . . Every week had its spawn of periodical publications; feeble, but of desperate fecundity. . . . . . Of magazines alone, weekly and monthly, I will enumerate the specimens which a very few weeks, between the close of 1759 and the beginning of 1760, added to a multitude already wearing out their brief existence. They were: the *Royal Magazine*, or *Gentleman's Monthly Companion*; the *Impartial Review*, or *Literary Journal*; the *Weekly Magazine of Gentlemen and Ladies' Polite Companion*; the *Ladies' Magazine*; the *Public Magazine*; the *Imperial Magazine*; the *Royal Female Magazine*; the *Universal Review*; the *Lady's Museum*; the *Musical Magazine*; and the *British Magazine*, or *Monthly Repository for Gentlemen and Ladies*.

[32] Forster John, *Life and Times of Oliver Goldsmith*, 6th ed. (London, 1877), ii, 199.

Goldsmith and Smollett were among the editors of and contributors to these magazines. Goldsmith edited the *Lady's Magazine* during 1760-1; he was also helping Smollett with the *British Magazine* which the latter edited and in which his novel, *The Adventures of Sir Launcelot Greaves*, first appeared in 1760-1; at the same time he was writing the *Chinese Letters* for Newbery's paper, the *Public Ledger*. Against so much and such gifted competition Mrs. Lennox's periodical must have had to struggle vainly, although we have no method of ascertaining this except from the fact that it ceased after eleven numbers and that it is exceedingly rare today.

The "History of Harriot and Sophia", later published by Mrs. Lennox as *Sophia*, was printed here and is usually the longest section in each number. "The Trifler" also appears in each number. I shall give below the contents of number nine as a typical number of the *Lady's Museum*.

The Trifler no. ix, pp. 641-644.
The History of Harriot and Sophia (cont.), pp. 645-666.
On Reading Hutchinson on the Passions, a poem, p. 667.
Shalum to Hilpa, poem, p. 668.
Hilpa to Shalum, poem, p. 669.
The Morning, poem, p. 670.
The Ode, p. 671.
The History of the Count de Comminge (concl.), pp. 673-685.
Treatise on the Education of Daughters (cont.), pp. 686-694.
Essay on the Original Inhabitants of Great Britain (concl.), p. 695.
The History of the Princess Padmani, pp. 697-709.
The Lady's Geography, pp. 710-720.

Sometimes there are fewer poems than in this number. In seven numbers there is a section entitled "Philosophy for the Ladies", which deals with such subjects as "The Natural History of the Swallow Tail'd Butterfly, and its Ichneumon" or "of the Ephemeron" or, more ambitiously, discusses methods of attack and escaping attack among animals. These articles are occasionally accompanied by one or more copper-plates as are the articles comprising "The Lady's Geography". This is made up of descriptions of the islands of Amboyna (one of the Moluccas) and the customs of the inhabitants. The number mentioned above deals almost exclusively with the strange fruits and extraordinary marvels which are to be found in that country. The information in the "Geographies" tends toward the fantastic and the wonderful. Of the other "instructive" parts is the "Essay on the Inhabitants of Britain", which begins in the third number and runs through the ninth. It aspires to be erudite and succeeds in being tedious. The style is flowery. As an example of these two points I give the following excerpts:[33]

As some period must be affixt to his reign, although the beginning and end of it are both very uncertain, let us suppose, . . . that it began in the year 465, and ended in the year 508.

Early in the fifth century, the Romans, now grown so weak as to perceive within themselves evident symptoms of dissolution, took a last farewell of our ancestors; and, like expiring friends, exerted their last efforts, amidst convulsive pangs, to assist and direct the Britons how to build a wall of stone . . . .

The treatises on the education of daughters abound in wise maxims. The theory of Locke is followed in so far as he urges against forcing the mind or the attention and recommends only such early reading as shall interest the child. Girls are to be brought up not to talk much in company, to be careful of expenditure, and not to dress above their rank. A girl's reading is to be concentrated as far as possible on the Bible stories.[34]

As for the heathen stories, it will be happy for a girl to remain totally ignorant of them all her lifetime; because they are impure, and abound with impious absurdities; but if you cannot prevent an acquaintance with some, do you endeavour to inspire an abhorrence of them.

[33] *The Lady's Museum,* ii, 516, 443.
[34] *Id.,* ii, 776.

Especially is she warned against too constant reading of romances.

"The Trifler" considers a variety of subjects: one number contains a tale illustrating the fate of proud beauty; another satirizes the trifling attitude and vanity of the ladies of the day; a third the smattering of education which a lady of the time receives; one of the last is supposed to be written by a grandmother who complains that young ladies no longer believe in witches and superstitions, and she blames the Methodists for taking the place of the witches; the last gives a translation from the Greek of a dialogue between Socrates and Aristarchus to illustrate that trifling is no modern invention; number four is a letter from Maria insisting that the author is not a trifler, but[35] "I am much mistaken if the Trifler is not written by the same moral pen that has given us so beautiful a picture of female virtue, in the history of Henrietta."

Mrs. Lennox draws upon some of her previous work for her magazine. The version in the 1752 *Proposals* of her poem, "On reading Hutchinson on the Passions", is reprinted in number nine. In the same number she reprints her poem "Shalum to Hilpa", and number one contains a song from *Philander*. "The Tale of Geneura", given in the last volume of *Shakespear Illustrated* as the source of *Much Ado About Nothing*, is reprinted in number ten. There is no mention that these are reprints. She does, however, note in the text that the "History of the Dutchess of Beaufort", which occupies forty-five pages of the first two numbers, is taken from *Sully's Memoirs*.

Other pseudo-historical tales of romantic interest appear in translation in "The Tryal of the Maid of Orleans" in number three and the "History of Bianca Capello" in numbers five, six, and seven. The latter, the story of the wife of Francisco de Medici, Grand Duke of Tuscany, purported to be a translation from the Italian. There was advertised

[35] *The Lady's Museum*, i, 244.

in *The Sun* for October 16, 1797, *The Life of Bianca Capello*, but it was translated from the German original. As I have not found a copy, I cannot say whether it was simply a reprint of this or not. Belonging in this group of tales is one oriental tale, "The History of the Princess Padmani", the scene of which is laid in India. It has little of the "true Eastern style . . . where all is great, obscure, magnificent, and unintelligible."

Two more serious articles are "An Account of the Vestal Virgins" in number two and "The Life of Anthony Van Dyck", "published from a Manuscript communicated to the Author of the Lady's Museum by a Person of Distinction", in numbers ten and eleven. The only contemporary comment is the account of the spectacular trial and execution of Lawrence Earl Ferrers in number four. The excuse for including such a scandalous tale in a magazine for the improvement of young ladies can only have been the great interest which it roused.

Most of the poems are Mrs. Lennox's own, reprinted from her early volume of *Poems*, or like them, conventional love ode or pastoral; one more original is in the last number and is entitled "A Poetical Epistle from Busy, the Lap-Dog, in London, to Snowball, the Buck-hound, in Windsor Forest." Although artificial in idea and execution it is not wholly without naturalness and vigor.

There is one letter in number six signed C. D.[36] and supplying an item of Shakespearean criticism which has interest in that Johnson doubtless based a note upon it. It has to do with the much-discussed passage in *Macbeth*, Macduff's line in the last act, "He has no children". The letter argues that the line refers to Malcolm, who therefore could not understand the feelings of a father rather than to Macbeth who had children. In his edition of Shakespeare (1765), five years after this letter was printed here, Johnson has this note on the passage:

[36] *The Lady's Museum*, ii, 409-413.

He has no children—It has been observed by an anony-
mous critick, that this is not said of Macbeth who had children, but of Malcolm, who having none, supposes a father
can be so easily comforted.

This is a neat summary of C. D.'s letter. If Johnson had
not read "Charlotte's book" himself, she called his attention
to this Shakespearean note from her publication.[37]

The only other work of importance appearing in the *Lady*'s
Museum is the "History of the Count de Comminge. Written by himself." This begins in the second number and continues through the ninth. Next to "Harriot and Sophia"
it is the longest tale in the magazine. It is a translation of
the well-known romance by Madame de Tencin written about
1726. It reappeared in Paris in 1764 with a drama on the
subject by M. F. T. M. D'Arnaud and this was translated
and published in London in book form in 1775, when it was
criticized in the February number of the *Critical Review*
(xxi, 163) as "Stories of romantic love carried beyond the
bounds of probability." I have never seen a copy of this
1775 publication and cannot say whether it was a new translation or Mrs. Lennox's. Hers appeared in book form in
1764, under the title *The History of the Marquis of Lussan
and Isabella*, with her name on the title-page

In summary, we see that in her magazine Mrs. Lennox
included one of the oriental tales which were popular and
whose influence may be seen in *Rasselas* and in some of the
essays from *The Bee* and *Essays of 1765* of Goldsmith.
Her translations of romantic tales were also much in vogue.
Beginning with 1755 constant announcements of such translations appeared in the newspapers and magazines. Usually
these were of novels or memoirs: Smollett's translation of
Gil Blas was a famous example of the former, and her own
translation of *Sully's Memoirs* of the latter. It is difficult
to believe that with the freshness of Dyer's *Grongar Hill*

[37] I have dealt with this subject in detail in "The Source of a Note
in Johnson's Edition of *Macbeth*", *Modern Language Notes* (January,
1928), xliii, 34-5.

and the sympathetic reality of Thomson's "disaster'd Swain" before them people could still enjoy the thin, chill lines which this magazine and others of the period present as poetry. Some of the instructive articles are refreshingly naïve, especially if they are accompanied by such surprising copper-plates as those of "An Inhabitant of the Island of Amboyna equipp'd for War" or the "Antient Britons". Generally the "Philosophy for Ladies" or "The Lady's Geography" contains more diversion for the modern reader than treatises "On the Education of Daughters", which are too general to give much information on contemporary customs. Finally, *The Lady's Museum* is interesting in that by its content it shows what was thought to appeal to the ladies of the day.

As we glance over Mrs. Lennox's entire selection of translations and the comments they roused, we may judge that in general she was wise in her choice. She did not do any fiction except *History of the Count de Comminge*. Instead, she specialized in memoirs and the more learned works. Her most successful choice was obviously the *Memoirs of the Duke of Sully*; her most learned, *The Greek Theatre of Father Brumoy*. Although the latter did not pass to a second edition and was less skilfully done by Mrs. Lennox, it is probable that in her own day it added tremendously to her prestige, both because of the dignified nature of the work and because of the well-known and respected writers who collaborated with her in the task of translating. The production of so many translations, though often obviously hackwork, did much to keep Mrs. Lennox's name in the public eye as well as herself and her family from distress; and since her choice was always dignified and serious, she thus added to her reputation for learning, gentility, and real literary worth.

CONCLUSION

There is no question that Mrs. Charlotte Ramsay Lennox was regarded with serious respect in her own day. This is shown not only by the favorable mention which was almost invariably accorded her in the literary reviews but also by the tributes of the writers of her time. Among those who expressed admiration for her may be numbered Johnson, Fielding, and Richardson. Farmer called her the "ingenious Mrs. Lennox". If we consider those who in some way helped or encouraged her, we find first of all Johnson, then Goldsmith, Garrick, the Earl of Orrery, and the Duchess of Newcastle. Sir Joshua Reynolds painted her portrait and Baretti taught her Italian. Fanny Burney evidently disliked her. So did Mrs. Thrale and Laetitia-Matilda Hawkins. We have expressions of disapproval of her or her works from Mrs. Carter and Lady Mary Wortley Montagu. It is a case where the sexes are divided, the men for Mrs. Lennox, the women against her. The only woman of prominence with whom she seems to have had friendly relations is Mrs. Yates, the actress.

Whatever we may think of Mrs. Lennox's writings today, we must certainly grant her the quality of versatility. She wrote poems, novels, a dramatic pastoral, plays, a critical work, translations; she edited a magazine. The productions of her pen number seventeen in all. Besides these she tried her luck as an actress, was the mother of two children, acted as governess to some young ladies of fashion, and is mentioned as enjoying moments of social relaxation with some important figures of the time. Although throughout her life hampered by financial distress, she managed to maintain a dignity and worth which permitted her to know people of distinction and be known by them. Her literary relations alone lend her interest.

If we seek to estimate the value of Mrs. Lennox's works, we find two which are important intrinsically: these are

The Female Quixote and *Shakespear Illustrated.* The latter is the first work in which the sources of Shakespeare's plays are given and an attempt made to compare them with his treatment; in other words, Mrs. Lennox is one of the first historical critics of Shakespeare. *The Female Quixote* is still an amusing novel, ingeniously conceived, with a charming heroine; it may be ranked as an important link in the chain of Quixotic imitations in the eighteenth century. Of the other novels *Sophia* and *The Political Quixote* alone contribute little that is significant. *Henrietta* depicts a sentimental heroine who in the midst of stereotyped situations salvages for herself individuality. *Harriot Stuart* interests us with incidents which are frankly autobiographical. In *Euphemia* the mellow memory of age faithfully outlines early Colonial scenes in America; these pictures of American life offer something peculiarly fresh and authentic. One of Mrs. Lennox's translations, *Memoirs of the Duke of Sully*, turns a French classic into English. *The Lady's Museum* may be taken as a fair sample of an eighteenth century *Ladies' Home Journal*. Thus were Mrs. Lennox's efforts disseminated over a wide field of literary types; if she did not show genius in any one branch, she at least demonstrated versatility, and skill in adapting herself to popular taste without an entire sacrifice of worth and originality.

APPENDICES

APPENDIX I

James Ramsay

I AM including here all the material which I have been able to find upon any James Ramsay between the years 1700 and 1768.

1. *Calendar of State Papers. Domestic.* (1702-3), 452.
   "James Ramsay to be Commissary of the Artillery Company in place of Colin Ramsay, who has demitted that trust."
   Calendar of State Papers. American and West Indian. (1708-9), 559, ii.
   A James Ramsey acted as one of the Grand Jury at the trial of a man at St. Kill's.

2. *Calendar of Treasury Papers.* (1708-1714), cxxxv, 16.
   "July 7, 1711. Selling of lands by James Ramsay, of Prentatoun (in the county of Edinburgh)."

3. Dalton Charles, *English Army Lists and Commission Registers,* 1661-1714 (London, 1904), v, (1702-6) 73.
   *"25 March, 1705. James Ramsey to be ensign in Brigadier Howe's Regiment of Foot. (15th Regt. of Foot)."
   Id. v, 253.
   *"Lieutenant Jas. Ramsay Commission as Lieut. renewed 1st June, 1715. Major-General Tidcombe's Regt. of Foot."
   Id. vi, 33.
   "The Royal North British Dragoons. James Ramsay to be Chaplain *vice* Ge. Anderson, 4 May, 1714 s."
   Id. vi, 209.
   "The Marquis of Lothian's Regt. of Dragoons (7th Hussars). Jas. Ramsay to be chaplain. St. James's. 29 March, 1711. *note,* Commission renewed by George I in 1715."

4. *Gentleman's Magazine*, iv, 573.
   "Capt. Ramsay Oct. 1734. Capt. Lieut. in Capt. Congreve's Company in the 2nd Regiment of Foot Guards."

5. Wilson, J., "An English Army-List of 1740" in *Notes and Queries*, 12th series, viii, 327.

**"Lt. Gen. Bissett's Regiment of Foot. First Lieutenants. James Ramsay. 26 August, 1736."

Id., 12th series, vi, 331.

"Independent Companies of Invalids. Four Companies at New York.

		Date of Pres. Commission
Captains........	Richard Briggs (1)	14 Feb., 1728-9.
	Hubert Marshall	4 July, 1736.
	Edward Clarke	ditto
**	James Ramsay	30 Dec., 1738.

6. New York State Library, *Calendar of Council Minutes*, 1668, 1783 (Albany, Univ. of the State of New York, 1902), 19: 132.

"October 29, 1741. Warrants: to contractors for victualling troops at Oswego; to Henry Van Rensselaer for same; to James Ramsay for salary as surgeon there; to Gov. Clarke for military transportation."

7. State of New York, *Report of the State Historian* (Albany, 1897), Colonial Series II.

"1768. 4th Regt. Col. Claus's. Ensign, James Ramsey Junior."

(These last two I have included, thinking they might refer to a possible brother of Charlotte Ramsay.)

I have marked with an asterisk those it is possible refer to the James Ramsay who was the father of Charlotte Ramsay, and with two asterisks those that I think it is probable refer to him.

APPENDIX II

Two Poems by Mrs. Charlotte Lennox

1. I AM reprinting here a poem by Mrs. Lennox which appeared in the *Gentleman's Magazine* (November, 1750), xx, 519. It is not to be found elsewhere.

AN ODE On the Birthday of Her Royal Highness the Princess of Wales. Written by Mrs. Charlotte Lennox, and presented to her Royal Highness, by the Right Honourable the Earl of Middlesex.

> Again the swift revolving year
> Returns the bright, th' auspicious morn,
> That shed its kindest influence here,
> When Britain's future queen was born.

Still may the sun on this blest day
With brighter beams indulgent rise,
Still emulate the glad'ning ray,
And milder glories of her eyes.

Those charms thy spotless youth adorn
Each rip'ning year shall more display:
So the soft blushes of the morn
Give promise of a brighter day.

The pomp of pow'r, the grateful awe,
And homage which on sovereigns wait,
Your eyes without that aid cou'd draw,
And not demand it, but create.

Yet not that all-commanding form,
That face where love's soft graces play,
Tho' bright in every female charm,
Shall claim alone the muse's lay.

She meditates a nobler praise,
And wings a far more glorious flight,
Drinks in thy virtue's fuller blaze
And basks in those fair beams of light.

First in the ever-smiling train
Religion sheds diffusive grace,
In thy fair breast confirms her reign,
And gives the sacred sweets of peace.

There every generous passion glows,
That can the human soul refine,
There soft material fondness flows,
And love so pure, 'tis half divine.

Well has it been decreed by fate,
A form so fair, so bright a mind,
Should grace the world's chief regal seat,
And bless the noblest of mankind.

2. "The Art of Coquetry" was first published in *Poems on Several Occasions Written by a Lady* (London, 1747), 61-67. It was reprinted in the *Gentleman's Magazine*

(November, 1750), xx, 518-519, with a few alterations to make the sense and metre smoother. In the volume of poems every important noun is capitalized, but in the later printing Mrs. Lennox deviates from this custom, and capitalizes only occasionally for emphasis. I am giving the poem here because it is typical in metre and form, and because it seems to me to be the most successful of her poems. I follow the text from the *Gentleman's Magazine*, which is revised and improved from the earlier one.

The Art of Coquetry. By Mrs. Charlotte Lennox.

  Ye lovely maids whose yet unpractis'd hearts!
  Ne'er felt the force of Love's resistless darts;
  Who justly set a value on your charms,
  Pow'r all your wish, but beauty all your arms,
5 Who o'er mankind would fain exert your sway:
  And teach the lordly tyrant to obey;
  Attend my rules, to you alone address't
  Deep let them sink in every female breast,
  The queen of love herself my bosom fires,
10 Assists my numbers, and my thought inspires:
  Me she instructed in each secret art,
  That first subdues and then enslaves the heart;
  The sigh that heaves by stealth, the starting tear,
  The melting languish, the obliging fear;
15 Half-utter'd wishes, broken, kind replies,
  And all the silent eloquence of eyes;
  To teach the fair by various wiles to move
  The soften'd soul, and bend the heart to love.
  Proud of her charms and conscious of her face,
20 The haughty beauty calls forth every grace,
  With fierce defiance throws the killing dart;
  By force she wins, by force she keeps the heart.
  The witty fair a nobler game pursues,
  Aims at the head, but the rapt soul subdues.
25 The languid nymph enslaves with softer art,
  With sweet neglect she steals into the heart;
  Slowly she moves her swimming eyes around,
  Conceals her shaft, but meditates the wound;
  Her gentle languishments the gazers move,

30 Her voice is musick, and her looks are love.
   To few tho' nature may these gifts impart,
   What she withholds, the wise can win from art.
   Then let your airs be suited to your face,
   Nor to a languish tack a sprightly grace.
35 The short round face, brisk eyes, and auburn hair,
   Must smiling joy in every motion wear,
   The quick unsettled glance must deal around,
   Hide all design, and seem by chance to wound.
   Dark, rolling eyes a languish may assume,
40 These, the soft looks and melting airs become:
   The pensive head upon the hand reclined,
   As if some sweet disorder fill'd the mind;
   Let the heav'd breast a struggling sigh restrain,
   And seem to stop the falling tear with pain.
45 The youth, who all the soft distress believes,
   Soon wants the kind compassion which he gives.
   But beauty, wit, and youth may sometimes fail,
   Nor always o'er the stubborn soul prevail;
   Then let the fair one have recourse to art,
50 Who cannot storm may undermine the heart,
   First form your artful looks with studious care,
   From mild to grave, from tender to severe;
   Oft on the careless youth your glances dart,
   A tender meaning let each glance impart.
55 Whene'er he meets your look with honest pride,
   And soft confusion turn your eyes aside,
   Let a soft sigh steal out, as if by chance,
   Then cautious turn, and steal another glance.
   Caught by these arts, with pride and hope elate
60 The destin'd victim rushes on his fate:
   Pleas'd, his imagin'd victory pursues,
   And the kind maid with soft attention views,
   Contemplates now her shape, her air, her face,
   And thinks each feature wears an added grace;
65 'Till gratitude, which first his bosom proves,
   By slow degrees sublim'd, at length he loves.
   'T is harder still to fix than gain a heart;
   What's won by beauty, must be kept by art.
   Too kind a treatment the blest lover cloys,
70 And oft despair the growing flame destroys:
   Sometimes with smiles receive him, sometimes tears,
   And wisely balance both his hopes and fears.
   Perhaps he mourns his ill-requited pains,
   Condemns your sway, and strives to break his chains;

75 Behaves as if he now your scorn defy'd,
    And thinks at least he shall alarm your pride:
    But with indifference view the seeming change,
    And let your eyes to seek new conquests range;
    While his torn breast with jealous fury burns,
80 He hopes, despairs, adores and hates by turns;
    With anguish now repents the weak deceit,
    And powerful passion bears him to your feet.
    Strive not the jealous lover to perplex,
    Ill suits suspicion with that haughty sex;
85 Rashly they judge, and always think the worst,
    And love is often banish'd in distrust.
    To these an open free behaviour wear,
    Avoid disguise, and seem at least sincere;
    Whene'er you meet affect a glad surprize;
90 And give a melting softness to your eyes:
    By some unguarded word your love reveal,
    And anxiously the rising blush conceal,
    By arts like these the jealous you deceive,
    Then most deluded when they most believe.
95 But while in all you seek to raise desire,
    Beware the fatal passion you inspire:
    Each soft, intruding wish in time reprove,
    And guard against the soft invader love.
    Not for the tender were these rules design'd,
100 Who in their faces show their yielding mind:
    Whose eyes a native languishment can wear,
    Whose smiles are artless and whose blush sincere:
    But for the nymph who liberty can prize,
    And vindicate the triumph of her eyes:
105 Who o'er mankind a haughty rule maintains,
    Whose wit can manage what her beauty gains:
    Such by these arts their empire may improve,
    And unsubdu'd controul the world by love.

The only changes of even slight importance from the 1747 version are lines 12, 13, changed from

    How to enslave, and keep the vanquish'd Heart;
    When the stol'n sigh to heave, or drop the Tear,   ;

lines 31, 2, changed from

    Tho' not to all Heaven does these Gifts impart,
    What's theirs by Nature may be yours by Art.   ;

and line 108, changed from the more balanced

> And what they lost by Nature gain by love.

to a last line more direct of meaning.

APPENDIX III

Poems to Mrs. Charlotte Lennox

1. *Gentleman's Magazine* (June, 1749), xix, 278.

To Mrs. Charlotte Lennox, upon seeing her Poems, and Proposals for printing them.

> What gentle strain invades my list'ning ear!
> What soft emotions move the melting tear!
> How is my breast with gen'rous warmth inspir'd,
> My soul enraptur'd, and my fancy fir'd!
> *Ardelia sings!*—she sings in melting lays,
> And admiration kindles into praise:
> Each hears delighted the enliv'ning sound,
> Love strikes the blow, and Beauty feels the wound.
> Not *Sappho* more the yielding soul could move,
> O'er ev'ry line I sigh, and melt in love.
> Smooth as the stream, thy flowing numbers glide,
> Inspir'd by nature, nature is thy guide;
> On thee profuse, she beams each shining grace,
> Wit in thy mind, and beauty in thy face:
> While fluent Fancy prompts the pleasing lay,
> Serenely wise, and innocently gay.
> Mild in thy train, the Virtues all attend,
> Refine the poet, and exalt the friend:
> But did no charms adorn that form of thine,
> And in thy eye no peerless lustre shine,
> Thy wit, the tender passion would impart,
> Steal on the soul, and captivate the heart.
> Still love attends on those who thus excel,
> And yields the tribute due to writing well.
> O be thou bless'd with all that's dear to name,
> Secure in innocence, and bright in fame.
> O may no care thy rising Muse suppress,

No sorrows sadden, and no want distress!
But gaily chearful may thy tuneful art
Enliven, soften, and enlarge the heart;
While bless'd with ease and happiness refin'd,
At once you ravish and instruct mankind.

2. *Gentleman's Magazine* (November, 1750), xx, 518.

To Mrs. Charlotte Lennox. On reading her Poems, printing by Subscription, in one Vol. 8vo. price 5s.

Admiring *Greece*, which boasts the *Sapphic* muse,
To thee the second wreathe would not refuse:
But *Britain*, emulous of ancient fame,
May equal honours for her *Sappho* claim.
Her genius, sure, thy youthful breast inspires,
But breathes into thy numbers purer fires,
Love, the inchanting subject of thy song,
Tender as chaste, and innocent as strong,
Yet glows with such a warmth in ev'ry page,
As might renew the fires of frozen age.
Thy pen at once *Love's* dart and pencil too,
At once the painter and inspirer you.
Your eyes into our souls that fire convey,
So well describ'd in thy harmonious lay:
Your verse creates, your form can fix desire,
Wishing we read, and gazing we admire.
                                        E. N.

Nov. 20, 1750.

3. *Gentleman's Magazine* (January, 1751), xxi, 35.

Advice to the Novice in Love. Occasion'd by reading the art of coquetry, by Mrs. Charlotte Lennox, in Nov. p. 518.

In tuneful numbers *Ovid* sweetly sung
How best the lovesick heart to disengage;
He, when fierce passion scorch'd the glowing breast,
And *Daphne's* coyness fann'd the rising flames,
Advis'd to quench 'em in *Corinna's* arms.
But this is not to conquer, but to fly;
Not so I counsel, tho' the tutor'd fair,
Now vers'd in coquetry of novel mode,
Inspir'd by *Charlotte's* pen, inforce their power,
And make captivity severe by frowns.—
But hence! ye voluntary slaves, to you

The muse disdains to prostitute her song.
You who first arm the tyrant, then obey;
Who sooth the frenzy of capricious pow'r
And fawning, lick the hand that gives the blow.
But there are honest wretches, who, tho' bound,
Still sigh for freedom, struggling to be free;
If therefore I, by long experience wise,
Apprentic'd in the subtle arts of love,
Teach these to bend the proud, and in their turn
Enslave the tyrant; if I wreath their brows
With laurel, twin'd with myrtle's gentler green;
Be mine at least the praise, be theirs the bliss.
First then be this deep-rooted in the breast,
By slow degrees thy passion to disclose;
Adapting words to times, and times to place.
For this gains unperceiv'd upon the heart,
Or, when the case requires, yields safe retreat.
But when in formal phrase you whine of love,
And supplicate compassion from the fair;
She, vain and flush'd with plenitude of pow'r,
Or studious to proclaim it to the world,
Will, tho' she sigh in secret for the joy,
Affect disdain, and spurn thee from her feet,
By *slow* advances, therefore, make *sure* speed,
For this will bring thee safer to the goal.
Mark the gay linnet! how with wanton wings
He forms the mazy round; now high in air,
Now lightly perch'd upon the leafy spray,
Or flutt'ring o'er the lawn his mate pursues;
'Till by those distant modes of courtship, he
Reigns the gay monarch of *Linetta's* breast.
But shou'd thy youthful ardour unawares
Proclaim thy love aloud, while reason nods;
If coyness then ensue, and killing frowns;
Then, then stand firm, or thou art lost indeed.
Then let the dauntless eye, the steady step,
The careless smile, and well affected ease,
Proclaim thy heart thy own, and veil the pangs
That rend thy breast, or they admit no cure.
Then, smooth with happy skill thy anxious brow,
Like mild *Winander's* stream, which gently flows,
And in soft mazes rolls a silver tide,
'Midst all her ragged rocks, and cliffy shores.
Observe the couching mastiff, how he eyes,

With aspect grim, the passing traveller:
If he with timorous steps steals softly on,
Or views askaunt the lurking prodigy;
Sudden he springs, and rends the trembling prey
But if with careless strides he stalks along,
Or whistles as he goes regardless by;
Instant he fawns, and waves the circling tail.
So thou by calm indifference shalt elude
Thy fair one's frowns, and win the dimpled smile.
These rules, tho' short, if thou observest right,
Shall safe conduct thee to the happy shores
Of hymeneal love; then shift thy sails
Obliquely to the wind, by compass steer,
Regardless how the raging billows roar.
So shall thy fair-one beckon thee to land
When she thy distant veering bark descries;
Shall wave her lily hand, and smiling say,
O sail back, sailor, tack about this way,
Safe and serene you'll find this winding bay.

APPENDIX IV

Alla Signora Carlotta Lennox   Oda

Or, che ti sei condotta
Quasi all' Aonie Cime,
Di retroceder pensi?
Come questi, Carlotta,
In menti sì sublime
Pusillanimi sensi?

Or che più pochi passi
Ti rimangono a fare
Su pel difficil Monte,
Rivolgere vedrassi
Una Donna tua pare
Sbigottita la fronte?

Or che la stessa Clio
Ti viene incontro, e vuole
Teco cambiar di cetra
Or che il lucente Dio
T'apre sue dolci Scuole
Carlotta il passo arretra?

Deh quai genj funesti,
E invidiosi della
Gloria del suol Britanno,
Ti suggeriscon questi
Pensieri, e Te rubella
A Febo, ad Amor fanno?

Scuoti, scuoti Te stessa
Torna a calcar col lieve
Piede il primo sentiero,
Tu timida? Tu oppressa
Per un tratto or sì breve?
Ah no, non sia mai vero!

Torna a cantar d'amore
Sulle placide linfe
Del paterno tuo fiume.
Torna ad empiere il core
Di dolcezza alle Ninfe,
Com-era tuo costume.

Ma tu non dai aseolto
Al dritto mio consiglio,
Non parli, non respondi?
Anzi arrossendo in volto
Chini turbata il ciglio,
E al mio dir ti confondi?

E che vuol quel silente
Insolito contegno,
Che vuol, Carlotta dire?
Perchè chiudi tua mente
A chi ver l'alto segno
Ti vuole incoraggire?

E che? Ma già indovino
Di tanta vitrosia
La segreta cagione.
So chi dal bel cammino
Distoglier ti vorria;
So, so chi a me s'oppone.

Johnson, rigido Inglese,
Che un grazioso nulla
Crede peccato, e vizio;
Che sta pesando un mese
Ogni sua riga sulla
Bilancia del guidizio;

Johnson, che pieno ha il petto
D'austere cose, e il capo,
Filosofante grave;
Che un innocente affetto
Del tempio di Priapo
Teme non sia la chiave;

Johnson, Johnson è quello
Che intorno a te s'è messo
Col suo parlar feroce;
E la mente, e'l cervello
Sento intronarmi io stesso
Dalla severa voce.

Ma, (perdonami o saggio
Inflessibil segnace
Del buon, marito Greco)
Ma (nè recarti a oltraggio,
Se mia Musa loquace
Osa or contender teco)

Ma non è ver, che sacra
L'arte Apollinea deggia
A virtute esser tutta.
Virtute nuda, e macra
Non abiti una Reggia,
Che amor solo ha construtta;

O se un'agiata stanza
Lassuso aver desia
Nell' Eliconio tetto;
Lasci l'aspra sembianza
E faccia compagnia
Con chi ne fu Architetto.

Si, il Figliuolo gentile
Del zoppo Siciliano
Sempre non sdegni, e fugga;
E per soverchia bile
Predicandoci invano
Da se stessa si strugga

Con alto stile Omero
Virtuosi dipinga
E Nestore, ed Ulisse;
Ma poi cantando il fero
Pelide, sogni, e finga
Come Amor lo trafisse.

Erga a Diana un Ava
Sull'inospito lido
Il religioso Enea;
Ma su gli occhi alla cara
Addolorata Dido
Prima lagrime bea.

Carlo, e Goffredo i saldi
Brandi vibrino cantro
Gente barbara infida;
Ma gli Orlandi, e i Rinaldi
Non sostengan lo scontro
D'Angelica, e d'Armida.

Che dico? anzi anzi in riva
Del solitario Sorga
Un amico di Plato
Narri per Laura schiva
Quanto pianto gli sgorga
Dal ciglio innamorato.

Narri le crespe trecce
Scompigliati, o sospese
Dal susurroso vento;
E dietro un Taggio un Lecce
Goda il Pastor Francese
Dello straniero accento.

E mente l'aure molce
Soavemente intorno
Colla divina Lira
E che al suo canto dolce
Nel silvestre soggiorno
Tutto amor sente, e spira;

Lo stesso Johnson zitto
I suoi teneri lai
Ascolti, ammiri, e lodi;
Ne virtute a delitto
Gli attribuisca mai
I non lascivi modi

Or da te si dilegui
Quella vana paura,
Che il dir d'Amor ti vieta,
Siegui, Carlotta, siegui
Impavida, e sicura
Il Toscano Poeta.

E se non hai più dramma
D'Amor per quel Pastore,
Che tradita ti lascia,
Crea tosto un altra fiamma,
E lagnati a tutt' ore
D'una supposta ambascia.

Sì, sì, una finta pena
Se non una reale,
Mai in te non s'estingua;
E la tua dolce vena
Renda tua lingua equale
All' Italica Lingua.

Giuseppe Baretti
to "mio carissimo Don Rimigo"
Casale, Italy. From a book
found there containing nineteen
selections of his poetry. Dated London,
May 30, 1754.

In the possession of Capt. F. L. Pleadwell.

APPENDIX V

Works Doubtfully Attributed to Mrs. Lennox

I. *Eliza* and *The Trifler*

In Nichols' *Literary Anecdotes* (London, 1812), viii, 435, there is an addendum to the life of Mrs. Lennox (Id., ii, 200-1), which gives a few facts about her death and this information: "Besides the works already enumerated, Mrs. Lennox is the Authoress of

> *Memoirs of Madame de Maintenon,* 4 vols.
> *Eliza* erroneously attributed to Dr. Young, and included in a publication of his works.

Harriot and Sophia, 2 vols. . . . .
The three first numbers of *The Trifler*."

Of these the first and third are undoubtedly by Mrs.
Lennox, as they are reprinted or announced with her name
on the title-page. *Eliza* I have been unable to locate. It is
not included in any of the following editions of Edward
Young's works which I have gone through carefully:

> Edinburgh, 1741, 2 vols.
> London, 1757, 4 vols.
> Edinburgh, 1774, 6 vols.
> London, 1778, 4 vols.
> London, 1792, 3 vols.
> London, 1798, 3 vols.
> American edition, Charlestown, 1811, 3 vols.

It is not mentioned under his works in the British Museum
Catalogue.

There are two novels by the name of Eliza, which came out
while Mrs. Lennox was writing. One is *The History of
Eliza*, written by a friend. 1767. 12°. This is in the British
Museum. The other is *The Distrest Wife*, or, *The History
of Eliza Wyndham*, "related in a Journey from Salisbury.
2 vols. London: Printed from W. Cooke, in Mayfair, and
Sold by J. Wilkie, in St. Paul's Churchyard. MDCCLXVII."
This is apparently the work of a man, as in the Advertisement appears "written to amuse the Author in an absence
from his wife." It is improbable that either of these is by
Mrs. Lennox. The reasons besides the one given, that the
latter is by a man, are two. In her later works, after the
Female Quixote, Mrs. Lennox includes on the title-page "by
the author of The Female Quixote". In the advertisements
of *Euphemia* (The *World*, Friday, May 14, 1790, No. 1049
and *The Times*, June 1, 1790, No. 1696) there is this list
of novels given: "By Mrs. Charlotte Lennox, Author of
the Female Quixote, Henrietta, The sisters, and Sophia,
Novels." If she had written another novel as late as 1767

or 1768, it seems extremely unlikely that it would have been omitted here.

In the *Lady's Museum* each number contains a section entitled "The Trifler". As there is no reason to question that this magazine is by Mrs. Lennox, at least edited by her (see *London Chronicle* for 1760, February 19-21, 178), as there is nothing in these articles inconsistent with her style, and as number four suggests that the author of "The Trifler" is the author of *Henrietta*, we may safely say they are by her. Whether this is *The Trifler* referred to by Nichols we cannot be sure. There were two other papers by that title in Mrs. Lennox's lifetime. One may be eliminated. That is *The Trifler*, "a new Periodical Miscellany by Timothy Touchstone, of Saint Peter's College, Westminster. London: Printed for the Authors and sold by Mess. Robinsons, Pater-Noster Row. 1788." I have been able to look at this magazine, and there is nothing either in style or content to indicate that Mrs. Lennox had anything to do with the first three numbers. It is a paper connected with the college at Westminster.

In the *London Chronicle* for 1770, December 1-4, 533, is this advertisement: "A New Periodical Paper. Saturday next will be published. Price 3 d. Dedicated by Permission, to her Grace the Duchess of Northumberland. *The Trifler* No. 1. By a Lady. To be continued weekly, consisting of Essays Moral and Entertaining. Pr. for J. Wilkie, at No. 71, in St. Paul's Churchyard; T. Durham, at Charing Cross; and Richardson and Urquhart, under the Royal Exchange." This advertisement is repeated weekly for four numbers. I have not been able to find any copy still existing of this periodical and therefore have no way of judging whether this is by Mrs. Lennox or not. From the date and the nature of the advertisement, it is not impossible that it be by her; on the other hand, the section in her own magazine would seem to rule out the necessity for looking elsewhere. Certainly we need not consider the novel, *The Trifler*; "or, *A Ramble* among the Wilds of Fancy, the Works of Nature, and the Manners of Men. The Second Edition. London. Printed for R. Baldwin, at No. 47, in Pater-Noster Row. MDCCLXXVII. 4 vols." "By Henry Man" is written in in pencil on the title-page. It is a novel which in chapter five stops to tell us that it is imitating Sterne and Addison and then goes on.

II. *Memoirs of Henry Lennox.*

This book was formerly catalogued in the British Museum as being by Mrs. Lennox. There are several reasons for not accepting the book as hers.

(1) Whereas all her other books have on the title-page her name or "by the Author of the Female Quixote", the title-page ascribes this to the Hon. Miss Lenox.

> *Memoirs of Henry Lenox, Interspersed with Legendary Romances.* By the Hon. Miss Lenox. London: Printed by D. N. Shury, No. 7, Berwick Street, Soho. For J. F. and G. Hughes, Wigmore Street, Cavendish Square. 1804.

(2) Mrs. Lennox died on January 4, 1804. She was in ill-health and helpless in January, 1802, as we may judge from Lady Frances Chambers' letter printed above, p. 60. Therefore it is not likely that she recovered sufficiently, at the advanced age of eighty-two, to write another book. During the last two years she received such liberal aid from the Royal Literary Fund that we may infer she no longer found it essential to write for her living.

(3) Nichols in *Literary Anecdotes*, ii, 200-1, and viii, 435, gives a complete list of Mrs. Lennox's works. In his capacities as bookseller, printer, and member of the Royal Literary Fund, it is improbable that even a posthumous publication of hers should have remained unknown to him. He does not mention the *Memoirs of Henry Lennox.*

(4) There is nothing in the content of the book itself to indicate that it is the work of Mrs. Lennox. It relates the adventures of Henry Lennox's father and mother, the latter

of whom died in misery in the London streets after deserting
her husband and child to elope with a neighboring gentleman
of wealth. It also tells the story of Matilda Osmington,
whose mother suffers hardships because of a marriage for
love. Henry and Matilda are brought together in London,
and, after various misadventures, are happily married. Certainly there is nothing of Mrs. Lennox's life here, or of her
style, for not only from its commonplace sentimentality but
also from its lack of skill and grace, especially in the abrupt
jumps from direct conversation to rapid summary of events,
it sounds distinctly amateurish.

For these four reasons I have omitted the book from a list
of Mrs. Lennox's works.

III. *The History of Sir George Warrington*; or, *The
Political Quixote.*

The only reason to doubt that this book is by Mrs. Lennox
is that a copy exists, attributing it to the author of the
Benevolent Quixote. Therefore my only attempt to prove
that it is by Mrs. Lennox, besides an examination of contents above, pp. 106-8, is to describe the two copies
bibliographically.

There are three copies of the book known to exist: one
at Yale; one in the possession of Sir Michael Sadleir, which
I take to be identical with the one at Yale, though I have not
examined it; and one in the Library of Congress.

The copy at Yale is printed in three volumes, bound in
two, in boards, with the watermark of J H or I H 1796 on
the two leaves put in by the binder before the title-page.
The title page reads

THE/ HISTORY/ of / SIR GEORGE WARRING-
TON; / or the POLITICAL QUIXOTE. / By the
Author of the *Female Quixote.*/ In Three Volumes. /
Vol. I. / London: / Printed for J. Bell, Oxford- Street./
MDCCXCVII.

On the upper outer margin is part of the watermark 1796, which recurs through the three volumes on the first, third, ninth, or eleventh leaf of some of the gatherings, which are in sixes. The volume begins with the signature B through B_6 and continues through the single L and one leaf. The second volume begins, with no title-page, on the next leaf with CHAP. I. and has bound in this volume from B through G, G_2, G_3. There are two leaves put in by the binder at the end. There are 207 pages of volume i and 126 pages of volume ii bound in this volume.

Volume ii also has two pages at the beginning and the end put in by the binder, but in this volume there are no watermarks on the first two pages. The title-page is similar to the one in the first volume with VOL. II instead of VOL. I. It begins with CHAP. VII., p. 127 and the signatures G_5 and G_6 and then has six unsigned leaves, the last three apparently cut off from the last three in the first volume and caught in the gathering without sewing or pasting. Volume ii has through L and one leaf, 219 pages. Immediately after it comes the title-page for volume iii, like the other two, and Vol. III, which begins with $B-B_6$ and goes through I_4 and four unsigned pages, 184 pages.

The copy in the Library of Congress, which I have seen and compared with the one at Yale, is bound in three volumes and with the exception of the title-pages is identical. There are watermarks, often on the same pages as in the Yale copy and occasionally identical except that the margin is a little wider or narrower, see pp. 61 and 183 of the third volume or pp. 69 and 109 of the first volume. In other cases the watermark is inverted or reversed. The watermarks on p. 47, vol. i and p. 39, vol. iii of the Library of Congress copy are like that on the title-page of the Yale copy.

So far as the texts of the three volumes go I have collated them and found no sign of change. The catchwords correspond; the line endings correspond; the signatures are in the same position with reference to catchwords; the capitals are the same; the italics used on the title-pages are of the same fount; and a rule placed between two full stops on a page invariably falls along the same letters.

The title-page of the Library of Congress copy reads

THE / HISTORY / of SIR GEORGE WARRING-TON; / or the / POLITICAL QUIXOTE. / By the Author of the *Benevolent Quixote,* / etc. etc. / SECOND EDITION. / In Three Volumes. / Vol. I / London: / Printed for J. Bell, Oxford- Street. / MDCCXCVII.

The copy is similar to the Yale copy in all three volumes. As the evidence of the texts points to the same impression and the same edition, I should judge that these title-pages were printed and added later. They are insets in both copies. There are several points that argue for the Yale copy being the original issue. Sir Michael Sadleir's copy, the only other copy known, has title-pages like it. The review of the book in the *Critical Review* for May, 1798, refers to it as by the author of the *Female Quixote*. It is advertised in *The Sun* for January 16, 18, 27, 30 as by the author of the *Female Quixote*. The copy "By the Author of the *Benevolent Quixote*" has on the title-page "Second Edition". That there is another copy giving it to the author of the *Female Quixote*, that it is reviewed as by her as late as May, 1798, lead me to conclude that the bookseller put together what was left of the first edition with a different title-page, perhaps with the hope that it would sell better, and called it a second edition. There were so few copies of this that it never found its way into the papers or reviews and apparently neither the author of the *Female Quixote* nor of the *Benevolent Quixote* (whoever he or she may be) ever saw it or troubled to correct it. It seems safe to assume that the bindings with the change in title-page to "By the Author of the *Benevolent Quixote*" were few and were merely the result of an attempt to dispose of the first printing for which there was little sale.

APPENDIX VI

The Works of Charlotte Ramsay Lennox

After each item I have put in brackets the library where it may be found, using the following abbreviations: BM for British Museum; BN for Bibliothèque Nationale; LC for Library of Congress; NYPL for New York Public Library.

1747 *Poems on Several Occasions*. Written by a Young Lady. London: Printed for, and Sold by S. Paterson, at Shakespear's Head, opposite Durham-yard, in the Strand. MDCCXLVII. (Dedication to Lady Issabella Finch, signed Charlotte Ramsay. 88 pages. 30 poems.) [BM; Yale; NYPL]

> 1750 "The Art of Coquetry" reprinted in *Gentleman's Maga-zine* (Nov., 1750), xx, 518-9. (Same no. lines and same end rimes as "The Art of Coquettry" in *Poems*, 61-7; some verbal changes within lines.)

1750 "Birthday Ode to the Princess of Wales" by Mrs. Lennox. In *Gentleman's Magazine* (Nov., 1750), xx, 518.

1751 *The Life of Harriot Stuart*. Written by Herself. In Two Volumes. London: Printed for J. Payne, and J. Bouquet, in Pater-noster Row. MDCCLI. (No dedication. Vol. i, 243 pages; vol. ii, 234 pages.) [BM; Yale; Harvard]

1752 The/Female QUIXOTE;/ or, The/ Adventures/ of /*ARA-BELLA*./ In Two Volumes./ Vol. I./ *London*:/ Printed for A. Millar, over-against/ *Catharine-street* in the *Strand*./ M.DCC.LII./
The /Female QUIXOTE;/ or, The/ Adventures/of/ *ARA-BELLA*./ *In* Two Volumes./ Vol. II./*LONDON*:/ Printed for A. Millar, over-against *Cathe-/rine-Street* in the *Strand*./ M.DCC.LII./

> (Decorations on title-page, first and last pages of text cheaper, less clearly outlined in vol. ii. Vol. i B-N₂, 271 pages; ii B-P₃, 325 pages. Dedication to the Earl of Middlesex signed "*The* Author?" written by Johnson, i, [iii]-vi. An-nounced in *Gentleman's Mag*. for March, 1752.) [BM; Yale]

> 1752 The/ Female QUIXOTE;/ or, The/ Adventures/ of/ *ARABELLA*./ In Two Volumes./ Vol. I./ The Second Edition:/*Revised* and *Corrected*. / *LONDON*: /Printed for Millar, over-against/ *Catharine-street* in the *Strand*./ M.DCC.LII./
> (Title-page of vol. ii different in size of capitals, spacing,

insignia, punctuation after The Second Edition, instead
of : ; otherwise the same. Vol. i B-N₂, 271 pages;
vol. ii B-P₃, 322 pages. Ded. as in first ed. Changes
rare and slight, within sentences. Announced in *Gentleman's Mag.* for June, 1752.) [LC; NYPL]

1752 *The Female Quixote: or, The Adventures of Arabella.*
In Two Volumes. Dublin: Printed for J. Smith, at the
Philosophers-Heads on the Blind-Quay, MDCCLII.
(Vol. i, 202 pages; vol. ii, 243 pages. Dedication.
Printed from the first ed.) [Yale; Victoria and Albert
Museum]

1754 *Don Quixote im Reifrocke, oder die abentheuerlichen
Begebenheiten der Romanen heldinn Arabella.* aus dem
Englischen übersetzt. Hamburg und Leipzig, ben Georg
Christ, Grund und Adam Hein. Holle. 1754. (i vol. 656
pages. Vorrede des Ubersetzere, 6 pages.) [BM]

1763 The / Female QUIXOTE:/ or, The/ Adventures/ of/
ARABELLA./ In Two Volumes./ Vol. I./ The Third
Edition./ *DUBLIN*:/Printed for W. Whitestone, at
Shakes-/peare's-Head, in *Skinner-Row*,/ MDCCLXIII./
The/ Female QUIXOTE:/ or, The/ Adventures/ of/
ARABELLA./ In Two Volumes./ Vol. II./ The Third
Edition./ *DUBLIN*:/ Printed for W. Whitestone, at
Shakespear's-/ Head, in *Skinner-Row*. MDCCLXIII./

(Vol. i, 202 pages ff. by page of advt. of books pr.
for W. Whitestone; vol. ii, 243 pages ff. by page of
advt. of plays. Dedication. Printed from the first ed.)
[NYPL]

1773 *Don Quichote (le) Femelle*, Traduction Libre de
L'Anglois. A Lyon. Chez les Libraires Associés.
MDCCLXXIII. (In 2 vols. Vol. i lost; vol. ii, 256
pages.) [BN]

1783 *The Female Quixote; or, The Adventures of Arabella.*
By Mrs. Lenox. In Two Volumes [in 1]. London:
Printed for Harrison and Co. No. 18, Paternoster-Row.'
MDCCLXXXIII. (Dedication. 219 pages. 4 plates in-
cluded: Strothard del. all 4; Walker sculp. I, IV,
Angus sculp. II, Heath sculp. III. Printed from the
second ed. Same ed. as that bound in vol. xii of *The
Novelist's Magazine.*) [BM; Yale; NYPL]

1799 *The Female Quixote; or, The Adventures of Arabella.*
By Mrs. Lennox. In Two Volumes. Cooke's Edition.
Embellished With Superb Engravings. London: Printed

for C. Cooke, No. 17, Paternoster-Row; And sold bp[*sic*] in vol. i; vol. ii title-page reads *by*] all the Booksellers in Great-Britain and Ireland. (Vol. i, 204 pages, 3 engravings: one painted by T. Kirk, engraved by W. Hawkins Mar. 9, 1799; one drawn by R. Corbould, engraved by C. Armstrong May 11, 1799; one drawn by R. Corbould, engraved by C. Warren Apr. 13, 1799, all printed for C. Cooke. Vol. ii, 228 pages, 3 engravings: one painted by T. Kirk, engraved by A. Raimbach Apr. 20, 1799; one drawn by R. Corbould, engraved by C. Warren Sept. 6, 1799; one drawn by R. Corbould, ornamented by R. W. Satchwell, engraved by C. Warren Aug. 1, 1799, all printed for C. Cooke. Dedication. Printed from the second ed.) [In my possession]

1801   *Arabella ou le Don Quichote Femelle*: traduit de l'Anglais. A Paris, chez Bertaudet, Imprimeur-Libraire, quai des Augustins, no. 32, 1801. (Vol. i, frontispiece, Préface du Traducteur, 2 pages, 214 pages; vol. ii, frontispiece, 224 pages.) [BN]

1808   *Don Quijote Con Faldas*; *ó Perjuicios morales de las disparatadas novelas*; Escrito en inglés, sin nombre de Autor; y en castellano por Don Bernardo Maíra de Calzada, Teniente Coronel de Los Reales Exercitos, é Individuo de varios cuerpos literarios. Con Permiso. Por Fuentenebro y Compānia. 1808. 3 vols. (El Traductor á Los Lectores, 3 pages. Vol. i, 260 pages; vol. ii, 224 pages; vol. iii, 180 pages.) [BM; LC]

1810   *The Female Quixote*; *or, The Adventures of Arabella*. By Mrs. Lennox. In two volumes. A New Edition. London: Printed for F. C. and J. Rivington; W. Otredge and Son; A. Strahan etc. [many names including W. Creech, Edinburgh; and Wilson and Son, York] 1810. (Ded. Printed from second edition. Vol. i, 233 pages; vol. ii, 270 pages. Last page vol. ii says J. Mc-Creery, Printer, Black-Horse Court, Fleet-Street. No engravings.) [BM]

1810   *The Female Quixote* in *British Novelists*; with an Essay, and Prefaces Biographical and Critical, by Mrs. Barbauld. London: Printed for F. C. and J. Rivington etc. 1810. vols. xxiv, xxv. (Preface by Mrs. Barbauld, commenting also upon *Henrietta*. Vol. xxiv, 233 pages; vol. xxv, 270 pages. No engravings.) [BM; Yale]

1820 The *Female Quixote* in *British Novelists* etc. 1820. vols. xxiv, xxv. [LC; NYPL]

1752 November 4, 1752./ PROPOSALS/ For Printing by SUB-SCRIPTION,/ POEMS/ ON/ SEVERAL OCCASIONS./ By The / AUTHOR of the FEMALE QUIXOTE./ SUB-SCRIPTIONS are taken in by/ MR. MILLAR, in the Strand; and MR. DODSLEY, in Pall-Mall./ (4to double sheet. Title-page, page with 3 conditions and signature Charlotte Lennox, two page reprint of "On Reading Hutchinson on the Passions", *Poems*, pp. 37-38, with verbal changes and alteration at the end to poem of 22 lines instead of 26 as in original.) [Yale]

1753 *Shakespear Illustrated*: or The Novels and Histories, on which the Plays of Shakespear are founded, Collected and Translated from the Original Authors with Critical Remarks. In Two Volumes. By the Author of the Female Quixote. London: Printed for A. Millar in the Strand. MDCCLIII. (The third volume with the same title-page save the date MDCCLIV appeared in 1754. Vol. i, dedication to John, Earl of Orrery, signed The Author written by Johnson, [iii]-xii, 292 pages; vol. ii, 274 pages; vol. iii, 308 pages. With each play the source is given and a comment on Shakespeare's treatment of it by Mrs. Lennox.) [BM; Yale; NYPL]

 1809 *Shakspeare Illustrated*: or, the Novels and Histories on which the Plays of Shakspeare are founded. Collected and Translated from the Originals. By Mrs. Lenox. Author of the Female Quixote, etc. With Critical Remarks and Biographical Sketches of the Writers, by Mordecai Manuel Noah. In Two Volumes. Bradford and Inskeep, Philadelphia, 1809. (The first volume only of this was published, the author "not being able to collect the materials for the other".) [NYPL; LC; Boston Public Lib.]

1756 MEMOIRS / of / MAXIMILIAN de BETHUNE,/ DUKE of SULLY,/ Prime Minister to/ HENRY the GREAT./ Containing/ The History of the LIFE and REIGN of that MONARCH,/ And his own ADMINISTRATION under him./ Translated from the FRENCH./ To which is added,/ The Tryal of RAVAILLAC for the Murder of/ HENRY the GREAT./ IN THREE VOLUMES./ LONDON,/ Printed for A. Millar, in the Strand; R. and J. Dodsley, in Pall-Mall; /and W. Shropshire, in New-Bond-Street./MDCCLVI./ (3 vols. 4to. Title-page of vol. iii has no ; after Pall-Mall. Advt. in *London Evening-Post*, Oct. 18, 1755, to be publ. Nov. 1. *Gentleman's*

Mag. notices it in Nov., 1755. Dedication to the Duke of New-castle, signed Charlotte Lennox, dated Sept. 5, 1755, written by Johnson. Preface to Fr. ed. of M. de L'Ecluse, xxxiv pages.) [BM; Yale]

1757   *Memoirs of Maximilian de Bethune, Duke of Sully,* Prime Minister to Henry the Great. Containing The History of the Life and Reign of that Monarch, And his own Administration under Him. Translated from the French, by the Author of the Female Quixote. To which is added, The Tryal of Ravaillac for the Murder of Henry the Great. In Five Volumes. London, Printed for A. Millar, in the Strand; R. and J. Dodsley, in Pall-Mall; and W. Shropshire, in New-Bond-Street. MDCCLVII. (5 vols. 8vo. 15s. Advt. in *London Evening-Post* 4595, April 19, 1757. Dedication. Fr. preface.) [BM; Harvard]

1760   *Memoirs of Maximilian de Bethune, duke of Sully,* etc. Newly translated from the French edition of M. de L'Ecluse. Illustrated with an accurate map of France. To which is annexed, the Trial of Ravaillac, for the murder of Henry the Great. Edinburgh, A. Donaldson. 1760. (5 vols. 12 mo. No dedication. Advt. asks considera-tion for translation but translator is not named. French preface. Map wanting.) [LC]

1761   MEMOIRS / of / MAXIMILIAN de BETHUNE, / DUKE of SULLY, /Prime Minister to/ HENRY the GREAT./Containing/ The History of the Life and Reign of that Monarch,/ And his own Administration under Him./ Translated from the French./ To which is added,/The Tryal of RAVAILLAC for the Murder of/ HENRY the GREAT./ In Three Volumes./Vol. I./ The Third Edition./ London:/ Printed for A. Millar, in the Strand; R. and J. Dodsley, in Pall-Mall;/ and W. Shropshire, in New-Bond-Street./MDCCLXI./ (Title-pages of vol. ii and vol. iii differ from i in the last three lines, which read: Printed for A. Millar, in the Strand; R. and J. Dodsley, in / Pall-Mall; and W. Shropshire, in New-Bond-Street./MDCCLXI./ . 3 vols. 4to. Dedica-tion. Preface to Fr. ed. xxiv pages. Advt. in *London Chronicle*, June 13, 18, 20, 1761.) [Yale; NYPL]

1763   *Memoirs of Maximilian de Bethune, Duke of Sully,* etc. Translated from the French. To which is added, The Tryal of Ravaillac for the Murder of Henry the Great. In Six Volumes. The Fourth Edition. London:

Printed for A. Millar, in the Strand; R. and J. Dodsley, in Pall-Mall; and W. Shropshire, in New-Bond-Street. MDCCLXIII. (6 vols. 12mo. Ded. Preface to Fr. ed. xxviii pages. Advt. in *London Chronicle*, July 19, 1763, explains change of format because of pirated edition in Scotland.) [Yale; Columbia]

1773 *Memoirs of Maximilian de Bethune, Duke of Sully*, Prime Minister of Henry the Great. Newly translated from the French edition of M. de L'Ecluse. To which is annexed, The Trial of Francis Ravaillac, for the Murder of Henry the Great. In Five Volumes. Edinburgh: Printed and sold by John Robertson. MDCCLXXIII. (5 vols. 12 mo. Vols. i, ii, iii, iv have this title-page; vol. v the same till the bottom of the page where occurs: Edinburgh: Printed for A. Kincaid and W. Creech. MDCCLXXIII. Vol. i, ded. to the Memory of Sir Joseph Yates, One of the Judges of the Court of King's Bench, by the Editor, dated Edinburgh, August, 1773. Preface of Fr. ed. slightly altered in the first few pages, which are the only ones given, the rest omitted as they "would afford little instruction or entertainment". Rest of translation altered only by an occasional change of wording.) [Yale]

1773 *Memoirs of Maximilian de Bethune, Duke of Sully*, Prime Minister of Henry the Great. Newly translated from the French edition of M. de L'Ecluse. etc. Edinburgh, A. Kincaid and W. Creech. MDCCLXXIII. (5 vols. 12mo. No ded. otherwise exactly like edition above, probably another issue of the same.) [LC]

1778 *Memoirs of Maximilian de Bethune, Duke of Sully*, Prime Minister to Henry the Great. Containing The History of the Life and Reign of that Monarch, and his own Administration under Him. Translated from the French. To which is added, The Tryal of Ravaillac for the Murder of Henry the Great. In Six Volumes. The Fifth Edition. London: Printed for J. Rivington and Sons, J. Dodsley, S. Crowder, G. Robinson, T. Cadell, and T. Evans. M.DCC.LXXVIII. (6 vols. 12mo. Ded., preface to Fr. ed. xxviii pages.) [Princeton; NYPL vols. ii, iv, vi]

1778 *Memoirs of Maximilian de Bethune, Duke of Sully*, Prime Minister to Henry the Great. Containing The History of the Life and Reign of that Monarch, and his own Administration under Him. Translated from the French, by the Author of the Female Quixote. To which is added, The Tryal of Ravaillac for the Murder of Henry the Great. In Five Volumes. A New Edition. London: Printed for J. Rivington and Sons, J. Dodsley, S. Crowder, G. Robinson, T. Cadell, and T. Evans. M.DCC.LXXVIII. (5 vols. 12mo. Ded., preface to Fr. ed. xxv pages.) [NYPL; LC; BM]

1805   *Memoirs of Maximilian de Bethune, Duke of Sully*, Prime Minister of Henry the Great. Newly translated from the French edition of M. de L'Ecluse. To which is annexed The Tryal of Francis Ravaillac, for the Murder of Henry the Great. In Five Volumes. Edinburgh: Printed for Alex. Lowrie and Co. For Bell and Bradfute, W. Martin, John Fairbairn, Ogle and Aikman; and Vernor and Hood, London. 1805. (5 vols. 12mo. No ded., preface to Fr. ed. shortened and verbal changes as in 1773 ed.) [Yale]

1810   *The Memoirs of the Duke of Sully*, prime-minister to Henry the Great. Translated from the French by Charlotte Lennox. New ed. rev. and cor., with additional notes, some letters of Henry the Great, and a brief historical introduction. London, W. Miller, 1810. (5 vols. 8vo. Ded. to Duke of Newcastle, preface as in Fr. ed., hist. introd. by Sir Walter Scott.) [BM; LC]

1812   *Memoirs of Maximilian de Bethune, Duke of Sully*, Prime Minister of Henry the Great: To which is annexed, The Trial of Francis Ravaillac, for the Murder of Henry the Great. Translated from the French. A New Edition. In Five Volumes. London: Printed for Lackington, Allen, & Co.; Longman, Hurst Rees, Orme, & Brown; White, Cochrane, & Co.; S. Bagster, and R. Scholey:— and for Bell & Bradfute; Silvester Doig & Andrew Stirling, and A. Constable & Co. Edinburgh. 1812. (5 vols. 12mo. No. ded., preface of Fr. ed. shortened and verbal changes as in Edinburgh 1773 ed.) [BM; Yale 5 vols. bd. in 3]

1817   *The Memoirs of the Duke of Sully*, Prime Minister to Henry the Great. Translated from the French by Charlotte Lennox. A New Edition, Revised and Corrected; with additional Notes, some letters of Henry the Great, and a Brief Historical Introduction. In Five Volumes. Philadelphia: Published by Edward Earle. J. Maxwell, Printer. 1817. (5 vols. 8vo. Ded. to Duke of Newcastle, preface to Fr. ed., brief hist. introd. by Scott.

Advt. states some changes made from Mrs. Lennox's translation to correct errors shown by French publication in 1778.) [Yale; NYPL]

1819 *Memoirs of the Duke of Sully*, Prime Minister of Henry the Great: with The Trial of Francis Ravaillac, for the Murder of Henry the Great; and An Appendix, containing Refutations of the Abbé de l'Ecluse's Correctional Notes, Exculpatory of the Jesuits. A New Edition, Carefully Corrected. Embellished with Portraits. In Five Volumes. Edinburgh: Printed for Stirling & Slade, and Archibald Constable and Company, Edinburgh; and for F. C. and J. Rivington; Longman, Hurst Rees, Orme, [long list] London. 1819. (5 vols. 8vo. No ded., preface to Fr. ed. [v]-xxix. Advt. states care has been taken, "by an exact revisal, to make it more accurate than any preceding" edition. Slight changes of wording and spelling; summary of books omitted; otherwise like 1778 5 vol. ed.) [NYPL]

1856 *Memoirs of the Duke of Sully*, Prime Minister to Henry the Great. Translated from the French. A New Edition, Revised and Corrected; with additional notes, and An Historical Introduction, attributed to Sir Walter Scott. In Four Volumes. With a general Index. London: Henry G. Bohn, York Street, Covent Garden. MDCCCLVI. (4 vols. 8vo. No ded., advt. by editor as in 1817 ed., preface to Fr. ed., hist. introd.) [Bohn French Classics series]

1756 *The Memoirs of the Countess of Berci*. Taken from the French By the Author of the Female Quixote. In Two Volumes. London. Printed for A. Millar, in the Strand, M.DCC.LVI. (Sub-title, The History of the Chevalier des Essars and the Countess of Berci. Advt. in *London Evening-Post* for April 6, 1756.) [BM; Yale; LC]

1757 *Memoirs for the History of Madame de Maintenon and of the Last Age*. Bonam facile crederes, magnam libenter. Tac. Translated from the French, by the Author of the Female Quixote. In Five Volumes. London: Printed for A. Millar, and J. Nourse, in the Strand; R. and J. Dodsley, in Pall-Mall; L. Davis, & C. Reymer, in Holbourn. MDCCLVII. (5 vols. 12mo. Dedication to the Countess of Northumberland signed Charlotte Lennox, all of it but the last sentence and signature on the first leaf, which is a cancel; the catchword on the leaf verso is wrong. Advt. in *London Evening-Post* for April 19,

1757. The book of assignments, BM Add. MS.38730, gives accounts for printing 1,000 copies, let out to two printers. There were six sets for the Translator.) [BM; Yale]

1757 *Philander.* A Dramatic Pastoral. By the Author of the Female Quixote. London: Printed for A. Millar, in the Strand. MDCCLVII. (Price One Shilling. Dedication to Lord Viscount Charlemont, signed Charlotte Lennox, dated Nov. 20, 1757, written by Johnson, [iii]-vii, 48 pages.) [BM; Yale; LC]

    1758 *Philander.* A Dramatic Pastoral. By Mrs. Charlotte Lennox, Author of the Female Quixote. Dublin: Printed for Richard Smith, at the Hercules in Dame-street. M.DCC.LVIII. (Ded. to Lord Charlemont, [iii]-v, 36 pages.) [Yale]

1758 *Henrietta.* By the Author of the Female Quixote. In Two Volumes. London: Printed for A. Millar, in the Strand. MDCCLVIII. (Advt. in *London Evening-Post* for Feb. 2, 1758. No dedication. Vol. i, 255 pages; vol. ii, 315 pages.) [BM; Yale]

    1758 HENRIETTA./ By the AUTHOR of/ THE FEMALE QUIXOTE./ In TWO VOLUMES./ Vol. I./ DUB-LIN:/ Printed for George Faulkner, in *Essex-street,*/ Sarah Cotter, in *Skinner-row,* and Hulton/Bradley, at the *King's Arms* and *Two Bibles* in/*Dame-street,* Book-sellers. MDCCLVIII./

        HENRIETTA./ By the AUTHOR of/ THE FEMALE QUIXOTE./ Vol. II./ DUBLIN:/ Printed for George Faulkner, Sarah Cotter,/ and Hulton Bradley, Booksellers./ M DCC L VIII./

        (No ded. Vol. i, pp. [1]-153; vol. ii, pp. [157]-346.) [Yale]

1760 *Henriette.* Traduit de l'anglais, par M . . . . [Insignia] A Londres; Et se trouve à Paris, chez Duchesne, Libraire, rue St. Jacques, au-dessous de la Fontaine Saint Benoît, au Temple du Goût. MDCCLX. (Préface, 4 pages, vol. i, 348 pages; vol. ii, 415 pages.) [BN from the Bibliothèque Royale]

1760 *Henriette.* en Deux Volumes. Traduit de l'Anglois [Insignia] A Lausanne, chez Antoine Chapuis Imprimeur. Aux depends de Marc-Michel Rey Libraire à Amsterdam. MDCCLX. (2 vols. bd. in 1. Vol. i, 298 pages; vol. ii, 355 pages.) [BM]

1761 *Henrietta.* By Mrs. Charlotte Lennox. The Second Edition, corrected. Printed for A. Millar, in the Strand. MDCCLXI. (2 vols. 12mo. Advt. in *London Chronicle* for March 19, 1761, and for March 7, 1769, after the production of *The Sister*, the play based on it. Dedication to the Dutchess of Newcastle, signed Charlotte Lennox, dated Nov. 20, 1760, probably written by Johnson.) [Harvard; Bodleian; BM 2 vols. bd. in 1]

1770 *Henrietta.* A Novel. By Mrs. Charlotte Lennox. In Two Volumes. Printed for T. Lowndes, at his Circulating Library in Fleet-street. Price 6s. bound. 12 mo. (Advt. in *London Chronicle* for March 24, 1770. On Sept. 20, 1769, there was an assignment of *Henrietta* (BM, Add. MS. 38730). W. and J. Richardson had bought it at Millar's sale on June 13, 1769, and on Sept. 20, they sold a third share to Lowndes, who promises, when the present edition is sold off, to use his influence toward getting the Richardsons the printing of a new edition. As I have been able to find no copy of a 1770 edition of *Henrietta*, I believe the advt. is merely an attempt to "sell off the present edition".)

1787 *Henrietta.* By Mrs. Lennox. In Two Volumes [in one]. London: Printed for Harrison and Co. No. 18, Paternoster Row, MDCCLXXXVII. (Ded. to the Second Edition, to the Dutchess of Newcastle, signed Charlotte Lennox. 160 pages. Vol. i, [5]-74; vol. ii, [75]-160. 4 plates. E. F. Burney del. Milton sculp. II and III, Auker-Smith sculp. I and plate bd. in first, opp. p. 50, but unnumbered, all Publish'd, as the Act directs, by Harrison & Cº. Aug., Sept., Oct., and Nov., 1787.) [NYPL; BM bd. with Letters from Felicia to Charlotte. By Mr. Collyer. 1788 and The Female Quixote. 1783.]
The Novelist's Magazine. Vol. XXIII. Containing Rasselas, Prince of Abyssinia. Henrietta. Nourjahad. Felicia to Charlotte. The Creole. The Invisible Spy. London: Printed for Harrison and Cº. Nº. 18, Paternoster Row. 1788. (Same in title-page, text, as edition above, only 2 plates bd. in, I and IV, so numbered here. Probably more than one issue of this edition.) [NYPL]

1759 *The Greek Theatre of Father Brumoy.* Translated by Mrs. Charlotte Lennox. In Three Volumes. London: Printed for Messrs. Millar, Vaillant, etc. MDCCLIX. (Dedication, written by Johnson, to George, Prince of Wales. Vol. i, Preface and first three essays by Earl of Cork and Orrery. Vol. ii, Plays and observations by Mrs. Lennox. Vol. iii, Advt. states: "In this volume the discourse on the Greek comedy, and the General Conclusion are translated by the celebrated *author of the Rambler*. The comedy of the Birds, and that of Peace by a *young gentleman*. The comedy of the Frogs, by the learned and ingenious Dr. Gregory Sharpe, Esq. The discourse upon the Cyclops, by John Bourryau. The Cyclops, by Dr. Grainger, author of the translation of Tibullus." Advt. in *London Chronicle* for Jan. 24, 1760.) [BM; Yale; Princeton]

1760-1 *The Lady's Museum.* By the Author of the Female Quixote. London, Printed for J. Newbery, in St. Paul's Churchyard; and J. Coote, in Pater-noster Row. (Bd. in 2 vols. 8vo. The first number was announced in the *London Chronicle* for Feb. 19, 1760, as appearing on March 1, 1760; the last appeared on January 1, 1761. The magazine contains 11 numbers of "The Trifler", the novel "The History of Harriot and Sophia", afterwards the novel *Sophia*, "History of the Count de Comminge" translated from the romance of Madame de Tencin, "History of the Dutchess of Beaufort" from the *Memoirs of Sully,* various Oriental tales, several numbers of a "Treatise on the Education of Daughters", poems, some of them reprinted from Miss Ramsay's_ *Poems* with a few slight changes, and articles on geography and natural history.) [BM; Yale]

1762 *Sophia.* By Mrs. Charlotte Lennox. London: Printed for James Fletcher, in St. Paul's Churchyard. MDCCLXII. (Reprinted without change from *The Lady's Museum* where it appeared as "The History of Harriot and Sophia". Advt. in *London Chronicle* for May 15, 1762. Vol. i, 227 pages; vol. ii, 237 pages.) [BM; Yale]

1764 *The History of the Marquis of Lussan and Isabella.* By Mrs. Lennox, author of the Female Quixote, and Sophia. Dublin: Printed by James Hoey, Junior. M.DCC.LXIV. (12mo. 197 pages ff. by page advt. The History of Sophia, etc. This is the "History of the Count de Comminge" from *The Lady's Museum,* with an interchange of names and a change of ending.) [Yale]

1770 *Sophie, ou Le Triomphe des Graces sur la Beauté.* An imitation de l'Anglois de Mistriss Charlotte Lennox. Avec Figures. A Londres, et se vend à Paris, chez la Veuve Duchesne, au Temple du Goût; Jay, au grand Corneille,

Rue Saint-Jacques; et Marigot Jeune, Quai des Augustins. 1770. (Vol. i, 209 pages; vol. ii, 244 pages.) [BN from Bibliothèque du Roi, Fontainebleau.]

1769 *The Sister*: A Comedy. By Mrs. Charlotte Lennox. London, Pr. for J. Dodsley, in Pall-Mall; and T. Davies, in Russel-street, Covent-Garden. MDCCLXIX. (Price One Shilling and Six Pence. Announced in the *London Chronicle* for March 4, 1769, the play having been performed at Covent-Garden the night of Feb. 18, 1769.) [BM; Yale; LC]

    1769 *The Sister*. London, 1769. A Second Edition. (Announced in *London Chronicle* for March 19, 1769, as also printed by J. Dodsley.) [BM; NYPL]

    1776 *Hamburgisches Theater*. Erster Band. Hamburg 1776. Gedrückt ben J. J. C. Bode, und im verlag der Theatral: Direktion. No. 4. *Was seyn soll, schickt sich wohl*: ein Lustspiel nach den Englischen the sister der Mistress Charlotte Lenox. Ein Lustspiel in fünf Aufzugen. (80 pages. No prologue or epilogue.) [BM]

1774 *Meditations and Penitential Prayers*, written by the celebrated Dutchess De La Vallière, Mistress of Lewis the Fourteenth of France. After her Recovery from a dangerous illness, when she first formed the Resolution of quitting the Court, and devoting herself to a Religious Life. Translated from the French. With some Account of her Life and Character, extracted from Voltaire, Sévigné, and other Writers of that Time. By Mrs. Charlotte Lennox. Printed for J. Dodsley, in Pall-Mall. MDCCLXXIV. (Contains 24 prayers. No dedication.) [BM]

1775 *Proposals* for Printing by Subscriptions, dedicated to the Queen, a new and elegant edition of the original works of Mrs. Lennox. Subscriptions taken by Mr. Dodsley, etc. (These proposals were written by Johnson and were announced in the *Public Advertiser for Monday*, March 27, 1775. The proposed edition was never published. I have located no copy of these Proposals.)

1775 *Old City Manners*. A Comedy. Altered from the Original Eastward Hoe, written by Ben Jonson, Chapman, and Marston. By Mrs. Lennox. As it is performed at the Theatre-Royal, in Drury-Lane. London: Pr. for T. Becket, the Corner of the Adelphi, in the Strand. 1775. (Price One Shilling. 66 pages. An advertisement after the title-page conveys Mrs. Lennox's thanks to Garrick. Announced as published in the *Public Advertiser*, Nov. 28, 1775. Performed seven times between

Nov. 9 and Jan. 8, 1775-6.) [BM; Yale; NYPL lacking title-page]

1790 *Euphemia*: by Mrs. Charlotte Lennox. In 4 vols. London: Printed for T. Cadell, in the Strand; and J. Evans, Pater-Noster Row. MDCCXC. (Advt. in *The Times* (bd. with *The Oracle*) for June 1, 1790. No dedication.) [BM; Yale]

1797 *The History of Sir George Warrington; or the Political Quixote.* By the Author of the Female Quixote. In Three Volumes. London: Printed for J. Bell, Oxford-Street. MDCCXCVII. (3 vols. bd. in 2. Vol. i, I, 207 pages, II, 126 pages; ii, II, pp. 127-219, III, 184 pages.) [Yale; Sir Michael Sadleir's Collection]

> 1797 *The History of Sir George Warrington; or the Political Quixote.* By the Author of the Benevolent Quixote, etc. etc. Second Edition. In Three Volumes. London: Printed for J. Bell, Oxford-Street. MDCCXCVII. (Vol. i, 207 pages; vol. ii, 219 pages; vol. iii, 184 pages. Identical with previous item except for binding and title-pages.) [LC]

APPENDIX VII

List of Periodicals Containing References to Mrs. Lennox or Her Works

Court Miscellany (1769), v, 101-2, 104. Rev. of *The Sister*; prologue and epilogue reprinted.

Critical Review (May, 1756), i, 312-4. Rev. of *Memoirs of Countess of Berci.*

———— (April, 1757), iii, 312-4. Rev. of *Memoirs of Maintenon* and summary of the text.

———— (Nov., 1757), iv, 468. Rev. of *Philander.*

———— (Feb., 1758), v, 122-30. Rev. of *Henrietta* with summary of plot and lengthy quotation.

———— (Feb., 1760), ix, 116-7. Rev. of *Brumoy's Greek Theatre* with outline and extracts.

———— (May, 1762), xiii, 434-5. Brief rev. of *Sophia.*

———— (March, 1769), xxvii, 223. Rev. of *The Sister.*

———— (Feb., 1775), xxxix, 166. Brief rev. of the *Meditations of Vallière.*

———— (July, 1790), lxx, 81-3. Detailed rev. of *Euphemia.*

———— (May, 1798), series II, xxiii, 112-4. Rev. of *The Political Quixote.*

European Magazine (May, 1789), xv, 349, 439. Anecdotes of J. Baretti: acc't. of his meeting with Mrs. Lennox.

———— (Aug., 1790), xviii, 121-2. Rev. of *Euphemia*.

———— (Feb., 1804), xlv, 158. Obituary notice of Mrs. Lennox with list of her works.

The Gazetteer and New Daily Advertiser (Feb. 17, 20, 1769), xiii, 469. Acc't. of the performance of *The Sister*.

The General Magazine and Impartial Review (1790), iv, 313-5. Rev. of *Euphemia*.

Gentleman's Magazine (1749), xix, 278. Poem to Mrs. Lennox.

———— (1750), xx, 518, 519. Poem to Mrs. Lenox on her poems. The *Art of Coquetry* and *Birthday Ode* to the Princess of Wales by Mrs. Lennox.

     575. Brief mention of *Harriot Stuart*.

———— (1751), xxi, 85. Poem occasioned by Mrs. Lennox's *The Art of Coquetry*.

———— (1752), xxii, 146. Rev. of *Female Quixote* written by Johnson.

———— (1753), xxiii, 250, 255-6. Announcement of *Shakespear Illustrated* and excerpt from it with comment.

———— (1754), xxiv, 99. Announcement of third vol. of *Sh. Illus.* 233-4. Letter from T. B. objecting to Mrs. Lennox's attack on Shakespeare. 311. Allusion to *Sh. Ill.*

———— (1755), xxv, 527. *Sully's Memoirs* announced.

———— (1756), xxvi, 200. *Memoirs of the Countess of Berci* announced.

———— (1757), xxvii, 191. *Memoirs of Madam de Maintenon* announced.

———— (1758), xxviii, 133. *Henrietta* announced.

———— (1760), xxx, 96. Brumoy's *Greek Theatre* announced.

———— (1762), xxxii, 243. Rev. of *Sophia*.

———— (1769), xxxix, 157. Announcement of *The Sister* and comment on its performance. 199. Rev. of *The Sister*.

———— (1775), xlv, 542. Prologue of *Old City Manners* printed.

———— (1776), xlvi, 176. *Old City Manners* announced.

———— (1785), lv(1), 87. Anecdotes of Dr. Johnson by T. T. He composed preface to *Sully's Memoirs*.

———— (1797), lxvii, 438. Death of Alex. Lennox.

———— (1801), lxxi, 129, 610. Letters on *Shakespear Illustrated*.

———— (1804), lxxiv, 89. Obituary acc't. of Mrs. Lennox.

———— (1843), N. S., xx, 132-3. Rev. J. Mitford on Johnson's share in the *Female Quixote*.

———— (1844), N. S., xxi, 41-2. Reprint of ch. xi, bk. ix of *Female Quixote* as chapter written by Johnson.

The Grand Magazine of Universal Intelligence and Monthly Chronicle of Our Own Times (Jan., 1758), i, 52. *Henrietta* announced.

Lady's Magazine (Nov., 1775), vi, 587. Acc't. of *Old City Manners*.

Lady's Monthly Museum (Je., 1813), new series, xiv, 313-5. Memoir of Mrs. Lennox, adding details of her meeting with Johnson. Cook engraving of her.

Literary Magazine, or Universal Review (Sept., Oct., 1756), i, 281-2. Review of *Sully's Memoirs*.

———— (1757), ii, 427-431, 469-473. Rev. of *Memoirs of Maintenon*.

Lloyd's Evening-Post and British Chronicle (1769), Feb. 20, March 1, 3. Account of performance of *The Sister*. Advt. of *Henrietta*.

———— (1775), Nov. 8. Rev. of performance of *Old City Manners*; Nov. 20. Prologue repr.; Nov. 13, 15, 27. Performance advt.

London Chronicle (1757), March 10. Advt. of *Memoirs of Maintenon*; July 19. *Sully's Memoirs* listed; Dec. 1. Advt. of *Philander*.

———— (1760), Jan. 24, 29. Advt. of *Brumoy's Greek Theatre*; Feb. 19, 21, 23, March 28, April 1, 29, June 3, 28, July 31, Aug. 30, Sept. 30, Nov. 1, Nov. 29. Advt. of *Lady's Museum*.

———— (1761), Jan. 31, Feb. 28. Advt. of *Lady's Museum*; March 9, 31. Advt. of *Henrietta*; Feb. 24, June 13. Advt. of *Sully's Memoirs*.

———— (1762), May 11, 15. Advt. of *Sophia*.

———— (1769), Feb. 18. Account of *The Sister*. March 7. Advt. of new ed. of *Henrietta*.

———— (1770) March 24. Advt. of *Henrietta*.

———— (1775), March 2. Advt. of *Proposals*; Nov. 9. Rev. of *Old City Manners* and reprint of songs; Nov. 14, 16, 25. Performance advt.; Nov. 18. Prologue printed; Dec. 5. *Old City Manners* publ. and first sc. of first act quoted.

———— (1790), June 1, 3. *Euphemia* advertised.

London Evening-Post (1755), Oct. 18. *Sully's Memoirs* Advt.

———— (1756), March 16, Apr. 3, 19, *Sully's Memoirs* Advt.; April 3, 6. *Memoirs of Countess of Berci* advt.

———— (1757), April 19. *Memoirs of Maintenon* advt.

———— (1758), Feb. 2, Apr. 13, May 2. *Henrietta* advt.

London Magazine (1747), xvi, 536. Advt. of *Poems*.

———— (1750), xix, 576. Advt. of *Harriot Stuart*.

———— (1752), xxi, 195. Advt. of *Female Quixote*.

———— (1755), xxiv, 599. Advt. of *Sully's Memoirs*.

———— (1769), xxxviii, 63. Advt. of *The Sister* and brief mention of performance.

Monthly Magazine (March, 1804), I, xvii, 189. Obit. notice of Mrs. Lennox.

Monthly Review (1750), iv, 160, art. xxiii. Brief rev. of *Harriot Stuart* by Griffiths. (Page ref. here for authors are to Nangle, *The Monthly Review First Series* 1749-1789. Index of Contributors and Articles.) p. 227.

———— (1752), vi, 249. Brief rev. of *Female Quixote*, art. xxx, by Rose, p. 227.

———— (1753), ix, 145. Brief rev. of *Shakespear Illustrated* 2 vols. art. 3.

———— (1754), x, 309, art. xxxi. Brief rev. of *Shakespear Illustrated* vol. iii.

———— (1756), xiv, 516-520. art. lxii. Rev. and summary of *Memoirs of Countess of Berci* by Berkenhoult, p. 157. 561-573, xv, 97-106, 209-216. Long rev. of *Sully's Memoirs* with outline and quotations.

———— (1757), xvii, 80-1, art. 3. Rev. of *Memoirs of Maintenon* by Goldsmith, p. 230; 168, art. 28. Brief rev. of *Philander*.

———— (1758), xviii, 273, art. 24. Brief rev. of *Henrietta* by Rose, p. 230.

———— (1760), xxii, 287-302, 452-467. Long rev. of *Brumoy's Greek Theatre* with outline and quotations by Ruffhead, p. 69.

———— (1762), xvii, 73-4, art. 10. Brief rev. of *Sophia* by Kenrick.

———— (1769), xl, 245-249. Most detailed account of plot and performance of *The Sister*.

———— (1774), li, 485. Rev. of *Vallière's Meditations*, art. 31 by Langhorne, p. 240.

———— (1790), II, iii, 89-90, art. 3. Rev. of *Euphemia* by Ogle and Griffiths.

Morning Chronicle, and London Advertiser (1775), March 22. Advt. of *Proposals*.

Morning Herald (1823), Sept. 25. *The Sister* as source of Burgoyne's *The Heiress*.

Morning Post, and Daily Advertiser (1775), March 22. Advt. of *Proposals*.

Nation (Dec. 25, 1913), xcvii, 614-5. Wm. E. A. Axon, "News for Bibliophiles." Johnson's part in the *Female Quixote*.

Notes and Queries, 12th series, vi, 331; viii, 227. "An English Army List of 1740." James Ramsay.

Oracle (1790), May 14, June 1. Advt. of *Euphemia*.

Public Advertiser (1775), Jan. 28. Publ. of *Memoirs of Count of Comminge*; March 25, 27. Advt. of *Proposals*; Nov. 9, 10, 11, 13, 15, 17, 28. Advt. of performance of *Old City Manners*; Nov. 25, 27, 28. Advt. of publication of *Old City Manners*.

Public Ledger (1760), Dec. 18. Advt. of Brumoy's *Greek Theatre.*
St. James's Chronicle, or British Evening-Post (1769), Feb. 21. Rev.
of *The Sister;* March 9. *The Sister* publ.
———— (1770), March 27. Advt. of *Henrietta.*
———— (1775), March 2. Advt. of *Proposals.*
———— (1790), May 31, June 1, 5. Advt. of *Euphemia* and other
novels; Je. 9. Apology for calling *The Sister* a novel.
Sun (1797), Jan. 16. Advt. of *Hist. of Sir George Warrington.* Repeated Jan. 18, 27, 30.
Town and Country Magazine (1769), i, 94. Rev. of *The Sister.*
———— (1790), xxii, 357. Rev. of *Euphemia.*
Whitehall Evening-Post or London Intelligencer (1769), Feb. 20.
Acc't of *The Sister.*
World (1790), May 14, 20. Advt. of *Novelist's Magazine: Henrietta,
The Female Quixote;* of *Euphemia.*

APPENDIX VIII

Iconography

Graves and Cronin, *A History of the Works of Sir Joshua Reynolds*
(London, 1899), ii, 579; iv, 1480. There was an unfinished
portrait of Mrs. Lennox done by Sir Joshua Reynolds in 1761.
Harding Sylvester and E., *Shakespeare Illustrated* (London, 1793),
vol. containing 137 plates. No. 12 is the portrait of Mrs.
Lennox engraved by Bartolozzi in 1792.
Lady's Monthly Museum (June, 1813), new series, xiv, 313. Opposite
p. 313 is the portrait of Mrs. Lennox engraved by Cook in
1813.
Craig W. H., *Dr. Johnson and the Fair Sex* (London, 1895):
Opposite p. 134 is a copy of the Cook engraving of Mrs. Lennox.
Fielding Henry, *The Covent-Garden Journal* (ed. G. E. Jensen, New
Haven, 1915). Opposite p. 280 of vol. ii is a copy of the Cook
engraving of Mrs. Lennox.
Wilson Mona, *These Were Muses* (London, 1924). Opposite p. 14 is
a copy of the Bartolozzi engraving of Mrs. Lennox. Opposite
p. 34 is a copy of a print in the British Museum of Richard
Samuel's *Nine Living Muses of Great Britain.* This print was
probably torn out of the *Ladies' Pocket-Book* for 1778. Mrs.
Lennox is one of the muses here painted.
The R. B. Adam Library relating to Dr. Samuel Johnson and his Era
(London and N. Y., 1929), vol. iii. Opposite Mrs. Lennox's
letter to Johnson is a copy of the Bartolozzi engraving of
Mrs. Lennox.

INDEX